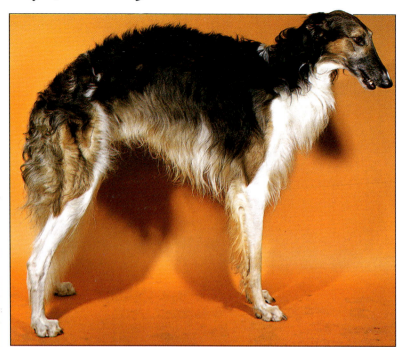

Left This Borzoi hound looks very elegant with its long legs and head. Borzoi hounds were originally bred for hunting.

Breed types

Type:	Purpose:	Examples:
Hounds	To hunt game from sight or scent.	Afghan Basset Hound Bloodhound Borzoi Irish Wolfhound Rhodesian Ridgeback
Working dogs	Herding livestock.	Collie Corgi German Shepherd Dog Old English Sheepdog
	Guarding livestock or property.	Boxer Bull Mastiff Dobermann Pinscher Great Dane Komondor Pyrenean Mountain Dog
Gun dogs	To find and retrieve game.	Labrador Pointer Retriever Setter Spaniel

Above The Airedale Terrier has become a very popular pet.

Below A pair of Cavalier King Charles Spaniels.

Type:	Purpose:	Examples:
Terriers	Hunting burrowing animals.	Airedale Scottish West Highland
Utility dogs	Bull-baiting. Escorting horse-drawn carriages. Guarding Dutch river barges.	Bulldog Dalmatian Keeshond
Toy dogs	Pets, lap-dogs and showdogs.	Cavalier King Charles Spaniel Chihuahua Italian Greyhound Maltese Papillon Pekingese Pomeranian Pug Yorkshire Terrier

Choosing the right dog

It is very easy to fall in love with a cute, tiny puppy and take it home only to find that in a few months' time it has grown into a giant and is eating you out of house and home. Dogs' homes are full of abandoned dogs to prove this point. I am a great believer in 'forewarned is forearmed', so let us have a look at some of the different sizes and breeds to illustrate the pleasures and the pitfalls of owning dogs.

Giant breeds

The term 'gentle giant' is probably the best way to describe most of the giant breeds. The group includes the Bull Mastiff, the Great Dane, the Pyrenean Mountain Dog, the Irish Wolfhound and the St Bernard. The giant breeds can weigh

Left This massive St Bernard has a gentle temperament, which is lucky as it probably weighs nearly 84 kg!

as much as 36 to 84 kg – that is heavier than most adult humans! So, it is a good job that they have loveable, quiet temperaments.

St Bernards are a great example of the gentle giant. They like people and are famous for rescuing lost travellers from snow-drifts. St Bernard puppies are lovely but you will find they grow very quickly.

Growing, giant breed puppies need a lot of food, so you will be spending a lot of money on food bills. You also have to be very careful about the diet of a giant breed puppy because they are prone to bone diseases which make their legs and hips go out of shape. They should be given the correct amount of minerals, such as calcium for healthy bones. It is a good idea to get your veterinary surgeon (vet) to give you proper feeding advice and to check your puppy – especially during the first six months.

This might all sound like a lot of trouble to go to but giant breeds like the St Bernard do make lovely pets. One of my clients has two, Lee and Shane, who love nothing better than to curl up with their owner on the sofa to watch television in the evenings. What a squash!

My pet dog

Right Many people think that the Golden Retriever makes the ideal family pet because of its quiet nature.

Below It is in a Golden Retriever's nature to fetch toys and pieces of clothing. You would have great fun throwing sticks and balls with a young Golden Retriever puppy like this.

Large and medium-sized breeds

The large breeds, such as the Afghan, the German Shepherd Dog and the Old English Sheepdog, can weigh from 23 kg to 36 kg. The medium-sized dogs, such as the Retriever, the Setter and the Pointer are all between 13.5 kg and 23 kg.

Both the large and medium-sized dogs need plenty of exercise every day as they were originally bred for their stamina to be hunting and gun dogs. Even if you have a big garden these dogs will have to be taken for walks. You should have a park or open space near you (that is safe from traffic) so that you can let your dog run off the **leash** for a while – once it has been trained to obey your commands of course!

The medium-sized Golden Retriever is a very popular family pet. Be careful with feeding Retrievers because they do tend to get a bit tubby quite quickly if they are overfed. They are also prone to hip dysplasia – a problem affecting the hips (see page 28), which is made worse if they are overweight.

A fit and healthy Retriever loves playing and they live up to their name by being really good at fetching balls and sticks. They will even fetch your old, smelly slippers. Pong! Now that is what I call devotion!

Small breeds and toy breeds

Small dogs, such as the Scottish Terrier and the Basset Hound are also ideal as family pets. They weigh between 4.5 kg and 13.5 kg and are a hardy, lively bunch. They love to play and although they do not need quite as much exercise as an Afghan or a Labrador, they should still be exercised *every* day with a walk on a leash or a visit to the park.

Toy breeds weigh between 1 kg and 4.5 kg. The smallest of all dogs is the Chihuahua. Toy dogs, such as the Pekingese and Pug are often called lap-dogs as some toy dogs love nothing better than to sit on their owners' laps and be pampered.

Toy dogs are great companions. I like the Yorkshire Terriers who are tiny but big-hearted. These small, lively dogs grow to about 5 kg and, like all terriers, are full of character.

Like most toy dogs, Yorkshire Terriers do not have great appetites so they are not expensive to keep but they can be fussy eaters. This can lead to problems if you give in and only feed them foods that they like – **offal** is a great favourite but this can affect the dog's bones and is not good for it.

Small terriers and toy dogs are quite excitable and do tend to snap a bit. In fact, like most vets, I have been bitten more often by terriers, like the Jack Russell and the Yorkie, than I have by huge dogs like the Great Dane.

Below Yorkshire Terriers can be very cheeky and have very strong characters.

Above Many of my favourite dogs are crossbreeds and mongrels just like these two.

Crossbreeds

So far we have only talked about recognized purebred dogs. There are of course a huge amount of **crossbreed** and **mongrel** dogs as well. Dogs of different breeds can **mate** together. Although some combinations produce very odd-looking results, I think mongrels can make great pets.

You will have to be careful when buying a mongrel pup because it is very difficult to guess what size the pup will grow into. Even if you know the size of the parent dogs, they might be crossbreeds as well and one of their parents might be a Great Dane!

A good place to find mongrels is at a Dog Rescue Centre such as those run by the **R.S.P.C.A.** Every year millions of perfectly healthy dogs are abandoned or made homeless for one reason or another and all of them deserve a kind, loving home. All good rescue centres, and especially those run by the R.S.P.C.A. make sure all the dogs that go up for adoption have been checked by a vet, have had all their **vaccinations** (see pages 27–8) and also have been **neutered** (see page 24) so that they will not be able to reproduce.

A home for your puppy and dog

Once you have decided on the size, breed and temperament of the dog that will suit your family, then it is time to find your puppy. For purebred **pedigree** dogs it is best to buy your puppy from a well-known, recognized breeder. You can find these through the relevant **breed clubs** or **the Kennel Club**. Your local vet will know how to put you in touch. Adult dogs can be bought from breed rescue associations. Crossbreeds and mongrels can be found through family, friends, advertising in newspapers or animal sanctuaries or rescue centres.

There are a lot of points to remember when you are visiting a **litter** to choose a puppy. Firstly, have you decided if you want a male (dog) or a female (bitch)?

Left All puppies are cute and loveable. It is very easy to fall in love with the first puppy that you see but it is a good idea to take a long time over your final choice.

Above Doesn't this Basset Hound mother look proud of her litter?

Make sure that you see the mother with the litter so that you can see what your puppy will look like later. Also you can check if the parent dogs have any **hereditary** problems such as hip dysplasia (see page 28) or progressive retinal atrophy (PRA) (see page 29).

Only agree to buy a puppy that has been completely **weaned** – around eight weeks old.

Watch how the litter behaves. Avoid picking a timid, shy puppy or indeed the really bossy and bullying puppy, because these will need careful handling later on.

The litter's owners should have the first vaccinations done on the puppies at eight and twelve weeks old. They should be able to supply a vaccination certificate which you will then keep up-to-date when your dog has its **booster injections** every year. Do not let your puppy outside or mix with other dogs until it has had its second vaccination at twelve weeks. When you have chosen your puppy have a vet check its health immediately.

Below Make your new puppy feel welcome in your home by having everything ready for it before it comes to live with you.

A new puppy in a new home

Before you take your puppy home you should already have some things ready for it – its own bed or a rug to snuggle into, its own food and water bowls, a collar with an identity tag and a leash.

Are you ready for the new arrival?

- Where will it sleep?
- Where will it eat?
- Where will it be allowed to go in the house?
- Where is off-limits?
- Is the garden or yard escape-proof?

Your puppy is going to miss its mum a lot when it first comes home with you. It is also going to be a confusing time for it. 'Where has mum gone? What has happened to my brothers and sisters? Who are these big people who want to cuddle me all the time?'

Let your puppy get settled into your home by letting it explore the room a bit. Show it its new bed or rug and give your puppy a little time to itself until it feels more confident. If you have other animals in the house, or younger brothers or sisters, then introduce them to the new arrival but do not leave them alone together yet.

If your puppy does not settle down to sleep for the first few nights, then a ticking alarm clock or a radio left on very low will be a comfort. Make sure that the alarm is not set or your puppy will be woken up with a shock!

Dog beds

Your dog's bed is very important to it because it is usually the only place in the house that is the dog's own. Where you put your dog's bed is also important. Dogs are **pack** animals and your family becomes its adoptive pack so it will prefer to be able to see the family from its bed. It should also to be out of the way of trampling feet so that it can get some peace and quiet as well! Make sure that the bed is not in a draught.

The bed, whether it is a basket, rug, mat or dog beanbag should be big enough for your adult dog to circle around in before settling down.

You can put an old towel in the basket or newspaper under the dog's rug or beanbag. Changing the newspaper and washing the towel regularly will help keep the dog's sleeping area clean. The bedding should be aired (shaken outside) every day and washed and dried thoroughly once a week.

Never let your dog get into the habit of sleeping on the furniture or the family's beds. This will spread dirt and fleas (see page 28).

Outdoor kennels

If you have a garden that is totally escape-proof then a kennel might be a good idea. You can buy them ready-made or, if you are good at woodwork, you could build one.

The kennel should be big enough for your adult dog to stand up in, turn around and lie down in comfortably.

It should have a slanted roof which overlaps the walls so that rain and snow will run away.

The floor should be 10 cm off the ground to avoid rising damp.

The dog's entrance should be on the side of the kennel not on the end – so that the dog has a corner of the kennel which will not have the wind and rain coming in. A timber-framed kennel may need lining boards inside for extra insulation. It is also a good idea to have a hinged roof that can be propped open in very hot weather.

Remember that you will have to clean out the kennel. If you cannot reach all the corners make sure there is a door you can open so that you can get to them.

Below It is hard work to make your own kennel.

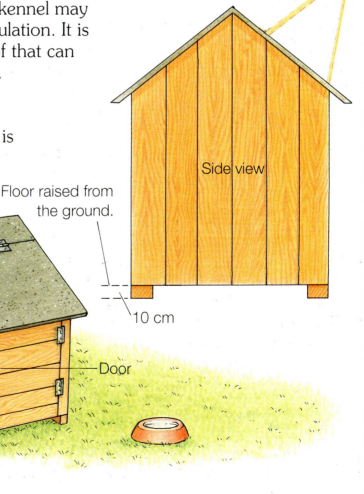

Hinged roof

Side view

Floor raised from the ground.

10 cm

Door

Entrance

Ramp

Feeding your dog

If you got your puppy from a breeder then he or she might have given you a detailed daily menu for your puppy. Sometimes they are very complicated and even I have been puzzled – and I'm a vet who is supposed to know about these things! They can be helpful as a general guide but ask your vet for his or her advice.

Puppies and dogs need a balanced diet. This means that they should get enough protein (from meat) for growth and strength, carbohydrates (from meal or dog biscuits) and fat to give your dog energy. Also vitamins and minerals, like calcium, are important to keep bones and muscles healthy. If you want to work out a fresh food diet or a vegetarian (non-meat) diet for your dog then *always* go to your vet for proper advice. I find that tinned food is very good for most dogs, but remember to add dog meal or biscuits.

You should follow the manufacturer's instructions, but as a guide for amounts that are suitable for your dog see the box on page 21.

Right All dogs have good appetites and really enjoy their food. This English Setter is certainly enjoying its bowl of food, isn't it?

A simple guide to feeding adult dogs tinned food

Breed:	Toy	Small	Medium	Large	Giant
Example:	Chihuahua	Fox Terrier	Bulldog	Retriever	St Bernard
Weight:	2 kg	7.5 kg	20 kg	30 kg	72 kg
Tins per day:	¼	½-1	1-1½	1½-2	2-3

Most tins of dog food weigh about 400 g. You should add an equal amount of mixer biscuits each day to balance your dog's diet.

Your puppy and dog should have fresh drinking water available to it at all times.

You should get your dog used to regular feeding times as soon as possible. Puppies have small stomachs and need to have several small feeds a day. Once they have been weaned you should gradually stop giving them cow's milk as this can upset their stomachs – but make sure that you give your puppy calcium tablets instead.

As the puppy grows older get it used to having the regular one or two meals a day – which will depend on the type of dog it is (see the box below).

Never give your dog chicken or lamb bones because they splinter, and never give them cooked bones. It is probably best not to give bones to your dog at all.

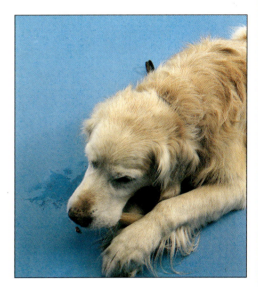

Above Give your dog special dog chews from the pet shop instead of bones.

Feeding times

Size:	Example:	Feed:	Amount:
Giant breeds	Great Dane	Twice a day	½ the daily amount in the morning and ½ in the evening.
Large and medium-sized breeds	German Shepherd Dog	Once a day	Daily amount in the evening.
Small, toy breeds and older dogs	West Highland Terrier	Twice a day	½ the daily amount in the morning and ½ in the evening.

Training your dog

It is never too early to start training your dog.

Most people start with **house-training**. House-training takes time and patience. Puppies have tiny bladders and they also find bowel control a bit of a problem. Lay down newspaper in your puppy's living area. Get it to go to the toilet on the newspaper only. Gradually reduce the area covered in newspaper and you should find that your puppy has got the idea that it must go to the toilet in only one area – eventually that is a litter tray or in the garden. If you find a mess somewhere else do not blow your top! A puppy cannot tell the difference between you being very angry or very happy. So if you do not watch out you will be encouraging just the sort of behaviour you want to stop.

Collars and leads

By the time your puppy is three months old it should wear a gentle, soft leather collar all the time. As your dog gets older it is probably a good idea to use a **choke chain**. Used properly, these collars put you very much in control of your pet. I find a lot of over-active dogs can be easily controlled using a **head collar**. All dogs should wear a collar of some sort and it is a very good idea to make sure your name and address is attached to it on a dog tag. Then your dog can be reunited with you if it gets lost.

All dogs should be trained to walk quietly on a lead and kept on your left side when out walking. It is a good idea always to have an adult with you to make sure that you and your pet are safe.

Head collar

Left Taking your dog for a walk is lots of fun. Make sure that you train your dog to stop and wait at road kerbs. You can join dog training clubs to make sure that you are able to control your dog so that both of you keep safe.

Your dog will soon start to respond to simple commands like 'sit' and 'heel'. Once your puppy has had all its vaccinations why not join a local dog training club? It is great fun and remember that one day a simple command like 'stop' might well save your dog's life if it is just about to race out in front of a car.

Choke chain

Grooming
Grooming gets the dust and dirt out of your dog's coat. Long-haired breeds, such as the Old English Sheepdog, need daily grooming to keep their coats free of tangles. In fact most breeds can do with a good brush-up nearly every day to keep them looking smart. Your grooming kit should have a towel, dog nail clippers and combs for long-haired breeds, brushes for medium-length fur and wire brushes for short-haired dogs.

Occasionally you may even need to bath your dog. Use special dog shampoo and make sure the suds do not get into the dog's ears or eyes.

Below Most dogs love having their coats brushed.

Breeding your dog

There are so many unwanted puppies about these days that most vets will try to discourage you from breeding if possible.

Bitches come into **season** (or 'on heat') twice a year. Spring and autumn are the usual times. A season lasts about three weeks and as there is quite a bit of bloody discharge it is not surprising many people find it a messy nuisance. Neutering your bitch will stop her having seasons. Male dogs find bitches on heat irresistible and often camp outside the house, so make sure your bitch is kept inside or out of harm's way until she has finished her season.

Bitches can be neutered or **spayed** by the vet any time from about five months old. Spaying stops unwanted **pregnancies**, false pregnancies (that is when your dog thinks she is a mum even though she is not) and often stops unpleasant growths developing when she is older.

Neutering your dog

Unless you are hoping to show your dog or breed from it then it makes very good sense to have it neutered. It is a very simple operation and does not harm your bitch or dog at all.

Below A male and female Labrador during their courtship before they mate.

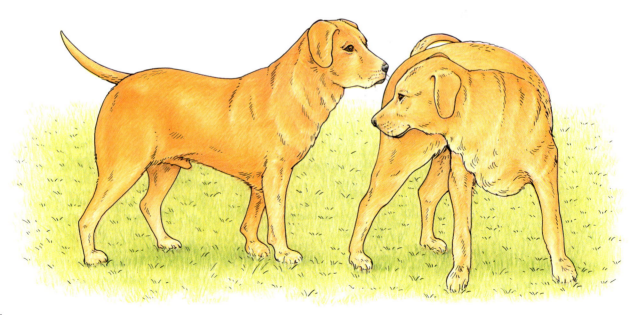

Pregnancy and young

A bitch that has mated is pregnant for about nine weeks. The bitch will start to put on weight after three or four weeks and her **nipples** start to stand out and go pink. Ask your vet to check her, as many bitches do have false pregnancies.

For most bitches whelping (or giving birth) is straightforward. Some get into difficulty though and your vet is there to give help if needed.

Some bitches, such as Rottweillers, have large litters of eight or more pups. Smaller breeds, such as the Cavalier King Charles Spaniel, may only have four or five pups. So whelping can be over quite quickly or take several hours.

Do not panic if the puppies are not born to the sort of regular timetable most books about whelping give. Puppies do not read and so they tend to be born when they want to and not before.

Above These Border Collie puppies are just two days old. The new mother and family look very peaceful and content, don't they?

A bitch will whelp best if left quietly alone – let her choose a place she feels safe and secure in. Do not invite the whole street in to watch; it will put mum off and she will take ages to have her pups.

Always get the vet to check over mum and her puppies a day or so after the pups have been born. Remember that you have to have all the puppies vaccinated. Your vet will advise you.

Now all that is left to be done is for you to find the puppies good, kind homes and keep mother and puppies safe and warm until the pups are weaned from their mother's milk.

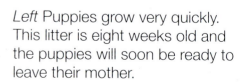

Left Puppies grow very quickly. This litter is eight weeks old and the puppies will soon be ready to leave their mother.

Keeping your dog healthy

Worming

Almost all puppies are born with worms. These are parasites inside your puppy's body which will make it very sick if you do not get rid of them. Your vet will give you some medicine to give to your puppy. I usually worm puppies every two weeks between the ages of eight to twelve weeks.

Major dog diseases

Distemper is very unpleasant. This virus causes lots of problems like diarrhoea (loose droppings), chest infections and sometimes fits. A sign of distemper is that the pads of the dog's paws thicken and go very tough.

Hepatitis is a serious disease which affects dogs' livers.

Another serious disease is leptospirosis which affects dogs' kidneys.

Keeping your dog healthy

- Vaccinate it against the major dog diseases every year.
- Feed it a good, balanced diet.
- Do not let it get fat.
- Exercise it every day.
- Check its teeth are clean and free from infection.
- Make sure your vet sees it regularly for a check-up.
- Wash it in special dog shampoos from the vet to keep its coat clean and free of **parasites**.
- Worm it frequently.
- Vitamin supplements are often very helpful.
- Give it plenty of love, affection and companionship.

Parainfluenza is one of the viruses which causes kennel cough – a rasping, harsh cough which is spread when dogs are kept together.

Parvovirus is a disease which can cause death through severe vomiting and diarrhoea.

All of these diseases can be prevented by having your puppy vaccinated and given the yearly 'booster injections' to keep up the level of protection.

Ears

Some dog breeds which have floppy ears, such as the Cocker Spaniel, always seem to have problems with their ears. Floppy ears pick up more dust and dirt than upright ears. There are also mites (parasites) that live in the lining of the ear which can irritate the skin. Your vet will be able to give you ear drops to clear up the infection. He or she will also be able to check if your dog has picked up anything else, like a grass seed, and take it out. Do not go poking about in there yourself though — a dog's ears are very sensitive.

Hip Dysplasia

Some breeds of dog, such as the German Shepherd and the Golden Retriever, are prone to this problem. The hips become misshapen, which causes discomfort and arthritis later on in life.

Fleas

All dogs suffer from fleas, I'm afraid. Fleas bite into the skin and make it very itchy and sensitive. When you are grooming your dog, remember to use a flea spray or powder. You could also buy your dog a flea collar. I would also use the flea powder when cleaning your dog's bed and kennel. Everything helps in the daily battle against fleas. This is war!

When grooming your dog, dust it with flea powder or flea spray.

Upset stomachs

Vomiting and diarrhoea is a common problem. If your dog is sick then do not feed it for one day. Then on the next day feed it very plain food, such as a little boiled fish or chicken with rice, for five more days. If your dog does not improve or there are signs of blood in the vomit or diarrhoea then go to your vet immediately.

Eyes

If your dog's eyes become red and sore then it is likely to have conjunctivitis. This is an infection which makes the skin around the eye very itchy. Your vet will be able to give your dog some ointment or eye drops.

PRA

Progressive retinal atrophy, or PRA, is a disease which affects the eyes and gradually makes a dog go blind.

Your vet

What with vaccinations, booster injections and ear infections you will be seeing a lot of your local vet. He or she will be glad to give you any advice and tips you need. If your vet gives you medicines to give to your dog, ask him or her to show you exactly what you have to do. Getting a dog to take its tablets is a tricky business!

I hope you have fun with your pet. Your dog will be your best friend for all of its life.

Glossary

Booster injections The yearly injections which vaccinate dogs against diseases they can pick up from other dogs, like distemper. The vaccination does not last for ever so your dog needs a boost or top-up of the protection.

Breed clubs The organizations which have formed with members who own or breed a particular breed or type of dog, for example the American Cocker Spaniel Club.

Breeding The mating of a male and female dog to produce puppies.

Breeds The many different types of dog. Each breed can be recognized because of very strong features, such as the pointed nose of the Greyhound.

Crossbreed The type of puppy which comes from the mating of two different purebred breeds of dog.

Choke chain A type of link-chain collar which is used to control your dog. It needs to be fixed correctly so that you can give one swift tug at the chain to stop your dog pulling, but then the collar loosens again. Beware that it does not really choke!

Head collar A type of collar which also has straps that fix over your dog's head and face.

Hereditary Something which is passed from one generation of dog to another. It can be a good feature or a bad health problem.

House-training Teaching your puppy only to go to the toilet in a litter tray or outside the home.

Kennel Club, the A major dog-owners and dog club organization in Britain. Most countries have an organization like the Kennel Club which is the best authority on dog care and information on breeding and breeders of purebred dogs.

Leash Another word for a lead which is fixed on to your dog's collar when you take it for a walk.

Litter A group of young puppies.

Mate Male and female dogs mate to produce puppies.

Mongrel A dog which has a very mixed family background – at least three different breeds.

Neutered The operation that a vet performs which stops dogs being able to produce young. It is called castration for male dogs and spaying for female (bitch) dogs.

Nipples Also called teats, these are the two rows of slightly raised flesh which run along the belly of your bitch. Puppies drink their mother's milk through these teats.

Offal The organs of dead animals which are used as food. Although many dogs love to have helpings of liver, kidney or heart it can be bad for them.

Pack A group of dogs which live and hunt together.

Parasites Animals which live on other animals' bodies.

Pedigree A dog whose family's history has a long line of purebred dogs of the same breed.

Pregnancies When female dogs are carrying litters of puppies inside their bodies.

R.S.P.C.A. The Royal Society for the Prevention of Cruelty to Animals. A leading British animal welfare organization.

Season The period of time when a female dog (bitch) is ready to start a litter if a male dog mates with her during this time.

Spayed When a female dog has been neutered so that she cannot produce any puppies.

Trained When a dog has been taught to obey your commands.

Vaccinations The series of injections which put a weakened form of a disease into your puppy and dog which will stop your pet from getting the full-blown disease.

Weaned When a puppy has stopped taking its mother's milk and is eating solid foods.

Further reading

For younger readers:
All About Dogs, by Katherine Tottenham (Ward Lock, 1986)
Care for your Dog, by Tina Hearne (Collins, 1985)
My First Puppy, by Nigel Taylor (Firefly Books, 1991)

For older readers:
Dogs (Know Your Pet series) by Anna and Michael Sproule (Wayland, 1988)
The Going Live! Pet Book, by Nigel Taylor (BBC Books, 1989)
The Ultimate Dog Book, by David Taylor (Dorling Kindersley, 1990)

Useful addresses

American Society for the Prevention of Cruelty to Animals (A.S.P.C.A.), 441 E. 92nd Street, New York, NY 10028, USA
The Kennel Club, 1-4 Clarges Street, Piccadilly, London, W1Y 8AB, England
National Canine Defence League, 6a Pratt Street, London, NW1, England

The Royal Society for the Prevention of Cruelty to Animals (R.S.P.C.A.), The Manor House, Horsham, West Sussex RH12 1HG, England
The Toronto Humane Society, 11 River Street, Toronto, Ontario, M5A 4C2, Canada

Index

Picture acknowledgements

Bruce Coleman Ltd/(J Burton) 25, 26/(F Prenzel) 15/(H Reinhard) 10; Frank Lane Picture Agency/
(S Kerscher/Silvestris) 13/(J Watkins) 9 (bottom); Oxford Scientific Films Ltd/(L E Lauber) 12/
(R Pearcy/Animals Animals) 9 (top)/(B Osborne) 7/(S Osolinski) 6; Tony Stone Worldwide/*cover*,
title page, 14, 16, 20, 23 (top); WPL/(Z Mukhida) 5, 21, 23 (bottom), 28.

FOCUS ON DANCE XII

Dance in Higher Education

Wendy Oliver
Editor

A Project of the
National Dance Association

An Association of the
**American Alliance for Health,
Physical Education, Recreation and Dance**

Editor's Note on Focus on Dance XII

This monograph, *Dance in Higher Education*, was compiled during 1991. A Call for Papers was made public over a six-month period, and the deadline for submissions was January 31, 1991. Papers submitted were then blind-reviewed by a panel of four highly qualified readers from the field of dance in higher education. I wish to thank these readers for their time, dedication, and insight. This volume would not have been possible without them.
Wendy Oliver, Editor

COVER CREDIT: Mark Wheeler teaches a dance class in
the Department of Health, Physical Education,
Recreation and Dance, University of Georgia, Athens.

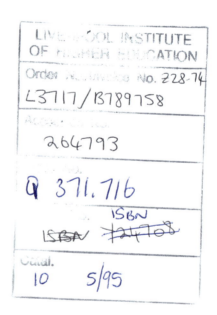

Contents

Introduction

Wendy Oliver

Brief Historical Overview of Dance in Higher Education

It has been a little over a century since the earliest dance programs were established in higher education in the United States. Since that time, dance in higher education has seen tremendous growth and change. Each era of university dance education since 1887 had a dominant issue, or issues, around which educators rallied. The record of these concerns has been kept in the publications of their respective times.

1887–1900

Most dance educators associate the year 1926 with Margaret H'Doubler's great accomplishment of establishing the first dance major in higher education at the University of Wisconsin, Madison. However, fewer of us are aware that in 1887, Dudley Sargent established the Harvard Summer School, a normal school which included dance within its physical education program. This school and others like it were established for the sole purpose of physical education preparation for female teachers; although men taught the courses, only women took them. The rationale for including dance (called dancing calisthenics or aesthetic dancing) in the curriculum stressed grace, manners, and physical fitness (O'Brien, 1966).

However, grace and fitness were not the only qualities valued during this time. The influence of Francois Delsarte's ideas of expressiveness through movement were strongly felt at the Harvard program, and this notion was "at the leading edge of ideas about dance" (O'Brien, p. 216).

1900–1930

1905 was the first year dance was the main subject of discussion at the conference of the American Physical Education Association. It was also the year when seven articles about dance appeared in the physical education literature. Henry Taylor, in his article "The Dancing Foot," said:

> . . . the new dancing must be hygienic; it
> must be gymnastic; it must be recreative; it
> must be expressive and it must illustrate the
> highest standards of beauty. (in O'Brien, p. 218)

Educator Luther Gulick was leading the reform of physical education for children, advocating dance as a beneficial and necessary activity (Chapman, 1974) and was the first educator to write a book about dance (O'Brien, 1966). During the years between 1905 and 1917, folk dance became popular in higher education, co-existing with aesthetic dancing. This was a change toward social rather than personal expression. Meanwhile, Isadora Duncan was performing in Europe, but her work did not appear to directly affect dance education at that time (O'Brien). In 1915, Jacques Dalcroze's eurythmics, or music interpretation, came to the fore in dance education. The importance of expressiveness in dance eclipsed the notion of physical fitness or grace.

During the years 1918–1932, dance expanded significantly through the "new" physical education, which valued what was natural, expressive, and educational. The center of activity was Teachers College, Columbia University, where Gertrude Colby created and taught "natural dance," based on her synthesis of ideas from Duncan and Dalcroze (Chapman, 1974). It was at Teachers College that Margaret H'Doubler was trained.

H'Doubler's dance major, established under the auspices of the Physical Education Department at the University of Wisconsin, stressed creativity and personal growth, founded on a biological understanding of the body. Although she called her style "interpretive dance," it was actually a part of the emergence of what became modern dance, which rejected both ballet and aesthetic dance (Chapman, 1974).

Also during the late twenties, dance educators attended the performances of Martha Graham,

1

Doris Humphrey, and other artists, and enrolled in their courses. The teachings of these great dancers then began to permeate the schools. Communication through dance became the byword. However, not all educators agreed that an artist-based approach was appropriate in an educational setting (O'Brien, 1966).

1930–1950

The National Section on Dance was established in 1932, as a part of the American Physical Education Association, and signaled an effort by dance educators to determine what dance in education should be. The purpose of the Dance Section, as stated by Chair Mary O'Donnell, was

> . . . to promote the constructive develop-
> ment of all types of dance in education, and
> to provide the leadership essential to the
> success of such a program. It aims to serve
> all school levels and all non-school groups
> as well. (in O'Brien, 1966, p. 208)

The thirties brought about a period of consolidation and strengthening of the ties between professional artists and dance educators. Modern dance was seen as a vehicle for the physical, mental, emotional, and social development of the student, thus legitimizing its place in an educational setting. Although modern dance was dominant in higher education, tap, folk, square, and ballroom were also taught; there was disagreement as to the value of ballet (Griffith, 1975).

During the forties, WWII slowed but did not stop the development of dance in higher education. After the war, the Bennington program founded by Martha Hill moved to Connecticut College, where artists such as Martha Graham, Doris Humphrey, Hanya Holm, Erick Hawkins, and Jose Limon were on the faculty. H'Doubler's views on dance continued to be taught across the country, and Rudolph Laban and Aileen Lockhart each published influential books. Dance programs were almost always housed in physical education departments, which varied in their commitment to dance.

Walter Terry, dance editor for the *New York Herald-Tribune*, published a report on dance in higher education in 1948. While modern dance, folk, and square dance were on the upswing, tap and ballroom declined somewhat (Griffith, 1975). The need for a strong dance pedagogy generated efforts to create a framework that would prove useful to all educators, whether in dance, physical education, or general education (Evan, in Chapman, 1974).

1950–1980

In the fifties and early sixties, a major focus was the location of dance programs within the university setting. Many programs initially considered becoming departments on their own, later deciding that such action would be impractical. Soon after, dance educators expressed conflict over moving into fine arts areas versus remaining in physical education. The resolution of this issue was that

> . . . dance was an autonomous discipline
> and must stand on its own feet, hopefully
> maintaining good relations with all its asso-
> ciated areas. This did not mean that most
> dance programs went out of physical edu-
> cation, but that the position had been
> finally accepted intellectually, and the trend
> was in the direction of autonomy wherever
> dance was located. (Griffith, 1975, p. 331)

Merce Cunningham and Alwin Nikolais emphasized nonliteral dance, and as they toured college campuses with their companies, their ideas began to be reflected in the curriculum. Creativity was stressed.

In 1965, the Nation Section on Dance in AAHPER became the Dance Division, mirroring the trend toward autonomy in higher education. Dance programs continued to migrate out of physical education, and by 1973, only 50 percent of all dance programs in higher education remained in physical education departments (Stanich, 1981).

Many publications on modern and recreational dance appeared in the 1960s, including Alma Hawkins' *Creating Through Dance* (1964). However, older texts continued to be popular. According to a survey by Fannie Melcer (1970), three of the most used dance texts at that time were Curt Sachs's *World History of the Dance* (1937), Margaret H'Doubler's *Dance: A Creative Art Experience* (1940), and Doris Humphrey's *The Art of Making Dances* (1959). The academic aspect of dance began to be recognized when philosopher Suzanne Langer wrote about dance as an art form in the late 1960s.

There was great concern about the lack of research in dance. Educators became aware that without a body of research and publications, their field would not be highly regarded by the rest of the academic community. In addition to voicing its concern about research, the Dance Division also pointed to three other problems of the time: "training quality teachers, getting men into the field, and establishing dance as a discipline on all campuses" (Griffith, 1975).

An issue of concern during the sixties and seventies was the disagreement over what styles of modern dance technique should be taught in colleges. There were factions who espoused the "old-fashioned" techniques of Graham and Humphrey, and others who preferred the approach of Cunningham or Nikolais. During this time, according to researcher Diana Stanich,

> the literature indicated that an effective dance major should include a variety of dance forms. The problem lies in dance faculty being trained in only one specialty of dance, or trained in only theoretical or historical aspects of dance. The findings from this study suggest training teachers of dance to teach at least three types of dance. Some dance programs solved this problem by having professional dancers to teach workshops in specific dance forms. (1981, p. 157)

Another issue was that of academic degree requirements. Many professional dancers were teaching within higher education without the "proper credentials." This continued to be problematic in the eighties and was linked to the notion that dancers should be taught the academic side of dance, as well as technique and composition. The issue of research continued to be debated, with some educators feeling that all creative efforts should be directed toward performance and choreography and others feeling the need or desire to legitimize the field through publications (Stanich, 1981).

For students aspiring to perform, it was generally accepted that professional studios, not colleges, were the best places to train. Most dance programs up through the early 1970s believed that the main focus of dance in higher education was to train teachers, not performers, although there were some exceptions to this rule (Stanich, 1981).

Ethnic and jazz dance became more visible on campuses during the seventies, and ballet gained reacceptance as the decades-long feud between ballet and modern dance died down. Dance anthropology, dance therapy, and dance exercise became a part of college education.

1980–1991

Since the early eighties, ballroom, folk, and tap dance have continued to thrive, and jazz dance has zoomed to popularity; however, modern dance and ballet have continued to form the core of dance programs. More dance programs have been geared toward training professional dancers than ever before; however, there is an awareness that dancers must prepare for a "second career" (Collins-Head, 1987).

"Multiculturalism" became an important issue, the thrust of which is that dance education must begin to seriously incorporate dance concepts and styles from many cultures if it is to remain relevant to future student bodies. As it stands now, most dance programs are centered around modern dance, generally a white, middle-or-upper-middle class art form that does not necessarily reflect the values of other cultures. Since minorities in the United States will become more and more prevalent, dance educators have noted that it is important to create dance education that takes into account different frames of reference.

Hiring, tenure and promotion, and gaining legitimacy and recognition in academe have continued to be viewed as problematic. As "degree inflation" has taken hold, colleges and universities have upped their hiring requirements, some as high as the doctorate, for jobs that are primarily teaching service classes. The struggle to equate creative work with publications continues in faculty bids for tenure and promotion. Even at universities where creative work is accepted in rank and tenure decisions, the standards by which this work is judged are not always clearly defined.

Issues for the 1990s

The subjects chosen for this issue of *Focus on Dance* reflect the current concerns of its authors, and by inference of higher educators across the country. It is interesting to note that many contemporary concerns in the field actually have precursors in earlier times.

The discussion of what constitutes an appropriate education in dance at the college level (certainly an ongoing theme through the decades) is the focus of four papers. Edrie Ferdun writes about the current roles and future directions of dance in higher education, explaining her vision of a discipline that would recommit to social concerns as part of its overall mission. Betsey Gibbons advocates moving away from compartmentalization and technical training to embrace a more pluralistic framework. Lynn Matluck Brooks discusses the situation particular to dance in the small, liberal arts college. Jan Van Dyke reacts against the "conservatory approach" in dance training that effectively cuts dancers off from many of their intellectual capacities. All of these authors are suggesting that a holistic approach be considered—one that exposes students to more than "dance training."

Quality teacher education was mentioned as a strong concern for the National Section on Dance in the 1960s. Here, it is discussed by three authors who still see room for improvement. Sylvie Fortin calls for consistency among technical, conceptual, and pedagogical knowledge in teaching dance. Karen Clemente writes that dance education degree programs have actually *declined* in number in the recent past, and speculates on the possible causes behind this trend. Francine Lee Morin stresses the need for a discipline-based approach to teacher education carried out through inservice teachers.

Tied to the theme of multiculturalism is Julie Kerr's paper on Afrocentric dance. Kerr points out the strong influence that African-American dance has had on the history of dance in this country and suggests ways for incorporating this information into the curriculum. John Crawford asserts that integration among the arts promotes a better understanding of dance composition. He has designed an approach for improving aesthetic literacy through the combined study of art, music, and dance.

College and adult beginners are the subject of four papers. Susan Gillis-Kruman discusses her strategies for studio classes based on principles of learning. Gail Lee Abrams has introduced "self-teaching" into her technique classes with excellent results. Carol Soleau describes the particular challenges in working with adult-beginner ballet students, sharing with the reader her own personal design for teaching. Eleanor Weisman talks of her experience at the University of North Dakota and how she was able to involve the university community in dance.

In the area of teaching choreography, Carol Press takes a historical view of the dichotomy that has occurred between process and craft, and urges composition teachers to examine the philosophies underlying their curricula. Larry Lavender suggests that "Did you like it?" is an inappropriate question for composition class and carefully outlines an alternate way of proceeding.

Finally, faculty issues were the focus of three authors. Jessica Wood writes about the problems of tenure and promotion. Erlyne Whiteman presents her survey on dance administrators, and Kelley Pierce-Byrd discusses mentoring among dance faculty members.

References

Chapman, S. (1974). *Movement education in the United States*. Philadelphia: Movement Education Publications.

Collins-Head, S. (1987). *Theoretical foundations of dance in higher education from 1975–1985*. Master's thesis, California State University at Long Beach.

Griffith, B. R. (1975). *Theoretical foundations of dance in higher education in the United States: 1933–1965*. Doctoral dissertation, University of Southern California.

Melcer, F. H. (1970). Three surveys of dance resource material. *Journal of Health, Physical Education, Recreation, 41*(2), 87–88.

O'Brien, D. A. (1966). *Theoretical foundations of dance in American higher education: 1885–1932*. Doctoral dissertation, University of Southern California.

Stanich, D. (1981). *Theoretical foundations of dance in higher education in the United States from 1965–1974*. Master's thesis, California State University at Long Beach.

**Wendy Oliver served as editor for this issue of *Focus on Dance*.
She is a professor at Providence College,
Providence, Rhode Island 02918.**

Current Perspectives:
Overviews of the Field

Dance in Higher Education: Out of the Picture or Into the Fray?

Edrie Ferdun

The status of dance in the colleges and universities cannot really be separated from the status of higher education, the society, and the world in which we live. In fact, it is in the chill climate of war, economic recession, and suspect values that questions about the relative importance and position of dance in higher education now present themselves. As a means of participating in the stock taking that is going on across the country, the following questions are posed. How rooted and sturdy is the institutionalization of dance in higher education? Whose needs are being served? What functions and affiliations now characterize dance in higher education? How satisfactory are they in relation to higher education and the society as we attempt to understand them today? All of us inside the field of dance must surely spend some time reading our situations and looking for what might be the handwriting on the wall or the crack that signals new hope. Although each of us faces a unique setting, perhaps we sense the times together. The observations I share can be tested against yours. The process may help in finding the next steps toward the future of dance in higher education.

Institutionalization

The 1990s see dance institutionalized more fully than at any time in the history of higher education in this country. It is represented in courses, programs, and majors leading to undergraduate and graduate degrees, including the doctoral degree. This fact, however, is still noteworthy. Dance, unlike mathematics or philosophy, is not a subject automatically assumed to be a necessary constituent in academe. Dance performance has found expression and a degree of public attention and support in many colleges and universities. The other arts and athletics are more prominent, but dance is viewed as a legitimate art and a viable avenue to the community. In many parts of the country college dance productions represent the only opportunities for experiencing live dance performance. Inside the academic institution dance has developed research, service, and programmatic relationships and affiliations with a variety of departments. Core requirements in the arts and humanities that include dance have tended to move dance a little closer to the mainstream of educational consideration. Dance faculty and their work in teaching, research, creative production, or service appear to have achieved full standing in most institutions.

Although one must certainly conclude that dance is present, the question of its relative vulnerability is unanswered. The recency of its establishment may make it easiest to root out. There are a limited number of tenured faculty commitments, and it has not been tested philosophically and practically during various kinds of social stress. As well as being young, dance is marginal in its lack of traditional support and affiliation with higher status departments in the university. Outside higher education, and sometimes within, dance still carries controversy and suspicion in its association with the body, sexuality, and nondominant cultural groups. Its primary clientele is female. On the other hand, it is these groups who have animated the culture in recent years, including higher education and scholarship.

A conservative climate would seem to speak for either maintaining what has already been built or somehow reducing it in keeping with earlier and presumably more essential definitions of the university. A more proactive position might see dance as a source of vitality and seek to redefine and perhaps redeploy it toward purposes it now only suggests but has great capacity to address, such as multiculturalism.

7

Populations Served

One of the themes of scholars in the 1980s had to do with the political nature of knowledge, methods, and goals. Throughout all processes of perception, language and action locations and implications related to power are relevant. How this works in our everyday lives can sometimes be obscure, but someone in dance does not need much prodding to talk about the role of essentially political factors in the status of dance as a field. One of the facts that has been critical to the birth and growth of dance in higher education has been that women make up the primary, sometimes exclusive, population served by dance classes, programs, and professional enterprises. In H'Doubler's book, *The Dance and Its Place in Education* (1925), it is interesting to find a foreword written by F. Louise Nardin, dean of women at the University of Wisconsin at Madison. Presumably her support played a role in the accomplishment of the first dance major in that period. Nardin spoke exclusively of women's education in her rationale for dance. The alliance among women, often in women's colleges or in sex separated departments of physical education, generated the power to propel dance through its first stages.

In 1925, unlike 1991, the force of women was clearly circumscribed; unique opportunities for collective expression came together in the symbolic worlds of sport and dance. As women have become more integrated into the assumptions and activities of higher education, the role of dean of women has faded and most colleges and departments are not explicitly identified as male or female. The current affirmative action officers and special services designed for women and women's studies departments appear not to have agendas that include dance or dancers. There has been remarkable silence from women's studies in the realm of dance. Conferences and workshops, even in the arts, are repeatedly held with little or no coverage of dance. Like dance, which had to work very hard to define itself as a discipline and professional field distinct from the populations most involved in it, so women's studies seems to need to define itself in terms of the most recognized, potent, and explicitly useful departments and functions in higher education. Unless dance academics strive hard to construe dance into frameworks understandable and appreciated by the articulate and energetic leaders affiliated with women's studies, there is little to expect in the way of automatic support for dance from organized bodies of women on campus.

Although the dance profession may understand that it continues to have a role as a change agent and symbol for women's opportunities, achievements, and dreams of cultural transformation, there is little momentum from which to build. It is in the context of African-American studies where the surge toward dance seems now to have deep and social reasons. Beyond multicultural concerns, there is a dance, art, communication imperative in African-American culture that speaks for itself, and needs to be heard and appreciated. Dance in higher education is just beginning to address those who see and experience dance in its cultural roles and who seek to make visible and powerful the legacies and visions of their communities. The dance Nardin supported in 1925 was not only assumed to be for women, but was associated with "higher qualities," "good music," and the absence of "individual self-striving" (H'Doubler, p. xiii, xiv). How lingering is this elite concept in the institutional setting? Modern dance has worked its way toward multiple definitions. Various kinds of democratization have taken place, but the whole field of dance as a subject matter, method, and cultural practice needs to alert itself to factors that may bear on its definition, access, and appreciation. Race, social class, ethnic, political, and sexual orientations may be classifications that need special study not only to fill out the picture of who is being served in dance in higher education but also to ensure against the preclusion or promotion of particular groups or ideas simply by virtue of the unexamined traditions of the history of dance in higher education.

Functions and Affiliations

Although there are issues of power, social context, and historical moments and figures, these need to be seen in their translation into the functions, programs, and working units that make up our current enterprise. Dance in connection with physical education has a long history of concern for the well-being of students in colleges and universities. The need for activity, as such, and the basis for valued accomplishment have made studio work the most fundamental ground for thinking about dance in higher education. Professional dance artists, leading choreographers, and dancers outside higher education have been an integral and inspirational part of shaping the dance activities to the art of the times. It was Alma Hawkins who acknowledged the diverse and sometimes divisive energies of artists and teachers in the colleges and

Ballet students in the dance program at Kent State University's School of Physical Education, Recreation and Dance. Developing dance artists and dance art in relation to other arts has become a primary function of dance programs in higher education. *Photo by University Photographers.*

responded by placing dance clearly in the middle of the important educational thinking of the time in her book, *Modern Dance in Higher Education* (1954). Dance as a comprehensive subject was not assumed; college programs meant dancing experiences and creative experiences for a range of learners.

Continuing development toward the performing arts, however, is readily apparent today in our BFA and MFA programs. Developing dance artists and dance art in relation to other arts has become a primary function. Hannah Wiley, in an article in the *Chronicle of Higher Education* (1989), sees this function as having been our dominant agenda and makes a case for further development and integration of dance programs with the professional world. Bringing professional dance into greater relation to university programs seems laudible, but seeing the arts establishment as the primary or

exclusive ground with which to articulate needs to be questioned. MFA programs dream and work for a world where artists are valued and rewarded in some adequate measure for their contributions. Federal, state, charitable, and university support is very basic to this assumption; the current economic situation inspires little confidence.

While dance was booming as a performing art in recent decades, the institution of education and other more service oriented fields have undergone various kinds of decline. Colleges of education and professional preparation programs have often found themselves having to retreat and defend. Karen Clemente (1990) found in a national survey, which included 134 college and university departments, that many had discontinued their dance education degree programs because of limited job opportunities in public schools. The philosophy and practice of dance education, however, was still

9

considered important and 77 percent of the responding schools offered courses. The majority also danced for the public schools while interacting in only minor ways related to more fundamental programmatic exchange. Dance preparation in the context of physical education persists in some form, even though the connection to dance departments cannot be assumed. The Clemente survey corroborates the impression that the physical education curriculum in the public schools is the largest purveyor of dance.

There has, of course, been significant movement toward dance specialists and dance certification across the country, but progressive institutionalization remains to be seen. Positive development along this line has profound implications for dance in higher education. Despite the significant leadership from many dance educators in colleges and universities, it is not clear to what extent dance in higher education seeks to affiliate itself with education or with the social agenda that seeks to renovate and revitalize the nation's schools and children. Is dance strong enough as a subject matter and performing art in higher education to allow the kind of participation, commitment, and contribution that it might want to provide? Who will pay the bills for investing in the future of education? Are the affiliations with other arts educators, physical educators, and mainstream education sufficiently developed to predict a way for dance to work?

The commercialization of much of what in the past had been associated with public institutions has created for dance a wider marketplace within which to understand itself. Although I am not aware of dance programs shifting markedly toward preparation for exercise, aerobics, and fitness centers or toward media, advertising, and other businesses using dance as a matter of course, it is apparent that dance majors have a variety of new part-time jobs and interests. The exercise science industry, the focus on performance enhancement, and the role of technology in creating shoes and devices of economic consequence has changed the context of dance in society. Affiliation with the sciences, professionally in the form of dance science, begins again to take dance in the direction of its original relationships in the colleges, that is, with the health and medically oriented field of physical education. This time, however, it is with changed social values and experiences. The foothold physical education used to have in the public schools seems to have loosened in some ways, making it more open to successful dance, while also subjecting it again to exclusive preoccupation with exercise.

From another direction, the human potential movement, holistic health concerns, and the accumulating theory and practice from East and West that dancers often refer to as the body therapies, give another philosophic framework and career vision to socially and personally concerned dancers. In an earlier period dance therapy successfully institutionalized itself in relation to various medically oriented contexts, as well as individual practice. Somatic educators and dance scientists may well seek to define special programs that may or may not stay intimately associated with dance as we know it. Dance departments have not been particularly necessary for many of the developments that are surrounding dance. It remains to be seen how the dynamics of dominance at the institutional level will shape the framework and role of dance.

Possible Directions

These times can certainly be read in a variety of ways and can lead us to an array of strategies to meet the potentials we ascribe to ourselves. The old needs that arise out of looking at the health and vitality of the people not only remain but shout their claims on our attention. Fantasy and play, touch and physicality, live interaction, discipline and creativity, group work and appreciation of difference all seem even more necessary than in previous periods. The needs for sound somatic orientations and personal and social stability in the face of persistent stress suggest ritualized dance activities be valued. Needs for self-help and growth suggest creative, integrative approaches informed by an expanded base in psychology.

The virtuosity expected of the professional dancer suggests that long and systematic pathways be provided for dancers to follow. Yet the multiplicity of approaches characteristic of today's dance suggests breadth, creative flexibility, and principles that can be applied across the various worlds of body, movement, art, and culture. The latter orientation may find particular compatibility to university purposes because of the resolve of cognitive dissonances and perspective it presents. Performance and production, however, demand that preparation be somewhat stabilized at least for individuals or groups participating in the same kinds of choreography. The situation can be read as a call toward greater specialization along various lines or among the various roles of choreographer, performer, audience, teacher, and scholar or toward a more unified approach centered on the individual or culture. In any case, to provide alternative pathways and to represent different approaches means dance departments must have a full complement of faculty. Choices must be made. Numbers of students, the relative importance of various functions of the dance in higher education, the potentials for alternative avenues for dance in the society, and the situational realities and needs all must play a part in the choices. What will the values be?

Dance as a performing art, professionally conceived, seems to excite great numbers of aspiring students. Concern is sometimes expressed as to the advisability of thinking and planning programs in relation to a star path dream set in view of limitations on future opportunities and remuneration. Audiences for dance have certainly grown, but who and how many are involved in a satisfying, economically sustaining cycle? Placement of dance in the real fabric of society and educating for its enhanced functioning seems to be an emerging goal. The same could be said for the discipline of dance within the context of the university. Should it serve an arts function, be a service vehicle for selected populations and functions, or be a subject with the usual assumptions for participation in the full range of education and research missions? Is it time for dance to better fulfill its subject matter role in relation to the humanities and to assume more confidently its importance as a socially relevant phenomenon? There are many dance departments fielding courses for the general education curricula of their colleges and universities. Often, facing a broader range of students encourages fresh definition of dance. Much of the recent development and controversy in the humanities and general education has changed the ground and the appreciation of the knowledges and practices represented by the field of dance.

As I see it, dance does have special significance in higher education at this time. Part of that significance is based on the historic refusal of dance to abandon immersion in dance experience as a vital form of education. Academe is on the brink of new realizations relative to alternative modes and meanings. Dance offers a background of information and a new frontier in scientific, cultural, and clinical studies. What dance seems to have forgotten is the dynamism of commitment to social change and personal integrity that was so vital to its early years. The present period would seem to call for movement into the central currents of social concern. By this I mean to confront poverty, racism, sexism, homophobia, agism, fascism, and the general abuse of life and legacy. The full development of dance as a discipline and comprehensive undertaking involving goals in dance as art, humanity, and vehicle for education and other human social needs seems to be the most potentially enduring and responsible framework for dance in higher education. There is a room for a great deal of variety in emphasis among the various aspects of dance and dance programming, but the full house of consciousness seems to provide the necessary perspective and the checks and balances to support and direct growth.

Higher education, like the society, is looking around for ways to resolve economic dilemmas, not always with wisdom or foresight. My sense is that staying in the picture of higher education is very important to the development of an enlightened sense of culture and is imperative not only for the growth of dance as a field, but for the success of higher education. I have no doubt that this is a time for entering fully and directly into the fray. Our history has readied us to speak if we can connect purposefully to our visions and values.

References

Clemente, K. (1990). Dance in public education. *Spotlight on Dance*, 17 (1).

H'Doubler, M. (1925). *The dance and its place in education*. New York: Harcourt, Brace and Company.

Hawkins, A. (1954). *Modern dance in higher education*. New York: Teachers College, Columbia University.

Wiley, H. (1989, August 16). College dance programs must become more fully integrated with the professional world. *Chronicle of Higher Education*, B 2-3.

Edrie Ferdun is a professor in the Dance Department at Temple University, Philadelphia, Pennsylvania 19121.

A Prismatic Approach to Analysis of Style in Dance as a Paradigm for Dance Education

Betsey Gibbons

Dance depends on the artistic processes of performers and choreographers to bring its incandescent phenomenon to life. More and more, these artists are being educated in dance major programs in colleges and universities. Dance educators must examine the educative process and seek to answer questions such as: What constitutes an education in dance? What is considered knowledge? How are we educating dancers in institutions of higher education today? What are the guiding concepts for education in dance? What are the underlying suppositions?

Dance and a Postmodern Curriculum

In a discussion of postmodern curriculum, William Doll (1989) described three facets of postmodern thought that have implications for rethinking dance curriculum. These are the nature of *closed vs. open* systems, the structure of *simplicity vs. complexity*, and *accumulative vs. transformatory* change. The *closed* system, exemplified by the "teacherproof" curricular materials of the 1960s, attempts to "protect itself" from fluxes of nature. An *open* system, on the other hand, uses fluxes, perturbations, and anomalies as triggers that set off the individual's internal transformations and reorganizations. *Simplicity* attempts to ignore anomalies and other "bumps" on a smooth, linearly ordered path, whereas *complexity* assumes a web-like reality with multiple interacting forces and views individuals as participants inside the web, rather than as external observers. In complex situations, interactions among intertwined elements can produce sudden spontaneous reorganizations into newer and higher orders of complexity. *Accumulative* change assumes predictable, controlled, and well-defined incremental changes. *Transformative* change occuring in an open system is exemplified by quantum physics with its nonpredictable, spontaneous leap; it has three assumptions: *internality, spontaneity*, and *indefiniteness*. *Internality* refers to internal reorganization by an active, rather than passive, learner. *Spontaneity* is a strong element in this transformative process; when a transformation occurs that allows new perspectives, it may occur suddenly, spontaneously. *Indefiniteness* refers to the concept of ends perceived as ends-in-view rather than predetermined goals. The course must develop its own path along which students, teacher, and course material undergo transformation, with inquiry and creativity guiding the direction and process of development.

An education should be a thoughtfully organized, cohesive, interconnecting web of experiences rather than a collection of narrowly defined and discrete areas of study. Penelope Hanstein (1986) describes a postmodern curriculum for dance as one "which attends to, in explicit ways, the perception, exploration, transformation, and discrimination of artistic conceptions while cultivating historical and cultural perspectives, developing the discerning skills of the critic, and guiding our students as they seek answers to questions about the nature of dance as an art form" (p. 56). Dance curriculum is often, however, polarized into "technique" (also called "studio" or "activity") classes and "theory" (history, criticism, aesthetics, etc.) classes, which often seem to have little in common and even appear to be at odds with each other. How do we as educators create a sense of education rather than simply administer a series of courses?

The duality inherent in the concept of "training the body as instrument" does a great disservice to ourselves and our students. Dissecting the person into the three parts of body (which is trained in technique classes), mind (which is taught in theory classes), and spirit (which is generally not dealt with at all in the educative process) leaves three parts in search of a whole. Technique classes often fail to promote the imaginative thinking, inquiry, and discovery that lead to the ability to creatively order and make flexible worlds from experiences. Theory classes such as aesthetics and criticism often employ a polarized approach to choreographing and performing, elevating to a superior position the role of the choreographer and neglecting the concept of the performer as a creative individual who also employs artistic process strategies.

Students enjoy the immediacy, the "do-ingness" of technique class. Within the total student experience in a college dance major program, a student will probably spend from two to four times the number of hours in technique, repertory, and rehearsing with dance faculty as in theory classes. Such experiences are most often approached with the least openness as closed systems with preset and tightly controlled outcomes. However, technique, repertory, and rehearsal can all be opportunities for educating students in perception, exploration, transformation, and discrimination of artistic conceptions.

The globalistic, pluralistic approach of the postmodern paradigm for curriculum should form the basis for the approach to teaching and curriculum. The total curriculum and individual approaches to teaching must be harmonious and interactive; faculty and students in the dance program should strive to approach the educative process by attending to the perception, exploration, transformation, and discrimination of artistic conceptions, while cultivating discovery-oriented approaches to the study of dance as an art form. Thus curriculum becomes a process of development, a becoming, rather than a concrete body of knowledge to be covered; learning becomes "a by-product of inquiry, not a direct and exclusive goal in itself" (Doll, 1989, p. 252).

The Prismatic Approach

The prismatic approach (Figure 1), originally developed by the author as a model for the analysis of style in dance, is also appropriate as a postmodern approach to curriculum for dance. The prismatic approach has, as its central core and guiding tenet, the unique individual: a complex and

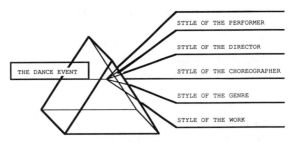

Figure 1. Pictorialization of the prismatic approach to the analysis of style in dance.

integrated person whose creative artistic processes stir a constant change in an ephemeral art form. The global model that the author developed from the prismatic approach is in the form of three-dimensional globe (Figure 2), which represents three interactive aspects of style (Gibbons, 1989). The first dimension concerns the artistic processes of the choreographer and the performer; the second concerns the qualitative features of the dance work and the genre with which it is associated; and the third concerns changes that occur in these aspects over time. The interaction of these three will produce, at any time, a dance event that is a unique gestalt. The first aspect, artistic process, holds the most fruitful information concerning dance education.

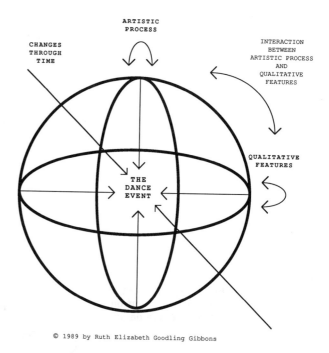

Figure 2. The interaction between the three dimensions of the global model: artistic processes, qualitative features, and changes through time.

13

The Nature of Artistic Process

Four aspects contribute to style in artistic process (Figure 3). *Disposition to act* refers to the initiative to discover and solve artistic problems; *schema* refers to how the artist conceptualizes the art form; *strategies* refer to choices made concerning the available possibilities; and *training and temperament* refer to the dancer's training in a form that is congruent with personal temperament.

Artistic creation is more than a matter of the artist skillfully manipulating the medium and is a much more involved process than simply reproducing or "expressing" an idea. The process of creation in art is a conversation or encounter between the artist and the medium, a discovery-oriented activity in which the artist seeks solutions within the medium. "Gradually the work 'tells' the artist what is needed. . . . The process itself yields ideas that were not a part of the initiating conception" (Eisner, 1982, p. 51). Through experimentation, investigation, and discovery, the artist learns about the work being created. The creative transactions that help to shape the idea are the result of the interactions among the idea, the medium, the choreographer, and the dancer. It is this process of creative transaction that is interpretation. The interpretation of ideas leads the choreographer and the performer to single out the qualitative aspect which is most intriguing.

Disposition to Act

The *disposition to act* involves formulating a problem. Jacob Getzels and Mihaly Czikszentmihalyi (1976), in a longitudinal study of creativity in the visual arts, differentiate between presented problem situations, in which the problem has a known formulation, and discovered problem situations, in which the artist must first identify or discover the problem itself: the task is given but the specific problem must be found. From an original vague idea, previously experienced only as diffuse tensions, the artist must create the concrete statement of a problem. The problem is discovered from within the situation itself, and each artist will perceive and resolve the problem in a unique fashion. This ability to formulate problems is the essential difference between the artist and the craftsman or technician.

Central to this process is the concept of thinking in the medium, what dance theorist Maxine Sheets-Johnstone (1981) refers to in dance as "thinking in movement." The painter may think in terms of line, hue, saturation of color; the dancer, in terms of the organic or geometric shapes of the body, the ineffable connotations of gestures, or the flow of move-

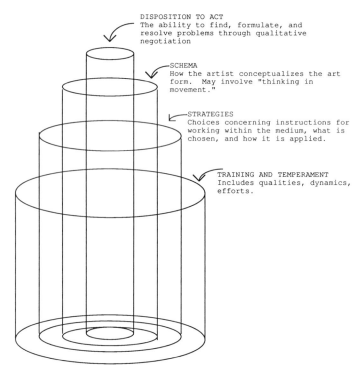

DISPOSITION TO ACT
The ability to find, formulate, and resolve problems through qualitative negotiation

SCHEMA
How the artist conceptualizes the art form. May involve "thinking in movement."

STRATEGIES
Choices concerning instructions for working within the medium, what is chosen, and how it is applied.

TRAINING AND TEMPERAMENT
Includes qualities, dynamics, efforts.

Figure 3. Ring model of elements that comprise artistic process in dance.

ment. The mental processes of a dancer are not merely a symbolic way of designating thought but are the very presence of thought, providing individually ordered information. "In such thinking, movement is not a medium by which thoughts emerge but rather, the thoughts themselves" (Sheets-Johnstone, p. 400). The act of dancing is an information gathering event for the dancer. Intelligence in dance includes kinesthetic and spatial intelligence; an awareness of abstract relations of space and time; concrete awareness of the movement phrases and body shapes in one part of the dance connecting with those in another part; the ability to discover new relationships between movements in various parts of the body while performing; and a sense of style to harmonize rhythmic spatial qualities of movement with expressive qualities and abstract ideas to create a sense of unity and order in a performance (Carter, 1983).

Schema

Schema refers to how an artist conceptualizes the art form. This is revealed as a constellation of qualitative features emerging through works and performances as reflections of personal schemata. In dance, each artist has a particular vision of art and the art form that helps to sculpt the developmental process. Each choreographer explores a unique conception of dance movement, of the dancer, and of the purpose of art, which will be consistent throughout the choreographer's *oeuvre*: "that is, the form the dances take is consonant with each choreographer's creative process, with each one's philosophy of the training and rehearsing required for dance performance, and with each one's expectations concerning viewers' responses" (Foster, 1986, pp. 1–2). In reference to the performer, Selma Jeanne Cohen (1983) stated that "for the dancer to execute the visible dimensions of the prescribed steps is not enough; that is only part of the style. The style lies also in the attitude toward the movement, which is also an attitude toward life" (p. 350).

One way of looking at schema in dance is to recognize the genres of modern dance, ballet, and jazz as general schemata. General schemata arise from the personal schemata of the individuals who work with and develop them; individuals develop personal schemata from the general schemata of the genres with which they choose to work.

Modern dance has been referred to as "a point of view" (Fraleigh, 1987; Martin, 1966) and is characterized by its individualistic spirit and individual discoveries, will, creativity, and imagination. Ballet, on the other hand, has often been referred to as a "system" characterized by a sense of tradition; its relatively long and strong collective history; and a movement vocabulary, pedagogical system, and rules for choreography developed over centuries. During the early development of the modern dance "a real dichotomy existed: the ballet dancers felt themselves disciplined instruments of precision; their counterparts considered themselves freely creative and self-expressive individuals. They moved differently, felt differently" (Cohen, 1983, p. 350). Jazz has often been characterized as highly skillful popular entertainment to be appreciated but not studied (Friesen, 1975; Giordano, 1975), dealing with the purely physical and sensual aspect of dance.

These genres exemplify but are not exclusively bound to such schemata. Performers or choreographers trained in any genre may conceptualize dance primarily as an individual point of view developed through individual discoveries, as a movement system embodying established ideals subject to stylistic interpretation, or as purely physical entertainment using highly skilled performers. This may not necessarily be a *result* of training in a particular genre; it is more likely that dancers *seek* training that closely resembles a personal schema.

Strategies

Strategies involve choices for acting upon the aspects of the medium the artist has selected. The particular nature of these strategies and how they are applied involves slightly different elements for each of the interpretive processes of the chorographer, director, and performer. The nature of the choices made during creation in the arts is extremely complex. The constraints or rules suggested by society and history still leave an enormous number of choices open to the artist, who would find it impossible to accept all such possibilities. However, what is chosen can also be seen as the result of what is *not* chosen. If each dance utilized the entire vocabulary of movements or range of qualities available, there would be little except syntactic arrangement to distinguish one work from another. Each dance and each performance is made unique by the artist's paring away those qualities that do not contribute to the work. During the interaction between artist, idea, and medium as the heuristic process of creation, the artist learns to discard what is not essential to clarify the developing idea. Each choreographer or performer chooses to eliminate from her or his particular style that which does not contribute to a particular artistic vision.

Strategies may be utilized on two levels: 1) as a genre imposing a tacit set of rules on choreographers and performers that define what is acceptable in that particular genre, or 2) as personally imposed delimitations, the self-imposed boundaries of the artist's choosing. The first strategical choice for an artist is whether to "follow the rules" of a particular genre or to stretch or break them. Originality or creativity may thus be of two different sorts. The first sort of originality is the invention of new rules; the second sort develops new strategies for realizing existing rules.

Most style changes have involved the use of novel strategies rather than novel rules, making possible subtle strategic plays. While some artists have invented new rules, some of the great choreographers have been incomparable strategists, developing new strategies for realizing existing rules. In general the ballet genre, with its strong rules, encourages strategists, while the modern or contemporary genres have been characterized by iconoclasts who sought to break the established rules.

However, certain modern choreographers such as Martha Graham, Erick Hawkins, and Merce Cunningham achieved longevity by successfully establishing a consistent, stable style and *developing* new rules, and then becoming strategists. Overall, successful choreographers in any genre are those who have explored and employed, in new ways, forms and procedures established by themselves or others.

Performers employ a similar process in the use of strategies; the difference lies in the nature of the material. For the performer, conveying the dance image is a more complex process than simply "expressing" oneself or "reacting" to the music. Conveying the work necessitates developing an understanding of it, then making choices about how to best convey that understanding. Each dancer approaches the art of performing differently and will find unique qualitative problems of interpretation and realization. Like the choreographer, the performer must find a way to express, through movement, a particular idea. Rehearsals represent a series of successive transformations during which the dancer transforms the subject matter, which may arrive as a movement vocabulary or "steps," into the very substance of the work of art.

Training and Temperament

Training and temperament are interactive and indivisible in dance. Training in technique is more than simply increasing speed, flexibility, and endurance. Addressing only the "body" aspect of the performer clouds an understanding of performance as an active artistic process and strips the performer of the role of artist. More than mere physical bodies trained in the motional habits of a particular school, dancers do not improve technique by sheer "physical" means, by mindlessly repeating the movement over and over. It is only when the dancer, working in the medium of motion, experiences a conflict, formulates a problem, and succeeds in resolving the conflict (usually on a wholly kinesthetic level) that technique is improved.

Training also helps to shape how the dancer conceives the act of moving and initiates or motivates movement. For example, a port de bras may be seen as a geometric shape, a relationship between body parts, or as a spatial investigation. Furthermore, training develops a dancer's view of the relationship between the studio educative process and the dance performance. According to Susan Foster (1986), "in [Deborah] Hay's class one performs dances, while in Balanchine's class one enhances skills; in Graham's class one trains the body, and in Cunningham's class one does the movement" (p. 46).

The interaction of training and temperament enables each dancer to develop a unique movement style. For the dancer, the link between self and style is individual temperament. If the dancer's movement propensities are not in accord with or not fulfilled by the general movement style studied, the dancer will often leave that style for another and will choose a general style which "fits" personal temperament. Sondra Fraleigh stated that "it is significant that movement is the medium of dance and the intentive human body its immanent source" (1987, p. 19). Here "intentive" is a key word to understanding the artistic process aspect of the performing dancer.

Summary

Dance education is often approached in a compartmentalized manner. Both the craft-oriented approach to choreography and the viewpoint of training the dancer's body as instrument often permeate a curricular approach to the dance discipline, from technique to philosophy courses. In history, criticism, and aesthetics courses, the roles of the choreographer and the performer are often given different weights or levels of importance: technique classes often focus on training the dancer's body as an instrument; choreography classes often focus primarily on the structural aspects of composition.

Recognizing artistic process and performance as heuristic processes is essential for a postmodern dance curriculum. In order for critics, aestheticians, educators, artists, and students to make cohesive whole from what are seen as many disparate parts, a cohesive, holistic framework is needed to provide a way of approaching the study of dance. The prismatic approach, which has artistic process as its core, can illuminate the vital roles that choreographers, performers, and reconstructors play in creating dance, enable analysis of each part in relation to the whole, and create a sense of wholeness in the production of this phenomenon. Such an approach also provides a framework for historians, theorists, and educators for the study of the various aspects of the discipline of dance (see Figure 4).

Whereas typically the academic system recognizes discursive thought, qualitative thinking as a form of knowledge in dance must also be recognized, cultivated, and explored in all parts of dance education. Disposition to act, schema, and strategies must be recognized along with training and temperament so that the students can learn to dis-

cover and understand the qualitative information inherent in dance, and avenues to creative problem-solving can be opened.

Concepts of artistic process must be applied to all classes in a dance curriculum. Artistic process should be applied and used as a basis for teaching choreography as opposed to traditional craft-oriented courses in composition (Blom & Chaplin, 1982; Hanstein, 1986). The concept of artistic process as applied to performance as well as choreography must form the approach to courses in criticism, aesthetics, and philosophy.

Recognition of the multiplicity of schemata for dance may enable less "competition" between dance styles. Why should a college student be compelled to choose a major in either ballet or modern dance, and why is jazz dance rarely given the legitimacy of its other two sisters? These schemata are not mutually incompatible. Each style offers a different "worldview" of dance, of the interaction of the roles of the performer and the choreographer and their relationship to the whole of dance.

Dance educators must seek to recognize and diminish compartmentalization within the discipline, and replace it with a sense of the interconnectedness of the art form as a whole. Dance curricula should be guided by the key characteristics of postmodern thought that include inquiry oriented toward discovery, a sense of the interaction of aspects of the dance discipline, and an understanding of process and transformation. It should be envisioned "not as a linear trajectory nor as a course (with hurdles) to be run, but as a multifaceted matrix to be explored" (Doll, p. 251).

Referring to the concept of complex reality as a web of multiple, interacting forces, we see that dance can be a means by which the individual moves in a variety of directions simultaneously: forward to the future, backward to synthesize and seek to understand former experiences, forward into a deeper understanding of the past; outward to connect and reconnect bonds between the self and others, inward to knit new internal connections among the selves of the self; upward to discover new depths of spirituality and intellectuality, downward to elevate the knowledge of the body. Learning can occur at any time. Life is a fundamentally heuristic process. Dance can be a way of accessing that deliciously interactive spiral of experiencing, learning from, and teaching the world.

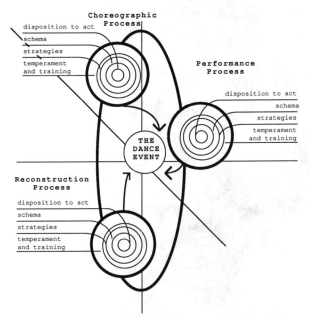

Figure 4. Aspects of style concerned with artistic processes and how they contribute to the unique dance event.

17

References

Blom, L.A., & Chaplin, L.T. (1982). *The intimate act of choreography.* Pittsburgh: University of Pittsburgh Press.

Carter, C. (1983). Arts and cognition: Performance, criticism, and aesthetics. *Art Education, 36*(2), 61–67.

Cohen, S.J. (1983). Problems of definition. In Copeland, R. & Cohen, M. (Eds.), *What is dance* (pp. 339–354). New York: Oxford University Press.

Doll, W. (1989). Foundations for a post-modern curriculum. *Journal of Curriculum Studies, 21*(3), 243–253.

Eisner, E. (1982). *Cognition and curriculum: A basis for deciding what to teach.* New York: Longman.

Foster, S. (1986). *Reading dancing: Bodies and subjects in contemporary American dance.* Berkeley: University of California Press.

Fraleigh, S.H. (1987). *Dance and the lived body.* Pittsburgh: University of Pittsburgh Press.

Friesen, J. (1975). Perceiving dance. *The Journal of Aesthetic Education, 9,* 97–108.

Getzels, J., & Csikszentmihalyi, M. (1976). *The creative vision: A longitudinal study of problem finding in art.* New York: John Wiley and Sons.

Gibbons, R.E.G. (1989). *A prismatic approach to the analysis of style in dance.* Eugene, OR: Microform Publications.

Giordano, G. (1975). *Anthology of American jazz dance.* Evanston, IL: Orion Publishing House.

Hanstein, P. (1986). *On the nature of art making in dance: An artistic process skills model for the teaching of choreography.* Unpublished doctoral dissertation, Ohio State University.

Martin, J. (1966). *Modern dance.* New York: Dance Horizons.

Sheets-Johnstone, M. (1981). Thinking in movement. *The Journal of Aesthetics and Art Criticism, 39,* 399–407.

Betsey Gibbons is in the Department of Health, Physical Education, and Dance at Washburn University, Topeka, Kansas 66621.

Students in the dance program at Washburn University. *Photo by Paul Goebel for Washburn University.*

Dance Education at the Selective Liberal Arts College

Lynn Matluck Brooks

Education in dance at the small, highly selective liberal arts college can, and should, have goals and methods distinct from dance in other higher education settings. These liberal arts colleges—with their small student bodies, high faculty-student ratios, selective admissions standards, limited yet student-accessible resources, and historically determined curricular focuses (Carnes, 1978; Carnegie Foundation, 1987, p. 22)—have a special mission in the preparation of students of dance. While these colleges may not be the most appropriate institutions for training the theatre dance professional, they can play a special role in the training of the crucial nondance population that supports the presentation and evolution of dance in America. Indeed, liberal arts graduates can serve as the main body from which educated board members, fundraisers, grants officers, publicists, and—most importantly—audience can be drawn. These roles might not be spotlighted in theatrical posters or in critical reviews, yet the dance artist cannot function in today's complex business world (and art *is* business, we have all learned) without an educated and articulate support structure.

The Liberal Arts Context: Goals for Dance

The history of higher education reveals several distinct philosophies that have, historically, determined goals, curriculum, and pedagogy. Bruce Kimball has lucidly analyzed these in terms of the "*artes liberales*" ideal, the "liberal-free" ideal, and the accommodations these two opposing ideals have made throughout the history of higher education in Europe and the United States. The liberal arts ideal concentrates on the handing down of knowledge, the appreciation of received wisdom,

and the study of great texts and classical sources (Kimball, 1986, pp. 107, 111, 237–238; Bennett, 1984, pp. 4–5). Devised and nurtured as training for the gentility in the Renaissance and later periods, *artes liberales* studies themselves were nontechnical, nonmarketable, indeed wholly nonprofessional (Kimball, 1986, pp. 182–183; Winter et al., 1981, pp. 2–4). But they led to the formation of a type of good citizen-statesman who could both lead and serve the government.

On the other hand, the liberal-free ideal is concerned with speculative investigations, free from "a priori" standards; it places stress "upon the volition of the individual rather than upon the obligations of citizenship found in the *artes liberales* ideal (Kimball, 1986, p. 119). This self-expressive and intently innovative search for truth, as characterized by the liberal-free ideal, is most evident in large research universities where departments prize experimentation and new findings. In the arts, this would translate as the creation of new works and the exploration of new aesthetic and technical frontiers. In dance programs at the higher education level, then, we see that training for the practice of the art and craft of dance can best be accomplished at conservatories or in large university departments with the resources and the philosophical tradition to support innovation and creative explorations.

Within the *artes liberales* tradition, however—characterized by the humanist concern for classical texts, language, and values—the student was and is traditionally prepared for a broad understanding of culture, aesthetics, history, and ethics and also for the articulation of values culled from this cumulative study. The study of the liberal arts, then, prepares the leading citizen for a role as statesman and orator, shaper and articulator of public policy, by establishing a historically justifiable basis for anal-

19

The liberal arts college provides a broad base of cultural knowledge and helps students develop skills in evaluation and discernment of quality. *Photos from Providence College by Alan W. Bean.*

ysis, evaluation, and integration of information. This base need not be forever backward-looking; it serves, rather, as a springboard for application, decision, and action *in the present*. The development in the student of taste, values, and mental acuity, which has been the ideal of liberal arts education, surely speaks directly to those in educational circles today who call for the nourishment of "critical thinking" and "values education" among students of all levels. These sorts of buzz words are not new in educational parlance. The ability of the liberal arts curriculum to meet these sorts of needs has been a longstanding argument of the defenders of the *artes liberales* ideal (Kimball, 1986, p. 151; Mayhew, 1962, p. 6; Winter et al., 1981, p. 27).

It cannot but be clear to any who are employed within the American higher education system that these two educational "ideals" are just that—ideals that are rarely achieved in reality. As Kimball stresses throughout his book, accommodations on both sides of the higher education divide have been made. For example, many faculty members and administrators within the institution of the liberal arts college now believe strongly in new research as a support for the good teaching and student preparation that they continue to prize.

Similarly, many large universities continue to champion some model of liberal arts education and to establish separate colleges of liberal arts or of humanities within the larger structure of the university. I do not intend here to argue for the superiority of any one model—be it an ideal or an accommodation. Rather, I would like to point out that returning to a traditional definition of the *artes liberales* can well serve our thinking in planning dance curricula and in devising goals for dance education at the selective liberal arts college.

The studies embraced by the liberal arts curriculum are the humanities, which include the history, criticism, and theory of art (Bennett, 1984, p. 3). This places the liberal arts curriculum in a sphere separate from the training of specialists, professionals, and technicians—those who actually make or produce the art. The liberally educated person, then, is skilled at "the analysis and discrimination of values"—including aesthetic quality (Kimball, 1986, p. 197), and is capable of asking penetrating questions about life, art, and ethics. William J. Bennett has articulated some of these questions:

> What is justice? What should be loved? What deserves to be defended? What is courage? What is noble? What is base? Why do civilizations flourish? Why do they decline? (1984, p. 3)

20

These are the questions the educated person must be able to ask and ponder if he or she is to have any appreciation of art as a sphere of legitimate inquiry and exposition. Performer-choreographer Meredith Monk, one of the great synthesizers of contemporary art in America, has wondered why art in our society has degenerated to the status of another "commodity," a "diversion rather than an essential need" (Monk, 1990, p. 30). Monk points out that, unwilling to make the effort to wrench themselves from their television sets, many Americans seem to find art too arduous a pleasure for their impatient, fragmented, tired lives. Monk concludes, "As artists, presenters, audiences, and lovers of art, we have a significant role in our society. We are responsible human beings" (p. 31). Monk rightly recognizes the crucial roles played not only by dance artists, but by those who must understand, appreciate, and support those artists' achievements. It is in this sphere that the liberally educated individual can be a vital presence.

Of course, liberal arts colleges face a tension in their own systems of values. Broad and lofty educational goals, which seek to provide a general and fundamental learning base, are in direct conflict with the concern expressed by parents, students, and college administrators for vocational preparation and placement (Astin, Korn, & Berg, 1990, pp. 54, 86; Mayhew, 1962, pp. 12–13). In this conflict, however, the field of dance can actually benefit within the context of the liberal arts college. Unlike the dance conservatory or the university dance department, which emulates a model of specialization established in such fields as the sciences, the liberal arts dance program need not be concerned with training for the profession of dance perform-

ance. This training is, in fact, generally best accomplished elsewhere and does not necessarily need to be gained within the realm of higher educational institutions at all.

While liberal arts colleges—like many other institutions of higher education—are busy trying to prepare their students for some sort of job proficiency or for graduate school in fields that draw the elite and financially ambitious student—fields such as law, medicine, business, government, and research (Astin, Korn, & Berg, 1990, pp. 48–49, 80–81)—they must also adhere to their historical mission. This mission includes providing a broad base of cultural knowledge and developing skills in evaluation of new material and discernment of quality. The fulfillment of this mission within the dance curriculum will allow graduates of these colleges—now professionals in their various fields—to serve on dance company boards of trustees, make arts policy, and be avid dance-goers. It is indeed the duty of these colleges to guide their now-educated alumni toward the effective and socially responsible exercise of their nonprofessional time (Mayhew, 1962, p. 6). Let us harness these resources for the support of the dance field.

There are certainly examples of small, liberal arts colleges such as Oberlin or Connecticut College that have effectively established conservatories within their educational structures. These schools have chosen to redefine themselves—or at least a portion of themselves—in pursuit of highly developed performance programs. Even liberal arts colleges that lack a focus on training for dance performance occasionally graduate individuals who choose to pursue dance as a profession. But liberal arts colleges, in general, are chosen by those stu-

dents whose professional goals lie elsewhere. These individuals, however, if provided with a sound liberal training and an appropriately designed dance curriculum, can prove vital to the sustenance of theatre dance.

Designing a Liberal Arts Dance Curriculum

In establishing arts policy—and thus support for the arts—education that moves beyond technical specialties is essential. With the diverse cultural forces affecting the arts at all times, but perhaps never more stridently or numerously than today, education in the liberal arts can help to establish a forum for "public discourse and the means to arrive at decisions that can be agreed upon" (Kinnan, 1989, p. 33). Richard Lyman points out that the establishment of a "shared knowledge base" is essential so that people have a body of learning from which to draw values, for it is indeed impossible to "expect people to learn to read in a vacuum of information" (Lyman, 1989, p. 57). Thus, the culling of classical sources and the analysis of great texts—the very stuff and method of the liberal arts ideal—is well suited to the formation of policymakers and arts supporters who can apply the appreciation developed by their training to the evaluation of new works.

Recently, much academic discussion has centered on the failure of American schools to provide students with a foundation in either critical, evaluative thinking or rudimentary cultural knowledge, resulting in an undiscerning and "culturally illiterate" population (see Bloom, 1987; Hirsch, 1987; also Bennett, 1984, p. 2). Dance educators can take responsibility for offering courses which do, indeed, provide students with a basis for knowledgeable evaluation in one portion of human behavior: dance—a behavior which manifests itself in art works as well as in ritual and social expression. To provide guidance in the choice of works or dance forms viewed and studied, it is the obligation, and the pleasure, of the dance educator at the liberal arts college to cull from the great body of dance history and ethnology those works that give the student a view of the evolution and role of dance as art and as vital human behavior. These works, supported by appropriate and accessible readings in aesthetics, analysis, and context, can provide the student with a foundation from which to apply judgments, to perceive evolutionary trends, and to

grasp meanings in works not studied before. Thus the teacher must be able to set aside a personal agenda regarding his/her own tastes and must offer a well-balanced, yet critically defensible program of study.

What are some criteria which such a dance-based liberal arts curriculum must meet? William Bennett has outlined some of the features that he finds can "mark the points of significance" in a field and ensure that a student "does not wander aimlessly over the terrain, dependent solely on chance to discover the landmarks of human achievement" (Bennett, 1984, p. 6). He urges care in balancing "breadth and depth" in the approach to the subject studied and urges the use of primary texts in a program that continues beyond one introductory-level course. Other requirements of good liberal arts teaching, states Bennett, include strong faculty, institutional conviction that the humanities are truly central to education, and the belief that they can be taught with rigor as "a means of inquiry that can convey serious truths, defensible arguments, and significant ideas" (p. 8). Course content and the quality of teaching, then, are the major constituents of a successful curriculum. In choosing course content, it is evident that any field of knowledge is far larger than even a full four years of study can encompass. Thus the choice of certain "blocks" of information must be made (Mayhew, 1962, p. 50), in order to balance demands of breadth and depth and to offer stepping stones toward continued independent involvement in the field.

Increased Attention to History

With careful thought, the features listed above can be applied to dance curricula with little difficulty. Dance is a field whose history can be easily lost, but in recent years increased attention has been given both to salvaging the past and to the preservation of current repertoire and related material for future generations. Such developments as the establishment of the Society of Dance History Scholars, the creation of a graduate program specifically in dance history at the University of California-Riverside, and the increased publication and quality of books and articles about subjects and methods in dance history and ethnology all attest to this concern among dancers and scholars for recapturing and sustaining the historical viability of the dance event and the life devoted to dance.

The materials are indeed becoming available for the founding of a curriculum in dance that follows the liberal arts ideal; great texts—dances and dance literature in our case—serve as a field for investigation, questioning, and the formation of critical judgment and aesthetic sensitivity. Also, access to filmed and recorded versions of dance works and to other audiovisual media now allows us to gain some experience of dances either lost to the repertoire or simply beyond the range of class field trips. While I certainly exhort students to see dance live and try to make live professional performance available to them—or to bring them to it—recorded dance is an important and relatively affordable way to introduce a large body of choreography and material for analysis in the classroom. The current commercial videotape market is dominated by ballet works, which allows some good coverage of great works in that genre, but leaves other masterpieces (e.g., in jazz and modern dance) unavailable. Distributors of educational and experimental films and videos must be investigated for coverage of areas not met by commercial distributors. The efflorescence and rising quality of regional dance groups is another means of bringing the experience of dance performance and viewing to colleges that may be far from such dance centers as New York or San Francisco. Many of these companies present works by masters of choreography, recreated through notated scores or set by designated artists; many regional troupes also commission work by renowned artists, as well as presenting their own material. Thus, it is truly possible today to create a dance curriculum that fits well into the liberal arts tradition.

Foundation courses in dance, then, can address a range of dance styles, functions, and criteria, using examples of fine performances and thoughtful analytical writing as the "great texts" for study. For example, under "styles" (or "forms" or "genres"), one might articulate such western theatre forms as jazz, ballet, and modern dance. These can serve as general categories for comparison, but also as umbrellas under which to group other subdivisions. Modern dance, thus, might be further studied in terms of historical periods, of individual techniques, or of national contributions. In terms of historical styles, the period of the forerunners, for example, might be discussed with film and video-recorded works of Ruth St. Denis used as visual texts (for example, *Trailblazers of Modern Dance* includes such excerpts, as does the 1958 film *Ruth St. Denis and Ted Shawn*), excerpts of St. Denis's own writings could be used as written texts, and Suzanne Shelton's *Divine Dancer* would be important for critical and contextual information and as a model of dance research. To study individual tech-

niques in modern dance, students could look at Doris Humphrey's style in her dances performed live in reconstruction or as recorded in the recently released video recording of *With My Red Fires* and *New Dance*; supportive written material might be chosen from Humphrey's autobiography, *Doris Humphrey: An Artist First*, as well as from Marcia Siegel's *Days on Earth* and Ernestine Stodelle's *The Dance Technique of Doris Humphrey*. A study of national contributions in modern dance might look at current American postmodernism, German dance-theatre, and Japanese *butoh*.

Functions and Purposes

The teacher might also choose to view dances by functions or purposes, so that "theatre dance" itself becomes a general category contrasted with ritual dances, folk dances, social dances, and so on. Choosing one culture or nation, such as Spain, might offer the teacher ample material with which to make such comparisons, with, for example, dances of the Escuela Bolera serving as theatre-dance works, the dance of los Seises used as a subject of ritual dancing, and the Andalusian Sevillanas studied as examples of folk dance. The interactions and common features of these dances and their functions can and should be articulated.

I believe it important to open students' minds about the range of dance that geographical, cultural, and historical considerations permit. Thus, I often place "classical dance" forms of different nations close together on a syllabus. Students might study classical ballet and then the classical dances of India. I ask them to reflect on what makes both forms "classical" despite their obvious differences in technique and performance. This leads to investigation of choreographic form, training, professionalism in dance, aesthetics, and social values in each culture.

At the same time, the very complex interplay of national styles that has influenced artists for centuries can be discussed within the context of any one dance form studied. For example, in a recent review of the work of Seattle-born modern dancer and choreographer Mark Morris, Arlene Croce points out that "multiculturalism exists and has always existed in American dance; there is scarcely an American choreographer of note who has not been influenced both by the pluralism of our society and by the way dance just naturally soaks it up" (Croce, 1990, p. 84). Morris, of course, draws on his background in flamenco, Balkan and Israeli folk dance, Hindu

Providence College Dance Co. photo by Alan W. Bean.

dance, modern and ballet, and others. He is hardly alone in this array of sources: Isadora Duncan drew from the ancient Greeks, St. Denis from the Orientals, Erick Hawkins from the American Indians, and so on, up to today's avant-gardists such as Molissa Fenley, whose upbringing in Spain and Africa has profoundly shaped her work (Dixon, 1989). Nor is this use of crosscultural material limited to Americans. Students should know that, for example, Diaghilev's Ballets Russes displayed national influences from old Russia, chic new France, exotic Spain, and the mysterious East.

Similarly, the influence of popular dance forms on "art" dance needs to be pointed out to students who may feel that they lack intellectual or aesthetic access to refined theatre dance. The evolution of ballet from European folk forms is only one example of this; Twyla Tharp's melange of boogying, baton-twirling, modern dance, and highly sophisticated ballet commentary is another such example. Thus there is literally a world and a wealth of subject matter for the shaping of a foundation course in dance at the liberal arts college. I advocate no one fixed syllabus here; there is great room for the individual teacher's creativity in course design.

The crux of the design, however, must be the quality and influence of the works (both visual and written) the teacher chooses, so that the most compelling themes, demonstrated by the finest examples of dance performance, choreographic styles, and aesthetic trends are presented to the students.

Criteria for evaluation can be introduced through introductory writings on aesthetics as a philosophical field, and on dance aesthetics specifically. For example, Betty Redfern's *Dance, Art, and Aesthetics* might serve as a text in this area, providing a basis for aesthetics in general and for dance aesthetics particularly (Carter, 1990, pp. 33–34). The writings of the best of dance critics through time—from Gautier to Edwin Denby to Deborah Jowitt—can serve as additional texts and examples of careful evaluation and articulate dance writing.

Earlier mention has been made of the need to choose "blocks" of material for presentation, rather than attempting total coverage of dance history, ethnology, and aesthetics. An example of such block design can be drawn from my syllabus. I try to discuss some examples of the great western theatre forms that I believe will be most available to our students-cum-dance supporters: jazz, ballet, and mod-

24

ern dance. I focus on certain great works or on certain great masters of the form; then, in close proximity, I introduce related forms, drawing on international folk dance, ritual forms from a variety of religious perspectives, current or historical social dances, and classical theatre forms with independent and powerful traditions. These subjects are supported by introduction to various methods of analysis, from effort-shape, to Adshead's "four stages" (Adshead, 1988, pp. 111–122), Allegra Fuller Snyder's "dance symbol" (Snyder, 1972, pp. 213–224), and others. Students learn that all of these analytical methods can serve as a "way" to a work that might be initially unfamiliar and puzzling.

In order to know which one(s) of these avenues of approach will be most fruitful, I encourage students to start with the most immediately available material: the movement that they are seeing. They must learn, then, first of all to engage actively in what they view, so that they *do* see it, rather than letting it wash superficially over them, as if they were watching a television sit-com. They must attempt to describe what they are seeing, both in terms of specific movements done and of larger group or temporal developments. Any assertions they make—aesthetic, analytical, or sociological—must be supported by evidence based on the dance itself. If students describe certain movements they see as "gripping" or "ugly" or "romantic" or "expressive," for example, I ask them to articulate why the movement appears that way to them. Which dancers moved in the low level primarily, and why was this choice made? Were the dances led only by women—or only by men—and why or why not? Many other sorts of questions of this nature can be asked regarding any viewed material.

Learning to "Read" Dances

The students, thus, must learn to "read" the dances—to make of them texts of which specific questions can be asked in order to glean particular information and to make sound personal judgments, supported by evidence. The need for the current generation of students to learn perceptive *reading* in the conventional sense of that word has been stressed by education authorities (Bennett, 1984, p. 11), and I believe that we must extend that demand and training to the "reading" of dances. It is all too easy for our students to regard all dancing as entertainment, relaxation, a pretty gloss on the human body; I hope to jolt them out of that position forever.

This foundation course can, and should, be followed by courses that study in greater depth specific subjects or questions raised in the earlier course. But now the students have developed both a bigger picture of the variety of dance and its functions and some language for the articulation of what they are seeing. Lest my curriculum seem unduly to slight craft in favor of context (Hobgood, 1990, pp. 22–23), I want to make it clear that among the subjects that might be studied beyond the foundation course, or together with it, I include technique. The foundation course should help students to develop awareness of the kinesthetic component of dance viewing as well as dance doing. I always bring students in my foundation course out of the lecture hall and into the dance studio for movement explorations, so that the technical terms they must learn are understood from within their own bodies. Thus, for example, they explore, feel, and express the various poles of time, space, weight, and flow and work out combinations of full efforts. This is excellent preparation for any dance technique course, and also perhaps, these first forays into the studio will encourage hesitant students to venture back for a movement course.

Curriculum in such areas of dance study as composition, criticism, anthropology, and history can all spring from the foundation course. If the teacher has carefully designed the choice of materials introduced initially—the dance works, the dance artists, the forms, the geographical coverage, and the supportive readings assigned to each day's topic—students not only learn much information about those particular dances studied, but more importantly, they learn a number of widely applicable skills.

1. How to view works in a continuum of creativity and innovation.
2. How to analyze and evaluate new material presented, including that of the current avant-garde.
3. How to find information about forms not previously encountered.
4. How to articulate both what they see and their response to it.

These skills will well serve the mature individual who leaves college, becomes a professional in a field other than dance, but maintains an interest in dance as a supporter. Such support translates into dance audiences, informed boards of trustees for dance companies, and voters who understand issues of arts policy. These people can become the "good citizens" for dance that the liberal arts education attempts to develop in a more general sense. Those graduates who enter such fields as government or business may have direct influence on arts policy, funding, and representation. Lawyers and doctors, too—and those in many other fields—can apply their special expertise to areas of concern to dancers, if they are liberally educated about dance. And certainly there will always be those individuals who graduate from such a liberal education and find that they are somehow "hooked" on dance; they may choose to pursue independent or graduate study of dance technique and composition. Surely, their foundation in dance as a broad field of study, their familiarity with great works and a range of traditions, and their understanding of how to analyze and articulate the movement they view can only serve them well in that study.

For the dance field, this is a curriculum that can lead us all to become the "responsible human beings" whom Meredith Monk called for in her statement above. This is a curriculum in dance for which the liberal arts college is ideally suited.

References

Adshead, J. (Ed). (1988). *Dance analysis: Theory and practice*. London: Dance Books.

Astin, A., Korn, W., & Berz, E. (1990). *The American freshman: National norms for fall 1989*. Washington, DC and Los Angeles: American Council on Education and UCLA.

Bennett, W. J. (1984). *To reclaim a legacy*. Washington, DC: National Endowment for the Humanities.

Bloom, A. (1987). *The closing of the American mind*. New York: Simon and Schuster.

Carnegie Foundation's Classifications of More than 3,300 Institutions of Higher Education. (1987, July 7). *Chronicle of Higher Education*, p. 22.

Carnes, B. M. (1978). *A profile of private liberal arts colleges*. Washington, DC: U.S. Department of Health, Education, and Welfare.

Carter, C. (1990, Fall). Review of *Dance, art, and aesthetics*. *Dance Research Journal, 22*(2), 33–34.

Croce, A. (1990, July 23). Dancing: Multicultural theatre. *The New Yorker*, pp. 84–87.

Denby, E. (1968). *Looking at the dance*. New York: Horizon Press.

Dixon, B. (1989). The Afro-centric aesthetic. Guest lecture at Franklin and Marshall College, April 4.

Guest, I. (Ed.). (1986). *Gautier on dance*. London: Dance Books.

Hirsch, E. D., Jr. (1987). *Cultural literacy: What every American needs to know*. New York: Houghton Mifflin.

Hobgood, B. M. (1990, Summer). The state of theatre in American education. *The Phi Kappa Phi Journal, 70*, 21–23.

Humphrey, D. & Cohen, S. J. (1972). *Doris Humphrey, an artist first*. Middletown, CT: Wesleyan University Press.

Jowitt, D. (1984). *The dance in mind*. New York: David R. Godine.

Kimball, B. A. (1986). *Orators and philosophers: A history of the idea of liberal education*. New York: Teachers College Press.

Kinnan, E. T. (1989). Liberal education in a post-modern world. In *New Perspectives on Liberal Education* (pp. 25–40). Seattle: University of Washington Press.

Lyman, R. W. (1989). Defining our future: The liberal arts in contemporary society. In *New Perspectives on Liberal Education* (pp. 41–60). Seattle: University of Washington Press.

Mayhew, L. B. (1962). *The smaller liberal arts college*. Washington, DC: Center for Applied Research in Education, Inc.

Monk, M. (1990, September). Some thoughts about art. *Dance Magazine*, pp. 30–31.

Redfern, B. (1988). *Dance, art, and aesthetics*. London: Dance Books Limited.

Shelton, S. (1981). *Divine dancer: A biography of Ruth St. Denis*. Garden City, NY: Doubleday & Co., Inc.

Siegel, M. B. (1987). *Days on earth: The dance of Doris Humphrey*. New Haven, CT and London: Yale University Press.

Stodelle, E. (1978). *The dance technique of Doris Humphrey and its creative potential*. Princeton, NJ: Princeton Book Co.

Snyder, A. F. (1972). The dance symbol. *CORD Research Annual, 6*, 213–224.

Winter, D. G., et al. (1981). *A new case for the liberal arts: Assessing institutional goals and student development*. San Francisco: Jossey-Bass Publishers.

Lynn Matluck Brooks is director of dance at Franklin and Marshall College, Lancaster, Pennsylvania 17604-3003.

University Dance: Some Questions

Jan Van Dyke

There was a time, not long ago, when, as a free-lance dance artist, I saw little need for dance-oriented theoretical work or a broad-based education in a field geared to performance. For twenty years, my life had been centered on dancing, on being active, making dance visible and possible, seeing that things happened. Today, after three years of doctoral study and one and a half years working as an assistant professor of dance, my point of view has changed. Slowly, I have become aware of the distinction between "training"—which most other serious dance students and I have sought over the years—and "education": the difference between how to produce a better dancer and how best to educate dancers as citizens and members of a culture. I have begun to view the dance studio as confining, and with it, the perspective of the performer, defined by its emphasis on personal readiness. And as my point of view slowly broadens to include more of the world, I glimpse the difficulties in trying to accommodate both approaches at once.

Over the past few years, in adjusting to life within the university, I have experienced a kind of culture shock, finding myself part of a system with its own values, strengths, and weaknesses, quite separate from the professional dance world. Many of my graduate classes were conducted as dialogues between professor and students. After a lifetime of silently taking dance classes, I found myself overcome by shyness and insecurity at having to speak. My initial feelings were of being radically out of context, of having nothing to contribute to the ongoing discussion, of having come from another world, of confusion and uncertainty about my own beliefs. After sitting in these classes I would explode into the technique classes I was teaching, filling the room with my relief at having something to say, being in control, having a voice. But as I continued working toward my EdD, I became aware of questions about technique within the university setting and I began trying to reconcile what

I know the profession demands with the realities and values of the university.

In dance, as in any physical skill, discipline is essential. Repetition is accepted as ritual and we work for years to learn control and precision, trying to get it right, rarely questioning the why but only the how to. Learning technique is not a creative process nor does it promote critical thinking. In fact, technical training can work against creativity physically in the sense that, with enough repetition, muscles become programmed to more in ways that feel right (we call it "muscle memory"), making it difficult to break out of habitual patterns into new stylistic areas. Wanting to be dancers, we imitate our teachers and accept this training as necessary to building a strong technique. The daily channeling of concentration through the same patterns again and again, the nonverbal acceptance of direction and correction, being pulled to a norm, trying to look right—these are familiar to any dancer who has undertaken serious training, and they are not elements that encourage creative problem solving or critical response. The latter, historically, have been the domain of higher education. Technical training and the philosophical premises of a liberal arts education have never fit comfortably together.

Because university dance programs have traditionally required creative and/or scientific work and theoretical study, while sometimes downplaying the importance of technical training, they have tended to attract and develop dancers more interested in ideas and individual expression than those trained entirely in professional studios. In the university, dance began within physical education programs and from early on was focused on using the form to serve the ends of education by stimulating the imagination and broadening the "social capabilities of the individual that he may at once profit from and serve the greater world without" (Margaret H'Doubler quoted in Ruyter, 1979, p. 102). My perception is that, before 1970, university dance students normally went on to become the

27

dancer/teachers or dancer/scholars of the field, with only a small percentage making a career of performing. This lack of emphasis on technique in the academic curriculum allowed universities and colleges to graduate students in four years, though many were, at that point, not employable as professional dancers. Thus, in spite of apparent common interests, a schism developed between the academic dance world and the professional field, reflecting a deep divergence of values centering on the question of whether one is trying to train the dancer or educate the person, to teach skills or build inner resources (Kraus & Chapman, 1981, p. 158).

Since the mid-1960s, the number of American colleges and universities offering dance has grown steadily. At the same time, an evolution within the academic dance setting has been occurring with longterm implications for the field: the point of view has shifted. In an effort to integrate professional with educational viewpoints, the trend has been to move away from an administrative base in physical education, becoming either an independent dance department or program, or part of a department or school concerned with other performing arts, such as music or theatre (Kraus & Chapman, p. 292). In addition, dance faculties have adopted professional equivalencies to academic degrees, allowing for the increased hiring of performing artists as teachers. Some have encouraged older dancers to return to school by permitting the transformation of professional career experiences into academic credit.

Moreover, there has been a move to institutionalize professional training standards. In 1981, representatives from academic dance programs met in Washington, D.C. to consider the establishment of an accreditation association for educational programs in dance. As a result of that meeting, the National Association of Schools of Dance was formed. Forty-eight institutions became charter members: ten professional dance training organizations and thirty-eight colleges and universities. NASD describes its function as one of finding

> ways of clarifying and maintaining standards in dance through the responsible education of dancers. By means of accreditation, it can encourage those institutions that consistently give students a sound basis for significant future accomplishments in dance. (NASD, 1987, p. 2)

Membership is based on criteria such as curriculum, admission policies, sequencing of classes, length of time in operation, faculty qualifications, facilities and equipment, advertising, financial policies, and student access to libraries. Standards and guidelines are described as having evolved from a synthesis of thought about professional training in dance and are to be used as part of the peer review process of accreditation, rather than as a set of rules and regulations. According to NASD literature, standards for admission to the organization are meant to provide the basis for dialogue on three levels: within an institution as the self-study (which is necessary for application) is being developed, between an institution and the Association (during the period of evaluation), and between the Association and the general public.

Rona Sande, former director of the dance division at the University of California at Santa Barbara, was one of the dance educators who formulated these standards. Sande says that the NASD has, in a real sense, given university dance departments permission to do what many now want to do anyway: to require an intensive studio component within their programs. Additionally, she says, accreditation has helped legitimize dance programs within the university community, particularly among administrators with budgetary and discretionary powers (Sande, 1989).

"Professional" and "Liberal Arts"

Today, the Association has three categories of accredited membership. Division I is for dance schools and studios seeking legitimation in the eyes of the profession and the public. Divisions II and III are for college and university departments looking for professional credibility. The separation between Divisions II and III marks the difference between a "professional" degree and a "liberal arts" degree. The associate of fine arts and the bachelor of fine arts degrees are both included in Division II and both "require that at least 65% of the course credit be in studio work and related areas" (NASD, 1987, p. 40). This describes a strongly focused course of study, narrowed to the development of technical skills and dance artistry, in essence, a vocational degree. The liberal arts degrees are called associate of arts or science and bachelor of arts or science with a major in dance. These degrees usually require that one-third to one-half the total course credit be in dance. NASD describes Division III as including "schools and departments whose predominant purpose and enrollment are in quality education in dance" (NASD, 1985, p. 3), a telling distinction from BFA (Division II), which has as "its primary emphasis . . . the development of skills, concepts and sensibilities essential to the dance professional" (NASD, 1987, p. 41).

The difference between Division II and Division III points to the dissimilarity in emphasis between educating dancers as people and training dancers for dance. In its listing in the 88/89 *Dancemagazine College Guide (Lawson, 1988)*, the University of California at Santa Barbara, a public, state-supported university, makes the distinction clear:

> The BFA degree is oriented toward training the dance student for a professional career in performance and/or choreography and the curriculum is centered around studio courses and related theatrical experiences. The BA degree is a less structured program and allows time for students to pursue course work that could lead to alternate careers. . . . (p. 87)

This distinction affects dancers throughout their lives, bearing on both the transition they must make at the end of a performing career and on their ability to survive in a field where a "job" as a dancer rarely provides a living wage. It also points up an issue that is becoming more important within the dance world itself: Can educators reconcile the demand from the field for excellence in technique with the simultaneous demand for choreographers who have both skill and vision? What is the relationship between intensive technical training and the development of choreographic ability? Most professionally trained dancers learn to think technically, narrowing their concerns to rehearsing, injuries, diet, physical mastery, and survival issues: how to get work, the critical response to current and future work, and who is doing what. Would this be different with a stronger background in the humanities? With a broader education, might we not become more resonant artists with a stronger sense of our connection to the society in which we work? Today's dance might then be less concerned with itself, with technique and dancing, and deal more with new ways of viewing the times.

I first encountered the distinction between education and training when I began doctoral studies in 1986. It was new to me and seemed to imply that by thinking in terms of training, the term we use to describe a concentration on technique and production, we in dance deny our students balance. Already, in my professional life, I had been aware of a lack of verbal confidence and my narrow range of abilities. I was also conscious of the passive acceptance among dancers of professional situations that are sometimes inhumane and the lack of power many of us feel in response to press coverage and the political dance establishment, or in simply being able to speak intelligently about work we are interested in doing. With many dancers, there is a notable lack of relationship with the world outside the dance studio. In fact, in my experience, many dancers willingly exchange a lack of general power within society for the very personal sense of power that comes from having strong physical skills.

This is a trade-off with serious implications. The precursors of modern dance, the two women who pioneered the field, were not technicians and did not grow up in dance studios. Isadora Duncan and Ruth St. Denis were largely self-taught (Page, 1984, p. vii). Both trained sporadically in assorted styles ranging from Delsartian interpretations to ballroom dance, acrobatic tricks, and a brief introduction to ballet (Ruyter, 1979). Since their time, many of the artists considered leaders in modern dance, the innovators, the more creative minds, also have not been people who trained intensively in technique. Doris Humphrey did start dancing at the age of eight (Humphrey, 1966, p. 17), but Martha Graham waited, because of parental opposition, until she was 22 to begin her studies (McDonagh, 1973, p. 52). Paul Taylor got "a flash, or whatever it is . . . telling me that I'm to become a dancer—not any old dancer, but one of the best" (Taylor, 1987, p. 26), when he was a sophomore in college with no previous dance experience. Merce Cunningham has had a lifelong interest in theatre and began intermittent dance study at the age of eight, but he came to the study of modern dance during his college years (Cunningham, 1985, p. 33). Erick Hawkins began studying dance after college graduation (McDonagh, 1976, p. 297), and Jose Limon, who thought he would be a painter, came to his first dance classes at the age of 20 (Gadan & Maillard, 1959, p. 214). Alwin Nikolais initiated his training at the Bennington College School of Dance as a young man (Gadan & Maillard, p. 242), and Alvin Ailey started studying with Lester Horton while in his teens (Mazo, 1984, p. 23). Yvonne Rainer says she began studying dance in earnest in 1959, when she was 25 (Rainer, 1974, p. 5).

How Do People Learn To Dance?

These experiences raise a number of issues on the broad question of how people learn to dance. Is there a relationship between technical training and creativity and leadership? As we train bodies to be disciplined and obedient instruments, skilled at following directions, accustomed to taking correction, working silently to become a vehicle for another person's ideas, are we also training minds in the same way? Are serious, long-term dance students put at a disadvantage in today's society, sacrificing language and social skills for movement and technical training?

Speaking as one who spent much of her youth in the dance studio, I find that the very questions and their implications are uncomfortable. Discipline and obedience are high on the list of values we instill in dance students, and they are, on the whole, not the makings of creative leadership and innovation. What would Yvonne Rainer's work have been like had she studied dance for ten years before arriving in New York? As it was, she was 25 before she began serious work. Understandably, she had no tradition to uphold, and though she was an earnest student, the realization that she would never fit the mold of "dancer" in this society gave her an ambivalence that developed into a radical response, an adversarial posture in regard to the dance establishment (Chin, 1975). "The choices in my work are predicated on my own peculiar

resources . . . and also on an ongoing argument with, love of, and contempt for dancing" (Rainer, p. 71), she said, and in this context, the extraordinary directions she pursued make clear sense.

> I suspected that I would never be "good enough" to dance in an official company. Although I was becoming more proficient in conventional technical matters, the chunky construction of my body and my lack of natural litheness did not fit the popular image of the female dancer. (Chin, p. 51)

So she made work that defied that image. More important, she was not so identified with dance that she could not defy it. Because she had a broad background to bring to it, her work was not about trying to fit in.

A point of view, necessary to the development of one's own voice as an artist, needs cultivation and stimulation, exposure to ideas, and faith in one's own ability to know the truth. Richard Kraus and Sarah Chapman (1981) state that most dance educators today believe their position in education is strengthened by a growing recognition of the need for educational experiences that will provide a sense of personal involvement, helping students become aware of their uniqueness and capable of making meaningful judgments within all areas of life. Perhaps these kinds of experiences occur in programs that include dance in a general curriculum, but are they reflected in the way professionally oriented dance students are being taught? In fact, the restricted focus of a professionally-oriented dance program cuts out the social and philosophical grounding needed to understand the world and form a response to it and, without doubt, affects both art and lives in the long run.

Excellence in any field requires some narrowing of focus. As a dancer, I have valued my own technical ability and worked hard to increase it, enjoying the power it gives me, the pride in myself, and the range of performing opportunities it has opened to me. The issue here is how to balance the concentra-

Broadening the education of dancers will transform the field of dance in unpredictable ways. *Photos at left and opposite page from the dance program at Mankato State University, Mankato, Minnesota.*

tion required for this kind of achievement with the breadth and scope necessary for an active participation in the culture around us. Our problem—and the problem of the university programs involved with meeting the demands of the dance profession—is that the technical requirements of a professional career are so consuming that time taken out for other areas of study necessarily inhibits energy, concentration, and momentum in a very competitive field. However, university programs are uniquely placed to offer dance within a context meaningful to both the person and the professional in each student and could, with thought to curriculum, begin to exert profound influence over the teaching of dance.

Teaching About Choices

If long-term, rigorous technical training is the only way to produce versatile and skilled dancers, should we not also from the beginning teach dance students to develop their minds and emotional beings along with their bodies? Beginning training after the age of ten, teaching nonjudgmentally while providing information on safety and style, and allowing time for students to work out problems with combinations individually and together during class are all ways in which we might begin. Allowing discussion of why things are done the way they are to be a regular part of learning technique is another. Providing a context for what is being taught will give students a clearer picture of a world in which they can make choices, as will linking a particular technique to a belief system.

Encouraging the development of a point of view can only help to balance the discipline built in to longterm technical training.

We must be sure that dancers can separate the person from the function and that we teach them to strengthen both aspects. We do want to give students the skills required for moving with power and articulation. That sense of control is, I think, what draws many young women to the field, giving them a realm where they feel a certain empowerment. But we do not want them to stop there. While teaching physical skills, we must watch that we do not also teach dependency, creating followers and giving freedom only within the restrictions of the studio or the confines of a role.

The unanswered question is: How much do we require dance to stay as it is? By broadening the education of dancers we will be transforming the field in ways that cannot be predicted. Certainly dancers will become less pliant, more questioning of how they are used, and more conscious of their own power, as well as more aware of the context and history of their art. Perhaps the form will evolve to fit the dancers rather than the reverse process, to which we are so accustomed. Today, both dancers and choreographers find themselves swept up in the culture-wide worship of success, spectacle, and mastery. Western dance has traditionally held these qualities to be important and has tailored its training programs to suit its values. For a time, it seemed that with the work of Margaret H'Doubler and Anna Sokolow and the early work of Martha Graham and others, individualism and democratic thought would have an influence on the art. The old values have withstood the intrusion, how-

31

ever, and continue to exert a profound influence on standards within the field, on methods of training, and on priorities in dancers' lives.

Serving dance students within the university system remains a challenging issue. How best can we join the demands of the field with the educational grounding necessary for the creation of an authoritative art that can help us see ourselves, make us aware of what we take for granted, and lead us to provocative questions about the way we live? What we all want is the best possible situation for dance and dancers. In order to achieve this, we must continue to examine what we are doing, reflecting not only on how to be excellent dancers, but on how to be active and responsive members of our culture as well.

References

Chin, D. (1975). Add some more cornstarch, or the plot thickens: Yvonne Rainer's *Work 1961–73. Dance Scope, 9,* 60-64.

Cunningham, M. (1985). *The dancer and the dance.* New York, London: Marion Boyars.

Gadan, F., & Maillard, R. (Eds.). (1959). *Dictionary of modern ballet.* New York: Tudor Publishing Company.

Humphrey, D. (1966, spring). New dance: An unfinished autobiography. *Dance Perspectives, 25,* 9–77.

Kraus, R.G., & Chapman, S.A. (1981). *History of the dance in art and education.* Englewood Cliffs, NJ: Prentice-Hill.

Lawson, W.J. (Ed.). (1981). *88/89 College guide.* New York: Dance Magazine, Inc.

McDonagh, D. (1973). *Martha Graham: A biography.* New York, Washington: Praeger Publishers.

McDonagh, D. (1976). *The complete guide to modern dance.* Garden City, NY: Doubleday & Company, Inc.

National Association of Schools of Dance. (1985). *A brochure describing the functions of the association.* Reston, VA: author.

National Association of Schools of Dance. (1987). *Handbook 1988–1989.* Reston, VA: author.

Page, R. (1984). *Class: Notes on dance classes around the world 1915–1980.* Princeton, NJ: Princeton Book Company, Publishers.

Rainer, Y. (1974). *Work 1961–73.* Halifax: The Press of the Nova Scotia College of Art and Design; New York: New York University Press.

Ruyter, N.L.C. (1979). *Reformers and visionaries.* New York: Dance Horizons.

Sande, R. (1989, February). Conversation with Rona Sande.

Taylor, P. (1987). *Private domain.* New York: Alfred A. Knopf.

Jan Van Dyke is in the Dance Department at the University of North Carolina, Greensboro, North Carolina 27412.

Teacher
Education

Content Knowledge in Dance Education

Sylvie Fortin

In recent years, considerable attention and debate have focused on educational reform. In higher education, many educational reformers have recommended legislation requiring teachers to complete more course work in their own subject matter. This recommendation is based on the assumption that content knowledge is a "logical precondition for the activities of teaching" (Buchmann, 1983). Parallel to that, many education researchers have started to investigate the nature, the sources, and the development of subject matter knowledge in teacher preparation, as well as the influences that teachers' subject matter knowledge has on student achievement. The result has been a dramatic change in the way in which the knowledge base for teaching is conceptualized, and the newly emerging paradigm reflecting that change has begun to influence how experts think about teaching, how teacher education curricula are structured, and how research agendas on teaching are organized. It is important that dance educators become aware of the issues raised by this paradigm. The meaning of a knowledge-based approach to dance in higher education merits investigation and critical examination.

Three texts, *A Nation Prepared: Teachers for the 21st Century* (Carnegie Commission Task Force, 1986), *Tomorrow's Teachers: A Report of the Holmes Group* (Holmes Group, 1986), and the *Handbook of Research on Teaching* (third edition, Wittrock, 1986), are examples of the effort to improve teaching. Educator Penelope Peterson (1988) observes that although the three reports reflect different perspectives, they converge on several common themes such as the conception of teachers as "thoughtful" professionals who define their knowledge bases in systematic terms. Educator Lee Shulman (1987) is explicit on this point:

> The advocates of professional reform base their arguments on the belief that there

exists a "knowledge base for teaching"—a codified or codifiable aggregation of knowledge, skills, understanding, and technology, of ethics and disposition, of collective responsibility—as well as a means for representing and communicating it. (p. 4)

According to Shulman, any organization of teacher knowledge should include the following categories: knowledge of learners and their characteristics, knowledge of educational contexts, knowledge of educational ends, curriculum knowledge, general pedagogical knowledge, content knowledge, and pedagogical content knowledge. While much might be said about each of these categories, I will direct my attention first to pedagogical content knowledge and then to content knowledge.

Pedagogical content knowledge "represents the blending of content and pedagogy into an understanding of how particular topics, problems, or issues are organized, represented, and adapted to the diverse interests and abilities of learners, and presented for instruction" (Shulman, 1987, p. 8). Pedagogical content knowledge is a pedagogical understanding of the subject matter, the key that distinguishes a teacher from a nonteaching peer in the same discipline. Shulman (1986) refers to it as a missing paradigm because he notices that research on teaching has established quite a sharp distinction between subject matter and pedagogy. Indeed, most research on pedagogical knowledge in the 1980s refers to the broad principles and strategies of classroom management and organization that appear to transcend subject matter. Directing research toward the investigation of pedagogical content knowledge could serve to reverse this tendency of discussing the teaching profession mainly in generic pedagogical terms.

Also implicit in the paradigm of pedagogical content knowledge is an enriching of the notion of content knowledge. To the lay person, it would seem that content knowledge is just what the future teacher will have to teach. But in the framework of a knowledge base for teaching, content knowledge means more than expertise in the subject matter, more than the "stuff" that is to be learned by students. In this use, content knowledge is made manifest not just in *what* the teachers teach but in the personal internalized understanding they have of *why* they teach what they teach. "To think properly about content knowledge," declares Shulman (1986), "requires going beyond knowledge of the facts or concepts of a domain." He continues:

> Teachers must not only be capable of defining for students the accepted truth in a domain, they must also be able to explain why a particular proposition is deemed warranted, why it is worth knowing and how it relates to other propositions, both within the discipline and without, both in theory and in practice. . . . Moreover, we expect the teacher to understand why a given topic is particularly central to a discipline whereas another may be peripheral. (p. 9)

Shulman stresses the importance of investigating content knowledge because it is a necessary condition to have pedagogical content knowledge.

In the area of dance technique, if we accept Shulman's concept of content knowledge, then we must assume that when dance teachers possess content knowledge, they have mastered to a high degree the practical skills of their art form and have gained a broad and deep understanding of dance as a subject matter. Because of the physical component of dance, I believe that it is helpful to discriminate clearly two aspects of content knowledge: conceptual content knowledge and technical content knowledge.

Technical content knowledge is the knowing *how*. It is the predominant kind of knowledge in dance education programs. A look at the *College Guide 1990–91: A Directory of Dance in North American Colleges and Universities* reveals that dance teacher education programs usually stress the physical pursuits by an audition at the entry and the requirement of a long sequence of technical courses throughout the program. At the end of their undergraduate program, most dance teachers master, at quite a high level, the main skills of different dance styles such as the fall/recovery of the Limon technique or the contraction/release of the Graham technique. According to Judith Gray (1989), this kind of knowledge, compiled from experience, "prepares the student to perform a specific technique or apply a certain knowledge to a singular dance setting" (p. 82). What Gray refers to as heuristic knowledge and what I call here tech-

nical content knowledge may also be related to Harry S. Broudy's (1977) concept of replicative schooling in which "the school input is recalled pretty much as learned" (p. 9).

On the other hand, conceptual content knowledge is the knowing *why* and the knowing *about*. A teacher with such knowledge is not only able to do the physical skill but also able to provide, with insight and understanding, a descriptive account of how it is done and why it is worthwhile to execute each movement in a particular way. A teacher with conceptual content knowledge is also able to generate alternative explanations, representations, or clarifications of the same principle. It is this kind of knowledge that enables a teacher to develop abstract theories that can be applied to a large number of different situations. For example, a dance teacher trained in Graham technique not only should know the Graham vocabulary and the progression usually presented in this technique, but should also be able to pinpoint the first principle of the technique, the Graham contraction, which is one important dance movement that strengthens the core muscles of the body. When the core muscles are strong, the entire spine and torso are supported, which improves the execution of the movements of upper as well as lower limbs. In addition, the teacher should be able to relate the Graham contraction to the concepts of "centering" that dancers of all styles have worked with in one way or another. Graham's contraction, Bartenieff's "hollowing," the navel radiation of Bonnie Bainbridge Cohen, the "chi" of Tae Kwon Do or

Aikido, to name just a few, all appear similar in terms of physical characteristics despite their different labels.

Both kinds of content knowledge, conceptual and technical, are desirable in a dance education program. Conceptual knowledge is useless unless students know how to apply it concretely in a particular setting, and technical knowledge is limited when students have to work in a setting different from the one where they received their training. Unfortunately, I believe that dance teachers often rely strongly on their skills mastery or technical knowledge when teaching and do not sufficiently emphasize the comprehension, transformation, and reflection of their own training in order to adapt to the characteristics of a particular setting. At least two reasons may partially explain this strong emphasis on technical knowledge.

One reason may be the historical development of dance teaching. While in North America the dance performances have continuously changed over time, the actual training of dancers did not follow the same pattern. According to Gray (1989):

> In many cultures, one person was assigned the role of conveying dance movements, usually without embellishment or innovation. Dance usually evolved over time and changed subtly rather than dramatically . . . the dancers have handed down pedagogical strategies and acted as dance teachers ever since leading and following became forms of teaching and learning. Dance teachers traditionally have taught as they themselves were taught; role modeling is still dominant in the training of dance teachers. (p. 3)

The consequence of teaching as one has been taught fails to answer the new and changing demands of our western society. The last ten years have seen an increasing demand for dance teachers in various settings such as public schools and recreational or professional studios (McLaughlin,

"Spell," choreographed by Dana Levy and performed by Dana Levy and Eoin O'Brien, representing the Ohio State University at the 1991 Midwest Conference of the American College Dance Festival Association. *Photos by Mark Teague.*

(1988). According to Madeleine Lord (1984), a dance educator, dance teachers have the tendency to reproduce the model of instruction adopted in professional settings while teaching in educational or recreational settings. I believe that dance teachers often reproduce the dominant model of teaching they have received in their training because they do not have enough appropriate knowledge to be able to make the necessary adjustments that a different context requires. If someone has learned dance as a certain repertoire of skills to master and does not have a broad competency in the subject matter of dance in general, his or her range of effective teaching is limited at the outset.

Aside from the power of tradition in dance teaching, another reason for the predominance of technical content knowledge in dance programs in general and in particular in higher education is the paucity of research. Data based research represents an important contribution to the development of conceptual knowledge but research evidence in dance is relatively new and scarce. Shulman (1979) wrote that there was relatively little research conducted on teaching in the arts. Gray (1989) indicates that the situation has not changed, especially in dance teaching: "Research in dance teaching has to date been restricted to isolated studies of teacher behavior and limited investigations of students' attitudes and achievement" (p. 9). The body of disciplinary knowledge based on systematic study is still quite new. This is not surprising when one considers that research is mainly conducted in universities and that Margaret H'Doubler established the first dance major in higher education at the University of Wisconsin in 1926 and departments of dance did not gain autonomy until the 1960s.

Beliefs and Behaviors Changing

In recent years, the situation has, however, changed rapidly. Dance scholars are developing a positive attitude toward systematic inquiry and are more and more appropriately trained to do so. From the limited focus stated above, research in dance now encompasses the areas of kinesiology, psychology, computer motion analysis, etc. The recent *Dance: Current Selected Research* journal testifies to the growing interest of the dance community in systematic studies.

New knowledge is emerging from a variety of sources, and it is prompting teachers to change their beliefs and behaviors. According to Martha Myers (1989), the general picture of dance education is beginning to change. For example, throughout the United States and Canada, more and more higher education programs are including some adjunctive training in their regular schedules. Known as body-therapy or somatic practices, these idiosyncratic practices were developed by individuals such as F. M. Alexander, Irmgard Bartenieff, Bonnie Bainbridge Cohen, and Moshe Feldenkrais. Marginal to the mainstream of traditional technical training, the priority of the somatic educators is experiential knowledge. Although having different assumptions from the systematic researchers, somatic educators challenge the tradition of dance training the same way systematic researchers do.

My point here is that the increasing attention given to scientific research as well as body therapies reveals an important change in the conception of relevant knowledge in dance. This should help foster the development of instruction of the highest quality while simultaneously encouraging varied and experimental approaches to the teaching of dance, which is one of the objectives of the National Association of Schools of Dance as stated in its *Information Bulletin* (NASD, 1989).

According to Tony Eichelberger (1989), knowledge comes from three different sources: tradition, systematic research, and personal experience. In dance, tradition that emphasizes technical content knowledge is the main guide for educators (Clarkson, 1988). However, people from two different allegiances are beginning to challenge what Clarkson refers to as the "dancer's close-minded approach to training" (p. 18). On the one hand, there are those scholars whose intent is to break the dance teaching tradition by introducing new conceptual knowledge based on systematic inquiry. And, on the other hand, there are somatic educators who pursue the same ultimate goal but who root their conceptualization in their personal observation of the moving body. Although Eichelberger notes that "in making decisions, or drawing conclusions, one of the weakest logical foundations for doing anything is an appeal to authority" (p. 13), I believe that any dance teaching decisions must be made on the basis of all three sources of knowledge. "Dance education is changing," writes Sarah Chapman (1988); "a new vision has begun to emerge, one which embraces the truth and integrity of earlier decades of our discipline while planning for and shaping an expanded dialogue to guide us toward a new century" (p. 57).

So far, I have addressed the issues of sources and types of content knowledge, distinguishing technical content knowledge from conceptual content knowledge. I would now like to turn to pedagogical knowledge. It is important to reiterate that, whereas the area of pedagogical knowledge may be well established in other educational settings, this is not the case in dance. Little attention has been devoted to the elements of the teaching process, and dance educators have thus far minimized training in interaction skills and the management of time and students (Frances-Fisher, 1989).

Here again I think that significant changes are emerging in the dance community. For instance, during the last two years, the school of Les Grands Ballets Canadiens in Montréal has been offering its instructors a course in the pedagogy of dance, a change from its previous policy of depending exclusively upon the mastery of a repertoire of movements. However, it is important to point out that the addition of pedagogical knowledge will not translate automatically into better teaching, just as content knowledge alone, whether it is technical or conceptual, does not translate directly into better teaching in the classroom. There is much that remains to be done in the area of dance pedagogy, and this is an important challenge facing dance teachers today. One of the most important tasks we face is to determine future directions.

Inquiry-Oriented Dance Curriculum

Shulman's notion of pedagogical content knowledge appears to be a worthwhile direction. Art education programs should have, according to Daniel Reeves (1987),

> not only pedagogy and content but also the
> practice of integrating the two as their
> undergraduate education matures. . . .
> Strong art education programs are ones
> that succeed in integrating professional
> studies and discipline content so that future
> arts teachers learn how to apply knowledge
> and skills to instructional settings. (p. 41)

Reeves clearly concurs with Shulman's view. Content knowledge and pedagogical knowledge inform each other and the blending of the two deserves specific attention from scholars. A pedagogical content knowledge approach results in a shift in the way we will ask questions. "What will I teach today?" would change to "Why and how will I teach that to this particular clientele today?" In other words, the knowledge base paradigm calls for a dance curriculum that is inquiry-oriented rather than focused on replication. As Penelope Hanstein (1990) states so appropriately, "when taught only

as the replication of steps, as a closed system in which the ends are preset and the outcomes tightly controlled, we fail to promote the kind of inquiry, imaginative thinking, and discovery necessary for ordering our experience and making sense out of our lived world" (p.56).

In the attempt to provide relevant knowledge to dance educators, it is important to maintain a balanced approach to conceptual content knowledge, technical content knowledge, and pedagogical content knowledge. In the field of physical education, for instance, the absence of such a balance has resulted in an alarming situation. Daryl Siedentop (1989) explains that there was a turning point in the mid-1960s when people started to wish for a more intellectual approach to physical education. This view has resulted in a proliferation of courses in undergraduate programs such as motor learning, motor control, sport psychology, sport history, sport philosophy, exercise physiology, kinesiology, and biomechanics, allowing less time for the actual practice of physical education. The situation now is that physical educators are demanding programs less oriented toward the theoretical mastery of physiological, historical, psychological, or pedagogical components of physical education. They want to restore technical content knowledge to a central place in the curriculum. The reason is simple: without a minimal technical content knowledge, it is reasonable to think that someone cannot teach effectively. The physical education teacher of youth sport teams, for instance, should be able to demonstrate the sport activities at a level beyond that at which the students are performing.

It is interesting to note that the broad concept of pedagogical content knowledge meets the interest of academic disciplines as well as physical education or dance, but each of them emphasizes different aspects. The concept of pedagogical content knowledge has emerged from research on academic disciplines moving the study of teaching from general findings on pedagogy to particularities of the subject matter. In physical education, this emphasis on the specific knowledge of the subject matter has driven scholars to call for programs with better consideration of the type of knowledge that is relevant to physical education. Unlike physical education, dance has kept its focus on technical content knowledge. This may have contributed to the move away of dance from the field of physical education 20 years ago when the latter field began to overstress its conceptual content knowledge, which was a different conceptual knowledge from the one appropriate to the discipline of dance.

In the dance community, where the metaphor "the teacher as artist" is very popular, a commitment to the importance of consistency among technical, conceptual, and pedagogical knowledge should be welcomed by dance researcher and education community. Both must understand the centrality of pedagogical content knowledge and the consequences of a lack of such knowledge. They must also understand that implicit in the concept of a knowledge base is the premise that knowledge is constantly in a state of evolution; it is not perceived as static. As Hanstein (1990) expresses so well,

> The increasing complexity of our society requires us, and the students who will shape the future, to function in tasks that demand imaginative thinking and the ability to suggest alternatives and formulate hypotheses. Education in general, and dance education in particular, should focus on developing the ability to see the connection between actions and their consequences and between means and ends, to take cognitive risks, and to extend thinking beyond the known in order to deal effectively with what might be rather than with what is. (p. 57)

References

Broudy, H. S. (1977). Types of knowledge and purposes of education. In R.C. Anderson & R.J. Spiro (Eds., *Schooling and the acquisition of knowledge*. Hillsdale, NJ: Lawrence Erlbaum.

Buchmann, M. (1983). *The priority of knowledge and understanding in teaching*. Occasional paper #61. Michigan State University Institute for Research on Teaching. (ERIC Document Reproduction Service No. ED 237-503).

Carnegie Commission Task Force. (1986). *A nation prepared: Teachers for the 21st century* (The Report of the Task Force on Teaching as a Profession). New York: Carnegie Corporation.

Chapman S. A. (1988). Shaping a new vision. *Journal of Physical Education, Recreation and Dance, 59*(9), 57.

Clarkson, P. (1988). Science in dance. In P. Clarkson & M. Skrinar (Eds.), *Science of dance training* (pp. 17–21). Champaign, IL: Human Kinetics.

College Guide 1990–91: A directory of dance in North American colleges and universities. (1990). [Special issue] *Dance Magazine*.

Eichelberger, R. T. (1989). *Disciplined inquiry: Understanding and doing social research*. New York: Longman.

Frances-Fisher, J. E. (1989). What student choreographers need to know. *Dance Teacher Now, 11*(44), 40–43.

Gray, J. (1989). *Dance instruction—Science applied to the art of movement*. Champaign, IL: Human Kinetics.

Hanstein, P. (1990). Educating for the future: A postmodern paradigm for dance education. *Journal of Physical Education, Recreation and Dance, 61*(5), 56–58.

Holmes Group, Inc. (1986). *Tomorrow's teachers: A report of the Holmes Group*. East Lansing, MI: Author.

Lord, M. (1984). Enseigner avec souplesse ou l'art de s'adapter à sa classe. *Magazine Danse au Canada, 39*, 26–27.

McLaughlin, J. (1988). A stepchild comes of age. *Journal of Physical Education, Recreation and Dance, 59*(9), 58–60.

Myers, M. (1989, Spring). *Dance science and somatic education in dance training*. Keynote address for the Australian Association of Dance Education biennial meeting.

National Association of Schools of Dance. (1989, May). *Information Bulletin*. Reston, VA: Author.

Peterson, P. L. (1988). Teachers' and students' cognitional knowledge for classroom teaching and teaching. *Educational Researcher, 17*(5), 5–14.

Reeves, D. J. (1987). Learning to teach art: An integrative process. *Design for Arts in Education, 89*(1), 41–43.

Shulman, L. (1979). Research on teaching in the arts: Review, analysis, critique. In G.L. Kneiter & J. Stallings (Eds.), *The teaching process and aesthetics: Third yearbook on research in arts and aesthetic education*. St. Louis, MO: CEMEREL, Inc.

Shulman, L. (1986). Those who understand: Knowledge growth in teaching. *Educational Researcher, 15*(2), 4–14.

Shulman, L. (1987). Knowledge and teaching: Foundations of the new reform. *Harvard Educational Review, 57*(1), 1–22.

Siedentop, D. (1989, April). *Content knowledge for physical education*. Keynote address to C and I Academy Conference on the Implications of the Knowledge Base for Teaching for Teacher Education, Boston.

Wittrock, M. C. (Ed.). (1986). *Handbook of research on teaching*. (3rd ed.) New York: Macmillan.

Sylvie Fortin is a doctoral candidate at Ohio State University, Columbus, Ohio 43202.

The author wishes to thank Daryl Siedentop, Judith Koroscik, Dixie Durr, and Alida Moonen for their suggestions on the manuscript.

Dance Education Degree Programs in Colleges and Universities

Karen Clemente

This article is based upon a comprehensive national research project conducted during the years 1989 and 1990. It included surveys to college dance departments, state departments of education, and selected dance educators in the public schools. Though the article is primarily based on the particular survey responses by college dance departments in the nation, references are made to individuals who provided information with regard to the larger research project via personal memos, letters, and phone calls.

Dance education as an option for study in higher education loses a great deal of its appeal if job opportunities in the field are nonexistent. The discontinuation of college dance education programs in many states throughout the nation is becoming commonplace. Reasons for this trend are varied. First of all, in the states granting certification, almost all distinguish dance from other areas of study by stating that dance should be the second area of teacher certification in addition to another recognized subject area (Gingrasso, 1987). Or, as in the case of Massachusetts, dance certification is shifting to become a fine arts certification that will, by 1993, include dance, theatre, and communications. California, too, which once had dance certification, now requires that a public school dance teacher must hold certification in another subject area, such as physical education or liberal studies. Similarly, in Minnesota, dance may only be combined with elementary education or theatre arts certification. Under such conditions dance specialist positions are not viable.

Second, in states which do hire dance specialists, few new positions have been created for those teachers; since dance is not mandated as a subject for all students in the schools, there are few job openings in the field of public dance education. For instance, in Wisconsin, approximately five to six dance specialist jobs existed and these had been filled for a number of years. For this reason, at the University of Wisconsin in Stevens Point, college students were discouraged from pursuing a dance education major since, practically speaking, no jobs in public education were available (Gingrasso, personal communication, November 3, 1989).

Mary Elliott, a dance educator in Wisconsin (Orchard Ridge Elementary, Madison), stated that there were only two dance educators in her school system and that her physical education certification was the reason for her job assignment. She further stated that even though the Wisconsin State Board of Education had approved the phasing in of one dance teacher in each elementary school, there was no funding for such an endeavor. Also, though the statewide curriculum guide had been approved by the State Board of Education, there was no forced compliance. The Wisconsin Dance Council was lobbying for such a state mandate, but this particular dance educator stated that the outlook was not encouraging. Without mandates with regard to dance education, the job prospects will remain bleak.

The dance department of the University of Southern Mississippi also reported via the survey that there were few college graduates in the area of dance education and no job opportunities. Furthermore, certification, which had been in effect for ten years in Mississippi, had been lost.

Even in a certification state such as Georgia, as of 1989, no certified dance educators were working in the public schools (Mark Wheeler, University of Georgia). Even though two universities in the state reported the offering of degree programs in dance education, the lack of jobs in the public schools would most definitely seem to threaten the existence of such programs.

At the University of Oregon in Eugene, dance majors who desired jobs in public education were faced with the reality of having to relocate to states with certification or to go on to get a master's degree and teach at a university according to Janet Descutner, University of Oregon Dance Department chair, as reported in the college newspaper (Gilmore, 1989). This department was working to promote dance in public education and to create a climate for the acceptance of dance certification in the state. It was currently providing workshops and lecture-demonstrations to nondance specialists in public schools. These workshops were sponsored by the Western Oregon Institute for the Arts and Education and by the Oregon Dance Association. Also in this state, Sharon Oberst, of Western Oregon State in Monmouth, reported on the 1989–1990 Oregon Dance Association Roundtable Discussion Panel, which focused on ways in which to enhance dance education in public schools (Oberst, personal communication, November 6, 1989). These examples indicate the kind of networking that should be created between teachers in higher education, state dance associations, and public education if certification and job opportunities are to be created in noncertification states.

Many other college dance education programs suffered from the lack of job opportunities available in their respective states. Specifically, according to survey responses, at Fort Hays State University in Kansas, dance education courses were on the books but not currently offered due to lack of student interest. Likewise, in New Jersey at William Paterson College in Wayne, a course in the practice of teaching dance was dropped due to the lack of enrollment. Reasons for such situations were obvious in states with no teacher certification in dance.

However, in New Jersey, a positive move in arts education was reported in February 1990, by Theresa Purcell, a dance educator at Brunswick Acres Elementary School. Purcell provided information regarding the recent appointment of a 25 member advisory council on arts education in New Jersey, of which she is a member. A local newspaper reported that the council had been established to strengthen arts education in the state and work toward the achievement of arts literacy ("Cooperman selects," 1990). Such an effort can be seen as a way to develop dance education programs in public schools and, subsequently, in college dance departments.

Another reason for the discontinuation of college dance education degree programs in many states may be that dance has been viewed by state board of education policymakers as strictly a form of physical education. In such states, dance was taught by teachers who may have possessed certification in physical education but who lacked the qualifications of a dance specialist. Particularly, in Utah and Virginia, dance was a component of the physical education program; however, in Utah dance certification was granted as well.

In Virginia, though the dance programs generally were under physical education departments in the local schools, Susan Damron, of the Arts and Humanities Center of Richmond Public Schools, reported that the center budgeted money for a variety of changing arts programs, which included dance.

The exception to the rule nationwide was the state of North Carolina, which initiated the Basic Education Program in 1984. This program mandated that dance, music, theatre arts, and visual arts become a part of the required curriculum, grades K-12. Unique as this situation was, as recently as 1988, there was a shortage of qualified dance educators to teach in the public schools of North Carolina. Of the four dance educators who provided information regarding their dance programs in North Carolina public schools (Kris Cross, Wake County Public Schools, Raleigh; Barbara O'Brien, Henderson County Schools, Hendersonville; Claudette Saleeby Miller, Charlotte-Mecklenburg Schools, Charlotte; and Cindy Hoban, Apex Elementary [magnet school], Apex), all based their programs on the Basic Education Program and the North Carolina Standard Course of Study (mandated by the state). All reported direct outreach by university dance departments to their programs in such areas as student teaching, teacher renewal credits, and staff development.

Changes in the way state departments of education view the certification issue will contribute to either the increase or the demise of dance education programs in local school districts and subsequently in higher education. If dance is interpreted as a designated subject area and is mandated to be taught, then the potential for jobs will increase; likewise, college dance education programs will expand to meet such needs. The entire issue may be likened to a tightly wound and well-oiled machine that needs the strength of every part for it to achieve its designated work.

University Dance Department Survey

Responses to 1989–1990 surveys mailed to chairpersons of dance departments throughout the nation indicated the degree to which dance education was a current area of focus in college curricula. Surveys were mailed to all four-year private and state colleges/universities with major and/or minor dance programs that offered at least one dance education course in their curriculum. A total of 235 surveys were mailed; 134 completed surveys were received, representing a 57.0% response rate. Questions were asked in the categories of: (a) university acceptance requirements, (b) certification, (c) course work, and (d) outreach. The following paragraphs represent the specific survey results.

University Acceptance Requirements

In the survey category on university acceptance requirements, in response to the question "Does your college/university require that all entering students have completed a high school arts course," 20.2% ($n=27$) answered "yes" and 76.1% ($n=102$) answered "no." Approximately seven years ago, since the College Board had recommended the arts as a requirement for high school graduation, the policy had not become widespread enough to be included in most dance department college admission requirements.

The second question in the category on admission requirements addressed whether or not the dance department identified specific high school arts requirements to be completed prior to admission into the dance major program. Only 2.2% ($n=3$) dance departments answered "yes." Examples listed for the required courses/areas of study were music appreciation, art appreciation, and the humanities. Most wrote that previous dance training was required, but that this training was received in private dance school settings. Of all respondents, 94.0% ($n=126$) answered "no" to the above question. Six schools listed that there was no dance major or at least no dance education emphasis in their department.

Certification

In the survey category on certification, the question, "In your state, is dance a certifiable subject area," yielded a 37.3% ($n=50$) "yes" response and a 59.7% ($n=80$) "no" response. Of the 42 states included in the mailing, 13 currently granted teacher certification in dance on either the elementary or secondary levels, or both. These were: Arizona, Georgia, Idaho, Illinois, Maryland, Massachusetts, Michigan, North Carolina, Ohio, Rhode Island, Texas, Utah, and Wisconsin. At the time of the survey, some states also indicated that dance certification was pending or being reviewed.

If the state in which the college was located granted certification, the question was asked, "Does your department offer a dance certification track?" Answers included: 17.9% ($n=24$) offered an undergraduate emphasis in dance education; 22.4% ($n=30$) offered an undergraduate major in dance education; 6.0% ($n=8$) offered a graduate emphasis in dance education; while 4.5% ($n=6$) offered a graduate major in dance education. These percentages reflected that dance education emphases and/or majors were not prevalent even in states that offered certification, suggesting that job opportunities in public education did not exist within those states.

Also, there seemed to be an apparent lack of interest on the graduate level in the field of dance education. This may have been due to the lack of dance specialist jobs in public education as well as to the practice of hiring graduates with master of fine arts degrees as college teaching personnel. Therefore, those who would be apt to pursue a degree solely in the field of dance education may have been redirected to other degrees or fields because of the dearth in vocational demand.

Course Work

The third section of the survey investigated dance education course work offered in the respective dance departments. Areas listed were curriculum development, movement analysis, philosophy/theory of teaching dance, and practice of teaching dance. Course work in the practice of teaching dance may have included one or all of the following: workshop, practicum, apprenticeship, and student teaching. Additional courses that were included in the category of dance education also could have been listed at the department's discretion as an "other" option.

Courses in curriculum development were offered by 35.1% ($n=47$) of the departments; courses in movement analysis were offered by 58.2% ($n=78$) of the departments; courses in the philosophy/theory of teaching dance were offered by 73.1% ($n=98$) of the departments; and courses in the practice of teaching dance were offered by 79.9% ($n=107$) of the departments, including 17.2%

($n=23$) in workshop, 37.3% ($n=50$) in practicum, 28.4% ($n=38$) in apprenticeship, and 47.0% ($n=63$) in student teaching. Other courses that were considered by the departments as part of the dance education curriculum were listed as "other," 23.9% ($n=32$). Examples of these included internships, choreography for public school students, field experience, general psychology, educational psychology, foundations in education, special education, ideokinesis, perceptual motor, kinesiology/injury prevention, preschool creative dance, biomechanics, aesthetics, dance history, rhythmic analysis, accompaniment for movement, teaching dance activities K-12 for physical education and dance, and residencies. Overall, there was a high percentage of theory and practice of teaching courses offered, an indication that there was enough interest to carry such courses in the dance department curricula.

Question number two in the area of course work inquired into the number of credits a student must carry for either a dance education emphasis or major. For a dance education emphasis, numbers ranged from 16 to 106 quarter hours and from 8 to 150 semester hours. For a dance education major, the range was from 32 to 130 quarter hours and from 6 to 136 semester hours. Credits for minor programs ranged from 18 to 33 both quarter and semester hours. One master's degree through a school of education required 36 quarter hours. The wide ranges depicted the varied degree to which dance education course work was approached in each department, even in those that responded they offered a dance education emphasis or major program. Also, some numbers reflected only dance course requirements; others included all requirements in general education courses, liberal arts courses, and dance courses.

Outreach

The last category of survey questions addressed the dance department policy in regard to outreach to public education. In 23.9% ($n=32$) of the responses, no outreach was reported. The question asked specifically about outreach to dance practitioners in the public schools. Though 66.4% ($n=89$) reported that outreach did occur, only in 26.9% ($n=36$) of the cases did it occur for dance practitioners in local school districts. Many of the respondents explained that no dance education practitioners existed in their schools; therefore, outreach was limited to lecture-demonstrations and performances for students.

In fact, all 66.4% ($n=89$) of those that indicated the practice of outreach included contact with the public school students themselves. Though such outreach is important, trying to locate dance practitioners, in order to offer in-service workshops as well as to create exchange opportunities between dance educators in public education and higher education, becomes a top priority for creating an atmosphere for dance as part of a public school's general curriculum.

In the 26.9% ($n=36$) of departments that did provide outreach to local dance educators, examples of type of support and/or instruction included: networking to offer teacher workshops through the California Arts Project, working with an aesthetics institute to train classroom teachers in the arts (Colorado), giving workshops for dance educators (Connecticut, Massachusetts, Michigan, North Carolina, Oregon, Texas, and Utah), meeting with a secondary education advisory committee (Illinois), offering workshops for awareness of dance as an art form and means of expression (Iowa), working with the Kentucky Department of Education on educating classroom teachers in creative dance (Kentucky), giving workshops through the Comprehensive Arts Education and other specially funded arts programs (Minnesota), giving weekend workshops in creative movement (Montana), providing for curriculum development and supervision (New York and Texas), giving staff development workshops (North Carolina), coordinating arts programs for physical education teachers (Ohio), and serving as consultants for school districts beginning dance programs, as well as serving on an Arts as Basic Curriculum project steering committee (South Carolina).

Table 1 highlights percentages of the above findings in regard to the areas of course work and outreach to public education by college/university dance educators. The table indicates that though course offerings in dance education are commonplace, the existence of dance certification education tracks is low. The lack of job prospects may be seen as a deterrent to attaining dance certification.

The table also shows the difference in the occasion of outreach to public school students (66.4% of all respondents) as opposed to that for public school educators (26.9% of all respondents). The difference may indicate that there is not enough interest and/or time on the part of college/university dance educators or by public school dance educators to initiate such outreach. It may also indicate a lack of support by public school administration. This especially may be the case

Table 1. College/University Dance Department Percentages with Regard to Course Work and Outreach to Public Education

Category	Percentage of respondents	n
Dance Certification track		
Undergraduate emphasis	17.9	24
Undergraduate major	22.4	30
Graduate emphasis	6.0	8
Graduate major	4.5	6
Course work		
Curriculum development	35.1	47
Movement analysis	58.2	78
Philosophy/Theory of teaching dance	73.1	98
Practice of teaching dance:	79.9	107
Workshop	17.2	23
Practicum	37.3	50
Apprenticeship	28.4	38
Student teaching	47.0	63
Other	23.9	32
Outreach		
To public school students	66.4	89
To public school educators	26.9	36

Total number of respondents in the survey = 134; n = number of respondents per question.

Summary and Recommendations

The survey results reveal that college dance education programs are declining throughout the nation. Reasons are varied, but most likely these include: 1) the lack of job opportunities in a state upon the completion of dance education degrees; 2) the lack of state mandates for dance education in public schools; 3) the trend toward combining dance with other subject areas for the purpose of certification; and 4) a state board of education practice that considers dance as a component of physical education rather than as a subject area in its own right.

Even though dance education degree emphases are reduced in number, in philosophy, dance education continues to be viewed with importance by college dance faculty and students alike. This idea is reflected by the presence of course work in the theory and practice of teaching dance in approximately 77% of the survey respondents. Such findings indicate the perceived significance of dance education as a field of study even when lack of certification and/or job opportunities are detrimental to its growth.

with regard to funding for outreach, including financial support for dance educator workshops and staff development course work through colleges/universities in the particular states.

With these survey results in mind, those who believe in the power of dance education should begin to lobby with more determination at the state board of education level for dance programs in the public schools as well as for dance certification. Furthermore, greater networking between public school dance educators and professors in higher education is needed. Two specific projects that would bring together dance educators for the goal of increased dance education programs in the public schools are described here.

State Dance Implementation Strategy Project

Based upon the identification of dance education leaders from the areas of higher education and public education in each state provided by the research study, it would be possible to develop an individual state dance education implementation project to bring together state arts representatives, state education officials, state college/university dance department professors, intermediate unit personnel, and local school district educators with interests in dance. The project would involve the development of dance education programs as part of the state's general curriculum. Issues such as the integration of dance with other arts or other subject areas, the regular offering of dance as an artistic experience within physical education programs, the dance curriculum, and scheduling and facilities for dance would be addressed.

In the first phase of the project, the above issues would be discussed in terms of their appropriateness for specific school districts in the state, which would, in turn, become model programs for other districts. Further, procedures for implementation of dance education in each school district represented would be discussed. Second, after having arrived at a suitable context for dance education within identified school districts, the network of individuals brought together would develop a strategy for the integration of dance education programs in the state with the goal of instituting dance in as many school districts as possible within a three-year period.

These strategies could address all or some of the following structural possibilities: state graduation requirements in the arts satisfied by a dance component (dance as a distinct subject area); dance education implementation via physical education programs; and dance education implementation as one area of study in a fine arts curriculum. Focus would also be placed on policies for hiring dance education personnel where no state dance teacher certification exists and methods for training teaching personnel currently in place.

State Teacher Certification Project in Dance Education

The purpose of the state certification project would be to develop a plan in order to lobby toward separate/distinct teacher certification in dance. The potential participants, who would become a state certification committee, would include interested dance educators such as college/university professors, local school district dance educators, companion personnel in drama/theatre education, and college students in the field of dance education.

The plan would include the following steps: 1) the development of a rationale for dance education in the state's core curriculum; 2) a review of national and/or statewide field test studies of dance curriculum implementation followed by a revision process of state curriculum/curricular guidelines for the arts/dance based on field studies; 3) the selection of a spokesperson(s) for dance education certification in the state; 4) the creation of a position paper by the spokesperson(s) to be delivered to state education officials; 5) the review and revision of the position paper by the state certification committee; and 6) the development of a strategy for the presentation of the position paper at a certification hearing with education officials at the state level.

As a result of this project, based on the committee's rationale statement and the results of the national or statewide field studies in dance education implementation, dance would be more fully perceived as a necessary subject area in public education. Subsequently, the need for qualified teachers potentially would facilitate the certification of teachers in dance.

Similar projects have been initiated in many states and are needed in all of the states so that the field of dance education—especially with regard to public schools, but likewise, higher education—grows stronger in the future.

References

Cooperman selects 25 to serve as arts education advisors. (1990, February 2). *The Times*, p. A-6.
Gilmore, B. (1989). Dancing students not flipping over job outlook. *The Emerald*, University of Oregon.
Gingrasso, S. H. (1987). Dance education certification: Current status and significance. *Design for Arts in Education*, 89 (1), 31–35.

Karen Clemente teaches dance in the Department of Physical Education and Health Science at Eastern College, St. Davids, Pennsylvania 19087.

Prospects for Planned Change in Dance Education

Francine Lee Morin

Over the past three decades, arts educators and scholars have used a variety of written and verbal forums to express the need for change in school arts programs. The prominent recurring theme envisions a transformation from the traditional studio emphasis in arts education to a sequential, comprehensive aesthetic education, more recently labeled discipline-based arts education. This movement is founded upon the structures of arts disciplines and contemporary visions of aesthetics and human cognition. Reformed curricula in the arts aim at balancing perceptual and conceptual funds of information, performance and technical skills, and creative and analytical facilities for all students. There are concerns for interdisciplinary arts learning and approaching instruction in a more serious and rigorous manner. Current dance education literature clearly demonstrates this shift away from a production focus in curriculum thinking (Chapman-Hilsendager, 1989; Côté-Laurence, 1989; George, 1989; Gray, 1989; Howe, 1989; Morin, 1988; National Dance Association, 1988).

Education is continually in need of planned change in order to improve curriculum and instruction and to respond to the reform initiatives that emerge within the professional community. Current professional commentaries and profiles of dance education offerings suggest that change is highly desirable, but continues to be an overriding problem in the field. Sarah Hilsendager (1990) describes present practices within American education: "There are thousands of teachers in public and private education who continue to teach dance as they were taught—as an isolated activity limited to the mastery of discrete movement skills" (p. 25). Although there are multiple factors exerting influence on the change process in any social system, this article focuses on one key factor in school dance reform, higher education.

The key entry point for educational change is teacher preparation and the continuing education of teachers. Reports put forward by the Holmes Group (1986), Carnegie Task Force on Teaching as a Profession (1986), and the National Commission for Excellence in Teacher Education (1985) confirm this point and hint that present mechanisms for our professional work with teachers might be weak. Teacher educators in the dance recognize this problem and call for a reexamination of current practice (Gray, 1989; Gingrasso, 1987; Hilsendager, 1990; Hoad, 1990). A representative comment is made by James Undercofler (1987): "Colleges and universities need to make a complete revision of their arts education curricula. Only through the training of preservice teachers and the ongoing training of inservice teachers can real change be effected" (p. 30).

Along with the initial development of theoretical and practical guidelines for aesthetic arts education, the realities of daily teaching and teacher needs would logically make it imperative that high quality mechanisms for teacher education be worked out. Bernard Rosenblatt and Rene Michel-Trapaga (1975) point out, however, that several years ago teacher education in aesthetic education was either completely ignored or attempted half-heartedly. They state: "The responsibility of educating and informing teachers, administrators, and the community has been passed off from agency to agency like the proverbial waif—none claiming total stewardship, yet everyone expecting great results at the end" (p. 44). Foremost in the literature is the criticism that teachers have not been helped to change through appropriate teacher education experiences (Courtney, 1979; Hamblen, 1983; Karel, 1966; Undercofler, 1987; Wilson, 1989).

The importance that dance teachers themselves

be aesthetically sensitive products of discipline-based dance education programs at the university level must be stressed. To this end, Brent Wilson (1989) criticizes higher education by stating that "the variation in quality and breadth of preparation of teachers in the arts approaches a national scandal" (p. 33). Judith Gray (1989) and Susan Gingrasso (1987) attest to the problem of dance that is taught by educators drawn from distinct groupings who possess different degrees of teacher training, expertise, and interest in the subject. These indicators point to the actuality that universities and colleges in North America have not kept pace with the changes necessary to instruct teachers how to use aesthetic theory to guide action in schools (Holmes, 1986; Reimer, 1989).

A Concept

The typical undergraduate dance program still tends to emphasize technical skills and the compartmentalization of subject matters. Sarah Hilsendager (1990) describes the state of teacher education in dance as philosophically barren and performance-centered. She states that "within dance departments the trend has shifted toward performance, choreography, criticism, history and ethnology as fields of study; teacher preparation has not kept pace" (p. 25). It follows then, that universities turn out graduates who might have had a cursory introduction to aesthetics, so perhaps believe in the principles of an aesthetic, discipline-based education and can speak on superficial levels about the notion, but are unable to teach it effectively because their professors fall back into traditional modes of teaching in applied classes and so do not demonstrate the concept. It is not surprising, since graduates are left to their own devices, that our whole concept of dance in schools is based on performance.

A national inquiry into arts education in Canada provided evidence that even the certification year that arts teachers typically take in a faculty of education is problematic. According to Richard Courtney (1979), during this year the student has little opportunity for methods training in dance. In describing teacher preparation in American dance education Hilsendager (1990) reports that less than 7 percent of those institutes of higher education offering dance programs list practical teaching experiences in public school settings. The methods course and student teaching practicum can and should provide current reformed views for student teachers to emulate, but in the case of dance educa-

tion it seems as though they do not. Our induction programs produce novice teachers who enter the classroom with a fragmented knowledge of dance as a discipline, a brief and theoretical introduction to an aesthetic education or discipline-based arts education philosophy, and little comprehension of how to integrate the two in practice.

Graduate students in arts education, particularly those who teach full-time, also express dissatisfaction with the lack of practicality and usefulness of course work in their teaching (Stencel, 1988). A graduate degree program is often perceived as "consisting of courses that are theoretical and abstract, or completely unrelated to individual teaching needs and professional goals" (p. 11). This perception is due to two basic problems. First, like their undergraduate counterparts, graduate students rarely have the opportunity to see reform ideas discussed in a university seminar put into classroom practice. Second, the limitations of many graduate department offerings result in the need for arts teachers to select courses necessary to finish programs whether or not these courses are relevant to their individual teaching responsibilities. It can be seen, then, that teacher educators in the arts espouse aesthetic or discipline-based philosophies for arts educators, but either leave these ideas in a vague and unstructured form or contradict them by adhering to traditionalism in their practical work with future teachers. This has resulted in the continual dominance of the studio model in school arts programs, which has set in motion a perpetual inhibitor of necessary change.

Immediate improvement and change can only be implemented by inservice arts teachers who are in frequent contact with large numbers of students. It is for this reason that professional development is that level of teacher education that tends to take on the burden of sustaining and shaping new movements. It is considered by many authorities as the most crucial element in the reformation and continual improvement of arts education (Courtney et al., 1985; Glidden, 1989; Hoad, 1990; Martin & Ross, 1988; Reimer, 1989).

The continuing education of dance teachers is a crucial function of higher education and will always be needed as new philosophies and methods pertinent to curriculum and instruction in the field are brought forth. Teachers require avenues of enlightenment regarding such topics as new advances in dance, new areas of specialty in dance teaching, or contemporary issues affecting dance, the arts, and education. It is also important to ponder the fact that most dance teachers have a potential career life of more than forty years. It would be totally unreasonable to expect that a preparation program could possibly equip a dance educator for all the new and changing situations that would undoubtedly need to be confronted during that time span. In addition, some writers have collected statistical evidence suggesting that the average age of practicing arts teachers is increasing (Guskey, 1986; McLaughlin, 1988; Rosenblatt & Michel-Trapaga, 1975). This only compounds the need for professional development as the most appropriate means for renewing the expertise of dance educators and potentially influencing change.

The impotence of much of the professional development efforts used for teachers of the arts is attributable not so much to teachers' resistance to change as to the ineffectiveness of the models used. One-shot workshops, training without technical assistance or follow-up, top-down plans, courses unrelated to classroom experiences, diffusion of products, isolationism, lack of attention to teacher perceived needs, and so on have little impact because they are not designed to provide conditions for professional change and adult learning to occur (Meyers, 1988; Morin, 1990). It is interesting to note that many of the scholars in arts education have been preoccupied with producing major learning theories for children but have not yet concentrated on producing a major statement on how arts teachers might learn and change (Courtney et al., 1985). Although we have a few exploratory projects in place, there is no evidence of any mutually shared or supported foundation for the professional development of arts educators.

The need for research and development into the foundations of professional development of arts educators has been established by authorities such as Kathryn Martin and Jerrold Ross (1988) and Michael Andrews (1983). Roy Edelfelt (1979), expert on professional development and arts teaching, addresses the issue:

> The teacher involved in any type of instruction, including staff development, should have some foundation for teaching, in addition to having competence in the content to be taught. By "foundation" I mean a base on which instructional behavior can be built. Ideally a foundation consists of notions about psychology, tempered by one's own philosophy of education. Such a foundation should be defensible, reasonable, consistent, based on solid thinking, and flexible. It should provide direction in all teaching situations. It should be clear enough to provide positive direction and yet not be restricted by a narrow interpretation that might dictate stereotyped thinking or teaching. (p. 131)

Professional development expert Michael Fullan (1987) establishes the point that regardless of the approach to our work with inservice teachers, foundational knowledge about change is also necessary. He said: "Until we understand that staff development is change, and that everything we know about what change is and how it occurs is critical to any approach, we will continue to waste resources, to create false expectations, and to sustain the confusion and frustration that surrounds staff development" (p. 214). Rita Irwin's (1988) research findings also suggest that arts education consultants and supervisors need knowledge of curriculum change strategies in planning professional development experiences for teachers in their school divisions.

A New Model for Professionals

Given that forces such as internal dissatisfaction, the socio-political mood, and climate of support for arts education are currently motivating positive change in dance education, this writer speculates that much of the problem of reform is due to weak models of teacher education at all levels. Based on the information gathered and considered by this author in a study completed in 1990, it is believed that the success of planned change depends on providing dance teachers with opportunities to learn under the guidance of higher education leaders who are able to provide optimal conditions for facilitating and sustaining professional change. A potential solution to the problem of reform at the school level in dance education is offered in Figure 1, a new model of professional development that integrates and applies knowledge of past practice, adult learning, and the process of change. Although it is not within the scope of this paper to provide readers with the detailed discussions contained in the main report, a synoptic account of the findings can be given. Essentially, the model consists of a sequence of three main components, which incorporate features that were found to be consistently associated with the potential for successful educational and teacher transformations.

Effective professional development programs are the product of meticulous and decentralized planning. *Component 1: Cooperative Planning for Change: The Conference Experience* stresses that important inputs are the unique orientations that dance educators, both as a target group and as individuals, bring to the professional development experience. Good programming depends on a well-conceived plan of action emanating from the criti-

Figure 1. Composite illustration of a professional development model for planned change in arts education.

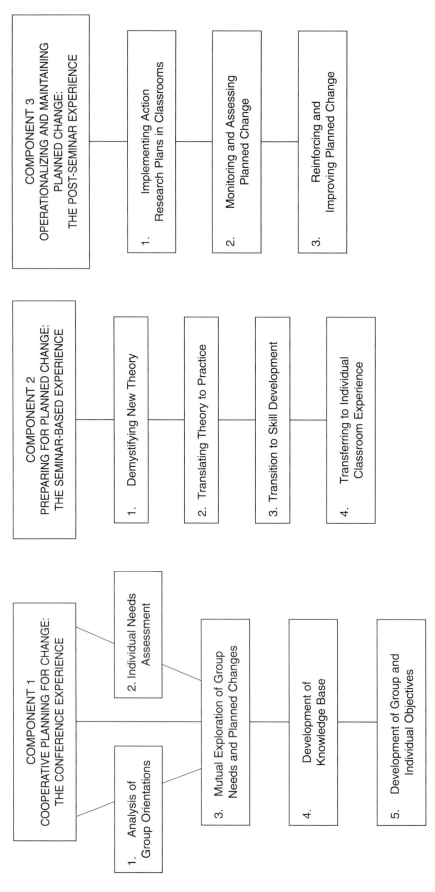

COMPONENT 1
COOPERATIVE PLANNING FOR CHANGE:
THE CONFERENCE EXPERIENCE

1. Analysis of Group Orientations

2. Individual Needs Assessment

3. Mutual Exploration of Group Needs and Planned Changes

4. Development of Knowledge Base

5. Development of Group and Individual Objectives

COMPONENT 2
PREPARING FOR PLANNED CHANGE:
THE SEMINAR-BASED EXPERIENCE

1. Demystifying New Theory

2. Translating Theory to Practice

3. Transition to Skill Development

4. Transferring to Individual Classroom Experience

COMPONENT 3
OPERATIONALIZING AND MAINTAINING
PLANNED CHANGE:
THE POST-SEMINAR EXPERIENCE

1. Implementing Action Research Plans in Classrooms

2. Monitoring and Assessing Planned Change

3. Reinforcing and Improving Planned Change

cal reflection and self-direction of teacher participants. Dance educators should be provided with opportunities to plan cooperatively with leaders, negotiate desired changes, articulate a concise base of essential knowledge, and establish clear group and individual objectives. Motivation should rely on the intrinsic rewards of progress toward superior group achievements and individual career goals.

The eventual generalization of desired reforms in dance education demands a continuing education experience that goes beyond the traditional one-day workshop model. Dance teachers need intensive seminar training which recognizes the distinct gradations from learning new knowledge and skills to the independent application of these as displayed in *Component 2: Preparing for Planned Change: The Seminar Experience*. Strategies should be designed to deal with the special challenges of illuminating change ideas via modeling methodologies, modifying the habitual practice and belief systems of participants, and solving problems related to the adult ego. Opportunities should be offered for continuous evaluation, peer support and dialogue, and exploring and developing materials that address context-specific needs. Dance teachers should work under sheltered conditions on problems of individual concern connecting the seminar in meaningful ways to the realities of the school.

Component 3: Operationalizing and Maintaining Planned Change: The Post-Seminar Experience addresses the overriding problem of sustenance common to reform efforts in the arts. The promise of enduring change calls for a professional development program that encompasses a component essentially based in the school. A period of trial and experimentation with change ideas will facilitate the reception of critical feedback about student learning that is so necessary for teacher change. Continued on-site support and technical assistance beyond the seminar training will help dance teachers persist with change efforts and tolerate occasional disappointments. Practitioners attempting to internalize change need to be further nourished by relevant follow-up workshops, collaboration with peers, and appropriate forms of written communication.

This paper sought to explore the critical connection between higher education and planned change in dance education. It was argued that present models of teacher education are falling short of meeting the challenges confronted by the reform initiatives of dance educators and their colleagues in other arts disciplines.

The writer has suggested that the most direct and promising route to facilitating and sustaining reform in dance education is through inservice teachers. Since higher education is responsible for offering programs to both prospective and practicing teachers, there is an obligation for leaders of these institutions to explore alternate, more potent professional development opportunities that are designed in light of the conditions necessary to help the present dance teaching force embrace change.

References

Andrews, M. D. (1983). Designing an arts education course for elementary teachers. *Journal of Creative Behavior, 17*(3), 175–180.

Carnegie Task Force on Teaching as a Profession (1986). *A nation prepared: Teachers for the 21st century*. Hyattsville, MD: Carnegie Forum on Education and the Economy.

Chapman-Hilsendager, S. (1989). *Under the big top: Dance education moves towards a new era*. Reston, VA: National Dance Association, American Alliance for Health, Physical Education, Recreation and Dance.

Côté-Laurence, E. (1989). In pursuit of dance literacy. *CAHPER Journal, 55*(4), 2–3.

Courtney, R. (Ed.). (1979). *The face of the future: The report of the national inquiry into arts and education in Canada*. Ottawa, ON: Canadian Conference of the Arts.

Courtney, R., Booth, D., Emerson, J., & Kuzmich, N. (1985). *Teacher education in the arts*. Sharon, ON: Bison Books.

Edelfelt, R. A. (1979). Staff development and teaching in the arts. In G.L. Knieter & J. Stallings (Eds.), *The teaching process and arts and aesthetics* (pp. 129–147). St. Louis, MO: CEMREL.

Fullan, M. (1987). Implementing the implementation plan. In M.F. Wideen & I. Andrews (Eds.), *Staff development for school improvement: A focus on the teacher* (pp. 213–222). Philadelphia, PA: Falmer Press.

George, L. M. (Ed.). (1989). [Special issue on dance]. *CAHPER Journal, 55*(4).

Gingrasso, S. H. (1987). Dance education certification: Current status and significance. *Design for Arts in Education, 89*(1), 31–35.

Glidden, R. (1989). The K-12 arts agenda: Next challenges for higher education. *Design for Arts in Education, 9*(1), 11–14.

Gray, J. A. (1989). *Dance instruction: Science applied to the art of movement*. Champaign, IL: Human Kinetics.

Guskey, T. R. (1986). Staff development and the process of teacher change. *Educational Leadership, 15*(5), 5–12.

Hamblen, K. A. (1983). An update on aesthetic education: Implications for teacher education. *Teacher Education Quarterly, 1*(2), 52–71.

Hilsendager, S. (1990). In transition—American dance education. *CAHPER Journal, 56*(1), 24–27.

Hoad, S. (1990). Dance in the context of Canadian schools. *CAHPER Journal, 56*(1), 20–23.

Holmes Group. (1986). *Tomorrow's teachers: A report of the Holmes Group*. East Lansing, MI: Holmes Group.

Howe, D. S. (1989). At the crossroads: The National Dance Association in the 1990's. *Design for Arts in Education, 90*(5), 44–47.

Irwin, R. L. (1988). The practical knowledge of a fine arts supervisor in educational change: A case study. Dissertation abstract (U.B.C.) *CSSE News*, XV(7&8), 5.

Karel, L. C. (1966). Teacher education in the related arts. *Music Educators Journal*, October, 38–41.

Martin, K. A., & Ross, J. (1988). Developing professionals for arts education. In J. T. McLaughlin (Ed.), *Toward a new era in arts education* (pp. 30–42). New York: American Council for the Arts.

McLaughlin, J. (1988). Arts education and school personnel: Renewal and retraining. *Design for Arts in Education, 89*(3), 31–34.

Meyers, D. E. (1988). The role of higher education in lifelong arts learning. *Design for Arts in Education, 89*(6), 37–42.

Morin, F. L. (1988). *Psychological and curricular foundations for elementary dance education*. Edina, MN: Burgess.

Morin, F. L. (1990). *A professional development model for planned change in arts education*. Unpublished doctoral dissertation, University of North Dakota. (Available from University Microfilms International).

National Commission for Excellence in Teacher Education. (1985). *A call for change in teacher education*. Washington, DC: American Association of Colleges for Teacher Education.

National Dance Association. (1988). *Dance curricula guidelines K–12*. Reston, VA: National Dance Association.

Reimer, B. (1989). Music education as aesthetic education: Toward the future. *Music Educators Journal, 75*(7), 26–32.

Rosenblatt, B. S., & Michel-Trapaga, R. (1975). Through the teacher to the child: Aesthetic education for teachers. *Council for Research in Music Education Bulletin, 43*, 36–49.

Stencel, P. L. (1988). *The value and feasibility of offering field-based courses as components of a master's degree program in music education for in-service teachers: The development of two models*. Unpublished doctoral dissertation, University of Rochester. (University Microfilms International Order No. 8814819).

Undercofler, J. G. (1987). An argument for a new college arts education curriculum. *Design for Arts in Education, 88*(3), 30–31.

Wilson, B. (1989). Reformation and responsibilities: A memo to members of the arts education establishment. *Design for Arts in Education, 90*(5), 27–35.

Francine Lee Morin is a member of the Faculty of Education at the University of Manitoba, Winnipeg, Manitoba, Canada R3T 2N2.

Afrocentric Forms in 20th Century American Dance History: Transforming Course Content and the Curriculum

Julie A. Kerr

Denial of the Afrocentric Presence in Dance

Many approaches to teaching dance history and related coursework in higher education reflect a Eurocentric bias. Often, course content and the manner in which it is disseminated suffer from the omission, unconscious or otherwise, of certain figures, conditions, and events, denying the influence of West Africa on 20th century dance. According to Molefi Asante (1988), an advocate of multicultural literacy and educational reform, and chair of African-American Studies at Temple University, the curriculum and its designers are "trapped in their monocultural paradigms" (p. 20). He further stated:

> . . . denial and omission are two of the most potent forces in the arsenal of those who would re-write the historical record to suit the ethnocentric conventions of the time. . . . Too often Eurocentrism has become an authentic ethnocentric view in education. The result is that many people who declare that they are educated are shocked to find that what they have learned is only a part of the human reality and is certainly not synonymous with human experience. (p. 21)

This is not to suggest that western European history is invalid. Rather, this author argues that *other* world perspectives, previously denied and/or omitted, need to be incorporated into the curriculum.[1]

Similarly, teaching dance history suffers from the same denial and/or omission of African-American dancers and choreographers whose contributions also have shaped the development of 20th century dance. Afrocentric forms have influenced American dance since the time Africans were transplanted on American soil through the transatlantic slave trade.

Robert Farris Thompson, African art historian (1984), stated:

> Since the Atlantic slave trade, ancient African organizing principles of song and dance have crossed the seas from the Old World to the New. There they took on new momentum, intermingling with each other and with New World or European styles of singing and dance. (p. xiii)

In a recent article, Brenda Dixon (1990 [aka Dixon-Stowell]) examined the magnitude of the Afrocentric basis in American dance. She stated:

> What is unacknowledged is dangerous! Reclaiming the Afrocentric tradition in the American dancing body means identifying the Afrocentric heritage in American dance by blacks AND whites, and acknowledging the broad significance of this tradition in American culture and American dance. WE NEED TO MAKE MAINSTREAM WHAT HAS BEEN *INVISIBILIZED* BY THE MAINSTREAM EUROCENTRIC *HISTORICAL ERASURE* OF AFRICAN-BASED INFLUENCES IN OUR CULTURE. (p. 4)

Dixon's point is well taken. The development of 20th century dance history is a shared history between people of all colors. To deny the contributions of one people only diminishes and limits everyone's perspective and understanding of the global society we have become.

A Eurocentric bias also occurs on a more subtle and systemic level in overall curricular design by compartmentalizing content that is non-Western European into separate units. Consequently, such content is isolated and fails to become integrated into an interrelated and intercultural whole. This procedure is referred to by James Banks, advocate of multicultural curriculum reform, as the "Contributions Approach" and was a popular

Left: Harriette Ann Gray—1938, Humphrey Weidman. From *Time and the Dancing Image*, Deborah Jowitt (University of California Press, Berkeley, 1988), p. 173.

Right: Dunham dancer Syvilla Ford. From *Caribe*, Vol. VII, No. 3, edited by Diane L. Jones.

method utilized in the 1960s to incorporate ethnic content into curriculum (Banks, 1988).

An approach that minimizes the limitations of the contribution method is the "Transformative Approach." In this approach, Banks (1988) contends the key issue is not the simple addition of ethnic content, "but the infusion of various perspectives, frames of reference, and content from various groups that will extend students' understandings of the nature, development, and complexity of U.S. society" (p. 2).

Banks' approach can be applied to the teaching of dance history. For example, by utilizing his perspective, the work of Katherine Dunham, Arthur Mitchell, or Alvin Ailey does not comprise a sepa-

rate unit on African-American concert dance artists. Rather, these figures and their works are integrated into course content and discussed relative to their European-American counterparts. In this way, students perceive the contribution of African-American artists to American concert dance as being equivalent to the contributions of Martha Graham, George Balanchine, and Paul Taylor. Consequently, *both* African-American and European-American concert dance artists are approached relative to their movement techniques and philosophy as well as their social, political, and historical context.

In a recent article, Joan Frosch-Schröder (1991) described the role dance educators and artists will play in revitalizing traditional approaches to dance. The outcome will ultimately broaden students' definition of dance. She stated:

> A fresh self-examination will translate with power into our presence as dance artists and educators. By examining the content of and ways in which we teach, we stand to invigorate ourselves, broaden the knowledge of our field and our world, and stimulate fresh approaches to learning, and creating new scholarship. Dance educators can address the challenges of the twenty-first century with knowledge, experience, and a heritage of diversity. We have within our discipline the opportunity to offer students a uniquely integrated perception of pluralism. (p. 62)

Clearly, 20th century dance is the product of a multitude of cultural influences—including Asian, European, Native American, and West African. However, the Afrocentric presence has, to a great extent, been denied, particularly in concert dance. This mindset or attitude is reflected in how we, as dance educators, perceive and teach dance—both in the classroom and studio. If we reexamine and subsequently rechart the development of 20th century dance history, what arises is the existence of Afrocentric forms throughout its evolution. The application of this perspective would transcend the teaching of dance history exclusively; it also transfers to courses in dance appreciation, criticism, aesthetics and philosophy, composition, and even technique.

The Evolution of American Dance History from an Afrocentric Perspective

Throughout the past century Afrocentric forms have been woven into American culture where they produced new forms. Afrocentrisms are particularly prevalent in both the visual and performing arts in varying degrees (Dixon, 1990).

John Golding (1968) credits the African influence in the work of such Cubist artists as Picasso, Braque, Derain, and Matisse. He stated that they were undoubtedly influenced by African masks and statues, particularly in the construction and use of space and in the artists' treatments of formal elements of the body.[2] (It is worth noting that these same properties, attributable to an African aesthetic, greatly affected the modern dance aesthetic.)

When jazz music emerged, it represented the fusion of European musical traditions with West African. This occurred through the use of syncopa-tion, improvisation, call and response, and poly-rhythmic arrangements that mark the African influence in jazz (Thompson, 1984). These same elements have continued to inform American musical forms such as gospel, rhythm and blues, rock 'n' roll, and, most recently, rap.

Twentieth century American dance history has been influenced by Afrocentric forms. These forms can be identified by examining movement content, choreographic theme, and aesthetic principles. The following section attempts to document the evolution of 20th century dance history through selected examples of the Afrocentric presence therein. (There are several recent publications that address this in greater depth. See the selected bibliography of sources.)

Plantation to Street Dances

As a result of the transatlantic slave trade, African-based movement patterns and performance traditions were retained and diffused into American culture where they affected the development of American dance. Through a complicated process of cross-fertilization and secularization, plantation dances of the southern United States evolved into America's popular dance. As African and then African-American based dances, they permeated American culture and produced such social forms as the Charleston, the jitterbug, the lindy, and disco. Many of these dances form the basis of jazz dance (Stearns & Stearns, 1968). An example of how jazz has retained elements of African-based dance forms is through the isolation of body parts. The isolation of body parts remained one of the defining features that links jazz to African dance. Through history, this element has been retained in the "body" of American folk (African-American) and social/popular dance through various transformations leading up to jazz dance.

Today, street dancing, a contribution from our nation's inner cities, is an example of the fusion of African culture with European. In the southern United States, buck dancing, a product of plantation culture, emerged among African-Americans.[3] Buck dancing was then transplanted to the industrial north when African-Americans left the rural south in search of better job opportunities. Once on city streets, it merged with the Irish jig and English clog to produce tap. Tap combined syncopated time and subtle body isolations characteristic of African dance and music with quick footwork characteristic of the Irish jig and English clog. The street corner became a viable environment for the fusion of these forms and the continual development of tap.

Rap is another form that emerged from the streets. Because of the interrelationship between African dance and vocal/rhythmic music, it is particularly worth noting the similar interchange that occurs between rap vocalists and their dancers.[4] This interrelationship is apparent in the dancers who often accompany many rappers. As popular forms, these dances are not only partially African-derived but also draw from a host of other dance forms. Consequently, they are constantly redefining and reinterpreting themselves to produce new forms. In both of these examples, the dancers' movement repertoire resembles a mixture of African dance,[5] the Nicolais Brothers of the 1930s and 1940s, and concert dance idioms such as jazz and ballet. The ballet vocabulary is often incorporated into these dances through the use of pirouettes (both en dedans and en dehors) that are performed from a parallel position in plié. From this perspective, the street informs the concert stage as the concert stage informs the street.

Concert and Popular Stage

Considered by many to be a "purely" European art form, the world of classical ballet has also been influenced by Afrocentric forms. Dixon (1990) noted that George Balanchine's early choreographic career began on the Broadway stage where he came in direct contact with African-American popular dances and African-American entertainers and performers such as the Nicolais Brothers and Katherine Dunham.

As a result of such experiences, Balanchine incorporated jazz-based movement into his ballet vocabulary that manifested itself in the use of a mobile spine and subsequently affected the placement of the hips. Particularly in his neoclassic ballets, Balanchine utilized jazz by allowing the hips to go off-center, for example, in the form of a side lunge into a parallel seconde position initiated by the hips. Because of the verticality of the classical ballet spine, Balanchine's displacement of the hips departed dramatically from that tradition. Arthur Mitchell, former principal dancer with the New York City Ballet and current director of the Dance Theatre of Harlem, stated that Balanchine was very intrigued with jazz-based movement (Pierangeli, 1989). Further, Balanchine often ventured into the New York City night club scene during the 1930s through the 1950s to extract jazz-based movement material from the performances he saw. He then incorporated these into his ballets. Mitchell cited such Balanchine works as *Four Temperaments* (1946) and *Agon* (1957) to exemplify the jazz influence in his work (Pierangeli, 1989).

Another American ballet choreographer to incorporate jazz in his ballets was Jerome Robbins. Evidence of this is in the work *Fancy Free* (1944) in which he not only utilized the jazz dance idiom but also musical forms such as the blues and Latin-based rhythms (Siegel, 1979). The final solo section of *Fancy Free* was set to a Latin beat. While the music is, in part, African-based, so is much of the movement Robbins incorporated. Many of the Latin dances, such as the rumba or the mambo, are based on extensions of African rhythms and movement from the Caribbean. Marshall and Jean Stearns (1968) noted:

> Today the Latin-American dances such as the Rumba, Conga, Samba, Mambo, Cha Cha, Pachanga, and so on, which have been imported from areas where a merging of African and European styles has already taken place, show the greatest African influence, both in quantity and quality. (p. 14)

Marcia Siegel (1979) described the final solo section of *Fancy Free* as follows: "The final solo . . . is Latin in beat, although the rhythms are again irregular. . . . He (the second sailor's dance) gives an exaggeratedly sexy version of a rhumba, hips swaying, glance tipping provocatively over his shoulder" [underline added] (p. 136). The use of the hips, displaced from the body's center axis in this fashion, is characteristic of African dance and was simply nonexistent in European-based dance forms.

In 20th century dance history, the Afrocentric presence is quite prevalent in American modern dance. With a direct departure from the criteria that had previously defined the European classical dance vocabulary, the development of American modern dance represented a new way of perceiving the body as a medium of artistic expression. Subsequently, this affected the body's potential for movement. The result was the invention of a new movement vocabulary that included baring the feet, allowing the spine to curve and become more supple, and working closer to the ground. All these characteristics can be linked to similar elements in African dance.

Throughout history Afrocentric forms have influenced American dance. In specific reference to American modern dance, Peter Wood (1988) supported this theory when he stated:

American modern dance, created largely in the urban North during the era of enormous social movement, owes more than it realizes to roots which are black, and southern, and ultimately African. During the first half of the 20th century, pioneer American dancers found it both possible and exciting to work closer to the ground, to plant their feet and bend their knees, to thrust their hips and point their elbows. And when troubled critics explained that these "new" movements had been "discovered" because American dancers and audience are a step removed from the balletic tradition of Europe, they were half right. They could have mentioned had they realized . . . that black and white were moving closer to the continent of Africa in body movement all the time [underline added]. (p. 8)

Ernestine Stodelle's (1984) description of Martha Graham's *Primitive Mysteries* (1931) and *Heretic* (1929) is laden with references to African influences. Her description of the Graham works is particularly relevant because Stodelle most likely unintentionally credits the movement and aesthetic principles that became a signature of American dance to sources outside the Western European classical dance tradition. Stodelle stated the following:

Then there was the movement itself: starkly simple, blunt, unadorned. Using the body as a total instrument was the main characteristic of the new dance. Louis (Horst) called it a "back to primitive urge." But he clearly differentiated between a "truly primitive approach [which] would be an affectation today" and the new aesthetic that emerged as a result of the modern dancer's appreciation of primitive forms. Asymmetry, reflective of the naiveté of primitive art, was favored over sophisticated symmetry. . . . Whereas the primitive dancer stamped on the ground with the whole foot, or in lifting the knee flexed the ankle angularity at the joint, the modern dancer, without actually reproducing those steps per se, uses their rough textures and broken rhythms to express the vitality of feeling behind such movements. An inner muscular awareness of weight and energy is manifest in every step, every lift of the leg, every turn of the body. Whereas tribal man moved in repetitious patterns without being conscious of movement as pure movement form, modern dancers use repetition knowingly, planting impressions like seeds so that their ideas will build cumulatively without recourse to overt or sequential gesture. The sheer power of repetition drove *Heretics* message of bigotry home. Repetition and purity of feeling also created the primitivistic ardor of *Primitive Mysteries* [underline added]. (p. 74)[6]

The previous descriptions by Wood and Stodelle represent evidences of African based movement content in American modern dance. The Afrocentric presence also manifested itself through choreographic theme in the works of both African-American and European-American modern dancers. Examples of African-American choreographers and their works include: Katherine Dunham's *L'Ag'Ya* (1937), *Rite de Passage* (1942), and *Shango* (1945); Pearl Primus's *African Ceremonial* (1944) and *The Negro Speaks of*

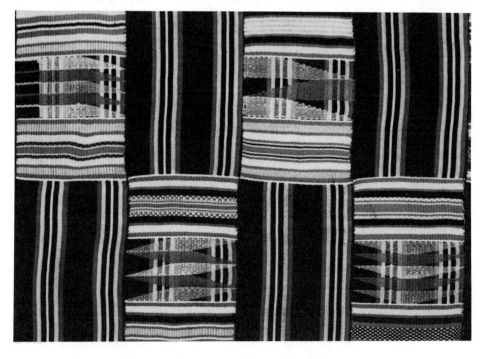

Kente cloth, Ashanti people of Ghana. From *African Art in Motion*, **Robert Farris Thompson (University of California Press, Los Angeles), p. ii.**

Rivers (1944); Alvin Ailey's *Revelations (1960)* and *Cry* (1971); and Garth Fagan's *From Before* (1978). Among European-American choreographers, some examples include: Ted Shawn's *Danza Afro-Cuba* (1935); Lester Horton's *Voodoo Ceremonial* (1932), *Xango* (1932), and *Dance Congo* (1934); Helen Tamiris's *Morning Ceremonial* (1931) and from *Negro Spirituals*, "Go Down Moses" (1932) and "Swing Low Sweet Chariot" (1929); Mary O'Connell's *Ritual* (1954); and Twyla Tharp's *Eight Jelly Rolls* (1971) and *Sue's Leg* (1975).

The Afrocentric presence in the above cited works manifested itself choreographically in two ways. The first was through a literal translation of Afrocentric content, for example, in Dunham's *Shango*, Horton's *Voodoo Ceremonial*, and Ailey's *Revelations*. These works depicted an actual story or narrative. In *Shango*, for example, Dunham based the work on the Yoruba god, Shango, and a theatricalized interpretation of the ritual surrounding this god. In works such as Fagan's *From Before* or Tharp's *Sue's Leg*, African and African-based movement content was utilized in an abstract or less literal sense. Thus, such works didn't follow a storyline. Fagan's work incorporated African and African-Caribbean rhythms that were embodied by the dancers through a multitude of polyrhythmic isolations and contractions of the torso and pelvis. Tharp drew from vernacular dancers or what Smith (1987) termed a "black vernacular wellspring" of material. For example, Tharp incorporated the lindy and tap—softened through the use of soft jazz shoes and the dancers' use of weight.

Influences on Modern Dance

African-based aesthetic principles have also influenced American modern dance. They are less tangible and more abstract in definition and in their manifestation in the idiom. Nonetheless, they have been woven into the modern dance aesthetic. Some examples include: 1) how energy is utilized in the body; 2) use of weight; and 3) improvisation.[7]

The modern dance idiom utilized energy in a manner that departed from classical dance by exploring new motion properties of the body. This exploration and unleashing of movement potentials and resultant kinetic energy in the form of momentum are exemplified in the techniques and philosophies of early modern dance. Although Walter Sorrell's (1969) choice of the word "primitive" is dated in his description of Hanya Holm's two works entitled *Primitive Rhythm* (1936) and *Festive Rhythm* (1936), it is suggestive of an African-based use of energy in Holm's work.[8] Sorrell stated:

> The first program closed with two dances in which the entire group was involved in an abandon of motor movement, stamping, leaping, and whirling. *Primitive Rhythm* was a perfect wedding of primitive music and movement. The usually rousing effect was obtained by the thumping of hands and feet on the floor in the excitement of the dance to supplement piano and percussive instruments. . . . The idea was one of *perpetuum mobile*, with the whole tightly knit group treading continuously, with arms thrust out like rhythmic accents, finally turning into a state of ecstatic exuberance. *Primitive Rhythm* led to *Festive Rhythm*, with overtones of a joyous celebration, a finale with the rich colors of a ritual. (1969, pp. 76, 77)

Use of weight or responsiveness to the body's natural use of weight also characterizes modern dance. The dancer is able to give into weight, into gravity, and thus, direct motion into the earth. In African dance, R.F. Thompson (1974) described this as a "get down" quality. The use of weight in this manner is distinctly different from classical ballet in which weight is directed away from the earth and into the air. As a result, in the modern dance idiom, the body's center of weight shifted from the chest, as in ballet, to the pelvis. This is particularly evident in Graham technique through the use of contraction and release of the pelvis—also characteristic of African dance. Hanya Holm (1966) made reference to this principle in her description of the Bennington years as the freedom to "Go down through the whole foot—going down into the areas of the body—there is no taboo. . . ." An example of this principle occurs in the depth of the grand pliés in seconde position of the dancers' side lunge in the opening section of Ailey's *Revelations* (1960). Another example is Graham's *Letter to the World* (1940) in which she descends to the ground in a deep contraction. In both works, the dancers must fully release into their weight and into the earth in order to achieve the depth of the grand plié or contraction to the floor.

Stearns and Stearns (1968) described the use of improvisation in African dance forms as follows:

> African dance also places great importance upon improvisation, satirical and otherwise, allowing freedom for individual expression; this characteristic makes for flexibility and aids the evolution and diffusion of other African characteristics. (p. 15)

Improvisation, as described by Stearns and Stearns, parallels many aspects of the modern

Left: "Letter to the World" 1940, by Martha Graham. From *Deep Song: The Dance Story of Martha Graham*, Ernestine Stodelle (Schirmer Books, New York), p. 170.

Right: "Revelations" (1960), by Alvin Ailey. From "Modern Dance Is Getting Hot," Ellen Cohn, *The New York Times Magazine*, April 29, 1973, p. 20.

dance aesthetic. From its inception to the present decade, modern dance can be characterized by the constant creation and re-creation of movement philosophies, movement techniques, choreographic process, and choreographic content. Improvisation has functioned as a primary vehicle in this process. The use of improvisation epitomizes the postmodern dance aesthetic. During the Judson and post-Judson years, improvisation was incorporated into the actual choreographic structure in that a given set of movement tasks or materials was explored, invented, and choreographed during the actual performance of the work.

Judith Dunn described this as follows: "Improvisation as I see it means composing and performing simultaneously" (Brown, 1979, p. 139). In effect, choreography took on a reflexive element in that properties of the medium and its own construction, or its seams, were allowed to show. Sally Banes (1987) described this when she stated that the task of the choreographer was to acknowledge the medium's materials and reveal the dancer's essential qualities in the process. An example representative of this improvisatory element is Yvonne Rainer's work *"Some Thoughts on Improvisation"* (1964). In this work Rainer's taped voice posed questions about choreographic process and the nature of "spontaneous determination" of movement design while she improvised (Banes, 1987).

Creating a Context for Change

What follows are some suggestions to assist dance educators who wish to incorporate Afrocentric content into existing dance history coursework. All sources cited appear at the end of this section.

1. Reconstruct your course syllabus to include the contributions of African-American dancers and artists. Develop this in such a way that is taught simultaneously with European-American contributions. In this way students will not perceive Afrocentric content as a separate entity but rather as equal in magnitude and influence to European-American dancers and artists.

2. Define dance as human behavior and relative to its cultural context. This will break down categories and fixed definitions of dance. When dance is situated in its cultural context, students will be better enabled to see dance relative to its social, political, economic, aesthetic, and religious dimensions. An excellent source is *To Dance Is Human* by Judith Lynne Hanna.

3. Include works that address African art and aesthetics. Identify and define for your students the term "black aesthetic" and its impact on the development of American dance. Discuss with students the cultural basis of aesthetic standards and values and how they shape and inform artistic process and product, for example, African-American or European-American. Identify the black aesthetic and discuss how it has been woven into the fabric of American dance relative to a European dance aesthetic. Some excellent sources include: *Flash of the Spirit, African Art in Motion,* and *An Aesthetic of the Cool: West African Dance* by Robert Farris Thompson.

4. Include film and video tape materials that provide students with numerous examples of African and African-American dance performance. This will facilitate awareness of the contributions of African and African-American dancers and choreographers.

5. Incorporate an experiential component into the course. This will enliven historical content and

function to personalize and maximize students' learning experiences. Some possibilities include: guest speakers/dancers who could teach students short movement sequences to acquaint them with a particular dance period or genre; attending a variety of dance performances by both Western and non-Western dance companies; and have students research, choreograph, and teach a short movement sequence reflective of a particular period or genre. As a result students will become more sensitive to the differences between the European dance vocabulary and those derived from West African or other world dance forms.

6. Include such sources as *Black Dance* by Lynne Fauley Emery, *The Black Tradition in American Dance* by Richard Long, and *The Black Tradition in American Modern Dance* published by the American College Dance Festival. These sources will help provide the missing pages of dance history. Create a context in your classroom that equitably identifies and discusses the contributions of African-American dancers and choreographers. Equity does *not* mean diminishing European-American contributions. Equity asks only that credit be given where credit is due; otherwise we run the risk of undermining what we have set out to rectify.

7. Discuss the interrelationship between popular and concert dance as a means to break down preconceived, finite definitions of what constitutes dance. An excellent source is the text *Jazz Dance* by Marshall and Jean Stearns. Another source is an article in *Katherine Dunham: Reflections on the Social and Political Contexts of Afro-American Dance* entitled "Folk Art and 'High' Art" by Joyce Aschenbrenner (1980). Engage students in discussion that asks them to reexamine terms, or better, labels, such as:
   a. "ethnic dance"
   b. "high" as opposed to "low art"
   c. "fine" as opposed to "folk art"
   d. "social" as opposed to "art dance."

8. Identify those movement traits and aesthetic principles that characterize West African and African-American dance relative to the European and European-American dance vocabulary. This will sensitize and help students identify how Afrocentric forms have influenced the evolution of American dance history. What follows are some identifiable traits characterizing the manifestations of Afrocentric forms in American dance.[9] Use them only as guidelines or as a "lens" through which to recognize the presence of these forms in dance movement content. They are as follows:

a. lower center of weight accompanied by movement directed toward the earth

b. knees that function as springs

c. improvisation—as part of either the choreographic process or performance context

d. contraction and release of the pelvis

e. embodiment of polyrhythmic structures in the spine, torso, shoulders, and pelvis

f. the bare, full surface of the foot.

Selected Bibliography of Sources

Listed below are sources that represent the Afrocentric presence in American dance. They will be valuable additions to dance history courses and other theory courses that acknowledge the Afrocentric presence in American dance.

Adamczyk, A. (1989). *Black dance: An annotated bibliography.* New York: Garland.

American Dance Festival. (1988, June). *The black tradition in American modern dance.* Durham, NC: American Dance Festival Publication.

Aschenbrenner, J. (1980). Katherine Dunham: Reflections on the social and political contexts of Afro-American dance. *CORD Dance Research Annual, XII.*

Begho, F. (1985). *Black dance continuum: Reflections on the heritage connection between African dance and Afro-American jazz dance.* PhD dissertation, New York University.

Brooklyn Academy of Music and State University of New York (1983, April 21–24). *Black dance in America.* Conference publication compiled in conjunction with the Black Dance America concert.

Dixon, B. (1990, February 13). Cultural identity and sociopolitical oppression: The Afrocentric basis of American concert dance! *The Faculty Herald,* pp. 4–6.

Dixon-Stowell, B. (1983, Spring). Between two eras: 'Norton and Margot' Afro-American entertainment world. *CORD Dance Research Journal, 15* (2), 11–20.

Emery, L. F. (1988). *Black dance: From 1619 to today.* Princeton, NJ: Princeton.

Friedland, L. (1983, Spring). Disco: Afro-American vernacular performance. *CORD Dance Research Journal, 15* (2), 27–35.

Goines, M. B. (1971–72). African retentions in the dance of the Americas. *CORD Dance Research Monograph, 1,* 209–229.

Hanna, J. L. (1979). *To dance is human: A theory of non-verbal communication.* Austin: University of Texas.

Hazzard-Gordon, K. (1990). *Atibas a'coming: The rise of social dance formations in Afro-American culture.* Philadelphia, PA: Temple University.

Long, R. (1989). *The black tradition in American dance.* New York: Rizzoli.

Nettleford, R. (1984). Caribe interview with Rex Nettleford. *CARIBE, 7, 1 & 2,* 24–38.

Small, L. A. (1989, June). Blacks enrich modern dance. *American Visions,* pp. 24–29.

Szwed, J. F., & Marks, M. (1988, Summer). The Afro-American transformation of European set dances and suites. *Research Journal, 20* (1), 29–36.

Thompson, R. F. (1984). *Flash of the spirit: African and Afro-American art and philosophy.* New York: Vintage Books.

Thompson, R. F. (1980). An aesthetic of the cool: West African dance. In Errol Hill (Ed.), *The theatre of black Americans* (pp. 99–111). Englewood Cliffs, NJ: Prentice Hall.

Thompson, R. F. (1974). *African art in motion: Icon and act.* Los Angeles, Berkeley, London: University of California.

Tucker, I. (1983). *The role of Afro-Americans in dance in the United States from slavery through 1983: A slide presentation.* PhD dissertation, New York University.

Multicultural Literacy in 20th Century American Dance History

The enduring presence and richness of West African cultural influences in American society have significantly contributed to the evolution of American dance. African sources in America have provided a wellspring of material that has constantly enriched dance forms in this country ranging from folk and vernacular to concert dance. Throughout history, because of the persistence and strength of this source, West African influences have had a dramatic impact on the development of American dance.

In its early history the United States was founded by a composite of peoples, most predominantly of African and European descent. Thus, Americans, of both African-American and European-American descent, share a common history. This very element makes this country unique, and the same factor has produced a remarkable dance history. There are several possible reasons why this may have occurred. One may be because of the distinct differences between African and European culture; another, because of the circumstances and conditions, however unfortunate, that have fostered their initial union.

By applying such methods as Banks's "Transformative Approach," dance history can be transformed. The examples presented in this paper represent only a small portion of the Afrocentric presence in 20th century dance. However, they set the tone for change to occur in our thinking. Subsequently, it is hoped that this paper will help cause dance educators to reevaluate their curriculums and, as a result, incorporate Afrocentric content where it has previously been omitted.

The potential role dance educators will play in this transformation process is tremendous. Previous definitions of dance need to be challenged beyond those framed solely by a proscenium stage and expanded to include other world views. If we do not we run the risk of even further marginalizing dance and diminishing any hope of bringing new information, vigor, and insight into our field, (Frosch-Schröder, 1991). We, as dance educators, hold the key to this transformation process. Our impact will be felt through input and action on curriculum committees and, more importantly perhaps, through our daily interactions with students in the studio, classroom, or on a campus streetcorner.

The implications of expanding our definition of dance apply not only to dance educators but to dance critics, scholars, and performers alike. Collectively we can no longer deny the impact of African culture on American dance by attributing the origins of dance solely to European sources. Such a monocultural perspective is biased, reductive, and inconsistent with the nature of this country's composition and historical development. Continued efforts must be made to incorporate this perspective into dance curriculums and thus broaden the understanding and scope of the origins of American dance.

Endnotes

1. It is worth noting the differences between the terms "denial" and "omission." In this context, denial refers to a conscious falsification of history while omission refers to negligence or ignorance, perhaps unwitting, which is reflected in certain institutional or structural preconceptions.

2. For example, in Picasso's painted work, *Les Demoiselles d'Avignon* (1907), the influence of African masks is apparent. Golding stated:

> The abrupt changes of style in the *Demoiselles* are due to the fact that while he was working on it Picasso came into contact with Negro art . . . the head at the left can be accounted for by a characteristic form of Negro mask, found on the Ivory Coast. . . . It was only in the series of paintings that followed *Demoiselles* that he began to grasp the intellectual and aesthetic principles of particular types of masks and to relate Negro culture more thoroughly to West Art. (pp. 55–57)

3. Buck dancing was a product of plantation culture and was performed only by men. It was also performed in hard soled shoes on wooden floors and represents the early beginning of what would later become tap dance. See *Black Dance* by Lynne Fauley Emery and *Jazz Dance* by Marshall and Jean Stearns for additional information about the origins and offshoots that emerged from buck dancing.

4. Akpabot (1986) reinforces these parallels between the two forms even further in his following analysis of African music:

> The idea of viewing a percussive instrument as having high, low or medium tone is borrowed from African speech which is inflectionary in character; and African musical instrumental music borrows much from vocal music which in turn is tied to speech melody and speech rhythm . . . Speech, melody, rhythm, and dance are usually interrelated in African music. . . . this interrelationship makes it possible for a dancer to take his cue from the rhythmic instruments and for a melody to be fashioned out of a sentence. (p. 3)

5. Most notably this is identifiable in the subtle contractions that occur in the rib cage, shoulders, and upper spine. Another identifiable trait is the use of weight that is often directed into the earth as opposed to away from it.

6. A portion of Stodelle's previous statement is untrue. Non-Western and/or African dance forms incorporated repetition on a very conscious level and were very aware of formal elements in choreography. African dance, like all dance forms, is governed by canons that determine aesthetic standards and values; included in these canons is the use of repetition. In addition, ironically, in Stodelle's analogy to modern dancers "planting impressions like seeds," she was unknowingly perhaps referring to an African basis to the movement because much of the thematic content of traditional African dance is based on agrarian motifs, which incorporate the full, flat surface of the foot in a stomping or planting action.

7. For a complete listing and definition of these African-based aesthetic principles see Julie A. Kerr (1990), *Parallels of African-based Movement Traits and Aesthetic Principles in Selected Examples of American Modern Dance*, PhD dissertation, Temple University.

8. Two excellent sources that discuss African-based energy and its manifestation in art and dance are: *African Art in Motion: Icon and Act*, by Robert Farris Thompson and *Wellspring: On the Myth and Source of Culture*, by Robert Plant Armstrong.

9. These movement characteristics are derived from *Jazz Dance* (1968) by Stearns and Stearns and the author's personal experiences in modern, African, and African-Caribbean dance classes.

References

Akpabot, S. E. (1986). *Foundations of Nigerian traditional music.* Ibadan, Nigeria: Spectrum.

Asante, M. (1988, fall). The case for multi-cultural literacy. *The Temple Review,* pp. 20–23.

Banes, S. (1987). *Terpsichore in sneakers: Post modern dance.* Middletown, CT: Wesleyan University.

Banks, J. A. (1988, spring). Approaches to multicultural curriculum reform. *Multicultural Leader, 1* (2), 1–4.

Brown, J. M. (1979). *The vision of modern dance.* Princeton, NJ: Princeton.

Dixon, B. (1990, February 13). Cultural identity and sociopolitical oppression: The Afrocentric basis of American concert dance! *The Faculty Herald* (published by Temple University), pp. 4–6.

Frosch-Schröder, J. (1991, March). A global view: Dance appreciation for the 21st century. *Journal of Physical Education, Recreation and Dance,* 61–66.

Golding, J. (1968). *Cubism: A history and analysis 1907–1914.* Boston, MA: Boston Book and Art Shop.

Holm, H. (Speaker). (1966). *Dance: Four pioneers* (Film). Bloomington, IN: Indiana University/National Education Television.

Pierangeli, C. (1989, August). Personal communication with Pierangeli, Department of Dance, Temple University, Philadelphia, PA.

Siegel, M. B. (1979). *The shapes of change: Images of American dance.* New York: Avon.

Smith, E. (1987, February 14). Jazz dance on film, tap and social: Films from the private collection of Ernie Smith (Lecture/Film Presentation). *Stepping out: Black American dance during the great migration.* National Museum of American History, Smithsonian Institution, Washington, D.C., February 14, 1987.

Sorrell, W. (1969). *Hanya Holm: The biography of an artist.* Middletown, CT: Wesleyan University.

Stearns, M., & Stearns, J. (1968). *Jazz dance: The story of American vernacular dance.* New York: Schirmer.

Stodelle, E. (1984). *Deep Song: The dance of Martha Graham.* New York: Schirmer.

Thompson, R. F. (1974). *African art in motion: Icon and act.* Los Angeles, CA: University of California.

Thompson, R. F. (1984). *Flash of the spirit: African and Afro-American art and philosophy.* New York: Vintage.

Wood, P. (1988, June). "Gimme de kneebone bent": African body language and the evolution of American dance forms. In *The black tradition in American modern dance.* Durham, NC: American Dance Festival Publication.

Julie A. Kerr is coordinator of the dance minor program in the Physical Education Department at Mankato State University, Mankato, Minnesota 56002-8400.

Dance MATERIAL
(Dance, Music, and Art Training and Education Resulting In Aesthetic Literacy)

John R. Crawford

Dance as an art form is related to the arts of music, painting, and theatre. The dancer learns visual and spatial forms and designs as well as musical counts, timing, and phrases. Thus, the dancer learns to perceive in visual, aural, and kinesthetic ways. These modes of perception comprise specific areas of knowing within the human being. Howard Gardner (1983) states that human beings have potential in seven areas. Music, visual-spatial aspects, and body-kinesthetic aspects comprise three of the seven areas of human potential. A study of the art forms of dance, music, and painting can effectively contribute to learning within these areas.

In particular, dance in education is able to facilitate aesthetic perception, which includes relationships within form and design. In the creation of dance, the student acquires an understanding of the organizational process of the artist. "Teachers gradually introduce elements of form (unity, harmony, contrast, etc.) and students attempt to incorporate these elements into their compositional work" (National Dance Association, 1988, p. 13). The abilities to think abstractly and to create concretely are both necessary to understand the forming process.

Concepts in the more recently published literature often refer to the fields of aesthetics and aesthetic education and support the idea that aesthetic literacy may be developed through the study of several art forms. Indeed, the aim of aesthetic education is the development of an individual's capacity to perceive, create, study, and evaluate art works in a variety of media. A study of interrelations among the arts in particular focuses on aspects of composition, the compositional process, principles of organization used by the artist, and theories within the field of aesthetics including both similarities and differences within the arts.

The field of aesthetics often focuses on relationships among the arts and posits theories as to possible commonalities. Although the arts may be related on either a formal or an ontological basis, dance, music, and painting all consist of organizational factors, and in every instance of art there exists a certain manner in which the totality is structured. "The art forms are similarly constructed . . . they are languages or symbol systems, aesthetically articulated and historically determined" (Karpati & Abonyi, 1987, p. 102). A study of the organizational principles within the arts engenders fuller comprehension of individual art forms and thus multiplies the possibilities of artistic expression.

Within the past two decades research in aesthetics and aesthetic education has revealed a need for workable teaching methods in the comparison of art forms. Theory that supports practice is advocated by educators. New curricular models and implementations are requested to provide teachers viable ways in which to present comparisons among arts. According to the Getty Center for Education in the Arts, "This means that university scholars will need to work closely with curriculum specialists and teachers to develop programs informed by the theory and practice of aesthetics, art criticism, history and production" (Getty Center, 1985, p. 6).

With such curricular materials, teachers are able to communicate ideas about art to students. Teachers can also more effectively convey the various roles and applications of art to their students. The arts constitute modes of communication that students can decipher as audience members and utilize as creators. The arts as a basic means of communication can be used to engender self-expression and creativity.

In order to transform aspects of experience that are part of the creative process into externalized form, the artist utilizes principles of organization. The artist orders, arranges, and organizes the material of the art form. A relationship between emotional feeling and ordered design may occur as part of the artist's compositional process.

Principles of organization used by the artist do not explain what artistic creation is or how it happens, Rather, principles of organization illuminate aspects of cause and effect utilized by the artist. In other words, the artist achieves a certain result through a certain organization of compositional elements. Whereas these principles do not dictate specific rules for good composition, they do serve as guidelines for the artist.

Dance MATERIAL (Dance, Music, and Art Training and Education Resulting In Aesthetic Literacy) was designed to identify, describe, and compare principles of organization that seem to be consistently used by the artist in dance, music, and painting. The significant literature regarding principles of organization in the arts was analyzed and as a result of this research, a synthesis of content areas was developed that interrelates these organizational principles and suggests a basis for curriculum development, incorporating dance as the disseminator of the organizational principles.

Dance MATERIAL is a curricular model which employs dance as the educational focus in order to teach aspects of unity, variety, contrast, balance, and their related components as used by the choreographer, composer, and painter in the process of composition. The content areas of this curricular model consist of the following headings, which are discussed in detail: *coherence* within the three arts; *dynamism* within the arts; *unity* and *variety; repetition* and *contrast; rhythm; emergence* and *recedence* (i. e., figure and ground); *balance,* including symmetry and asymmetry; and *development,* including transitions and flow to climax. Dance serves as the educational focus in a comparison of these organizational principles within dance, music, and painting. Additionally, Dance MATERIAL suggests a method of teaching major principles of organization as used by the choreographer, composer, and painter.

Dance MATERIAL is designed as a basis for a course of study in dance as an art form, with emphasis on dance composition. Within higher education, courses focusing on the basic understanding of aesthetics in the arts are increasing, and often such a course is offered as an elective within the basic liberal arts requirements of the university. Introductory dance courses designed for the general university student can benefit by including the content areas within this curricular model. Additionally, the content areas within Dance MATERIAL are applicable to units of instruction within college level dance composition courses.

Study of the content areas within Dance MATERIAL contributes to the individual's acquisition of information regarding choreographic choices and decisions, contributes to the student's acquisition of information regarding aesthetic judgment and justification, and relates the process of composition in dance to similar compositional processes in music and painting.

Dance MATERIAL presents specific principles of organization that are similar and comparable in the creation of dance, music, and painting, and which can be taught using dance as an educational focus. Through an analysis of the choreographer's use of these compositional principles, one is able to comprehend the process of organization interrelated in the three arts. The content areas, based on aesthetic principles discussed by Thomasine Kushner (1983), Karl Aschenbrenner (1985), and Alma Hawkins (1988), among others, begin with principles of organization in relation to dance. Next, dance is interrelated with the discipline of music and, finally, dance and music are interrelated with painting. Curricular development therefore progresses from dance (movement), to dance and music (movement and sound), to dance and music and painting (movement and sound and sight).

Content Area Summary

The following is a brief summary of the eight principles of organization that were synthesized from an analysis of the relevant literature in aesthetics, aesthetic education, and dance, music, and painting composition. These principles comprise content areas that can serve as the substantive information within a curriculum in aesthetic education: coherence, dynamism, unity and variety, repetition and contrast, rhythm, emergence and recedence, balance, and development.

Coherence

Coherence in art refers to the product of wholeness or consistency exhibited by the art work. In addition to the unification of constituent parts, all parts interrelate with all other parts. In an art work that exhibits coherence, nothing external to the work is needed for completion. The work exhibits an organic wholeness (Aschenbrenner, 1985; Broudy, 1972; Kushner, 1983; Weiss, 1961). As defined by Aschenbrenner, coherence is "the unique way in which elements belong to the art work and justify their place in it" (p. 7). He states that the artist in any medium works toward unification and coherence of specific elements, repetition, and development (p. 93). The concept that form or coherence exists in the arts can therefore be applied to all the arts.

Choreographer Doris Humphrey (1959) was in agreement with the concept of coherence when she stated that continuity is paramount to form in dance. In her view, nothing should threaten the cohesiveness of the dance (p. 149). Lynne Anne Blom and Tarin Chaplin (1982) also noted that no matter how wide the spectrum of variety and contrast used by the choreographer, those elements must exist within the principle of wholeness which binds the dance together (p. 109).

Dynamism

The theory of dynamism is based on the supposition that energy underlies all phenomena. Aestheticians such as Aschenbrenner (1985), W.A. Ball (1988), A. Hill (1968), Thomas Munro (1970), and Elizabeth Watts (1977) are among those who have described the concept of movement as an interrelation among the arts.

Dance theoretician Rudolph Laban (1971) considered movement as a basis for the creation of dance, painting, and music. "Movement . . . is present also in the playing of instruments, in painting pictures, and in all artistic activity." He continued to state that the significance of movement in the arts is varied due to the wide range of movement expression (pp. 99–100). In his view, human movement serves as a common denominator for the creation of the various arts.

Effort, which consists of the motion factors of weight, time, space, and flow, is both visible and audible. The effects of effort can be heard in the production of speech or song. Even if the effort action is not seen, it can be imagined and visualized when the resultant sound is heard (Laban, 1971, p. 24). Laban noted that if one watches a musician play an instrument, one can see and register the effort of the performance. Even if sound is not heard, the effort and rhythm can be discerned by

watching the movement of the performer (Laban & Lawrence, 1947, p. xiv).

Laban considered the painter's use of effort and movement at the time of creation to be still visible in the resultant art work, even though the work itself remained static. Movement and energy exist in static works of art (such as painting) as well as dynamic ones (such as dance). In consideration of the artist, Laban (1971) wrote:

> The movements he has used in drawing, painting or modelling have given character to his creations, and they remain fixed in the still-visible strokes of his pencil, brush, or chisel. The activity of his mind is revealed in the form he has given to his material. (p. 9)

Unity and Variety

Unity in dance attracts and holds the viewer's attention. Hawkins (1988) claimed that "the most essential attribute of a well-formed dance is unity or wholeness" (p. 88). When a dance possesses unity, each part contributes to the whole. Subsequently, the whole should be comprised of organic form and not arbitrary form. When visible form is evolved from internal responses, thoughts, ideas, or feelings, real unity emerges in the art work. "From a choreographic standpoint, unity means *selecting, limiting,* and *manipulating*" (p. 89).

Variety must exist within the unified dance. Variety consists of the dynamic tensions between the organization of forces within the dance. This results in contrasts that serve to differentiate between patterns, rhythms, and dynamics (i. e., the entire spectrum of the organization of forces). The interplay of organizational forces, however, must also be kept in balance. Balance consists of the controlled relationship between parts. The creator, or choreographer, controls these relationships in order to produce a unified and coherent work developed organically through the expansion and manipulation of the basic dance idea. If the aspect

of balance is neglected, the work may become distorted or incoherent. If the aspect of variety is absent, the dance may lack diversification and contrast and may become repetitive and monotonous.

Repetition and Contrast

Repetition is used in order to unify elements within the art work. Repetition is indispensable in all the arts and occurs visually as well as aurally. The function of repetition is similar in both spatial and temporal art forms, even though the manifestation of repetition differs in space and time (Aschenbrenner, 1985).

In a consideration of repetition in visual art, Nellie Arnold (1976) stated that the regular repeti-tion of a form contributes to unity within an art work. Rhythm in painting results from the repetition of forms. Repetition of the same sequence of forms, colors, lines, or sounds "reminds viewers or listeners that they have seen or heard that portion of the art work before" (p. 63).

Ideas are conveyed and emphasized through the use of repetition. The meaning or intent of a work is also conveyed through the creator's selection and manipulation of repeating elements or themes. Differences exist between repetition in dance, music, and painting, however. Repetition in visual art consists of repeated identicals, whereas in music repetition is a motif which occurs more than once. Either manifestation of repetition can exist in dance depending on the number of performers. If a soloist repeats a movement phrase or shape, the repetition is a singular motif that occurs more than once. If a group of dancers executes the same movement simultaneously, the repetition consists of multiplicity of identicals (Aschenbrenner, 1985).

Contrast exists in the arts in order to differentiate between extremes. Blom and Chaplin (1982) noted the difference between variety and contrast. Variety consists of an infinite spectrum of diversifications within an art work. Contrast, however, is comprised of differences that are more extreme. Variety may include transitions and gradients connecting parts of elements. Contrast deals with the comparison of opposites whereas variety may include a broader range of differentiations.

Rhythm

The element of rhythm as a visual, aural, and kinesthetic manifestation in all the arts has been expounded throughout the years by both theoreticians and educators. Dance educator Margaret H'Doubler considered rhythm to be manifested primarily through kinesthetic perception. In H'Doubler's perspective, rhythm can be manifested and sensed visibly, audibly, and tactually, but it is first perceived kinesthetically. H'Doubler (1940) cited rhythm as the basic and fundamental art form. She considered the study of rhythm to be essential to all art forms. The art form of dance especially, however, depended on rhythm due to its kinesthetic basis of perception. Doris Humphrey (1959) in her famous book on dance composition expounded that rhythm "might be compared to the ambience of existence" (p. 104). She stated that rhythm, which organizes our spatial, temporal, and dynamic existence, would not have developed as it has in music and visual art had it not developed primarily through movement.

Rhythmic organization within dance provides a framework that can contribute to the conveyance of aesthetic intent. Like H'Doubler, Hawkins (1988) maintains that rhythm is first perceived as kinesthetic awareness, after which the percipient equates rhythmic structure with musical symbols and notation. The kinesthesia created by the visible and audible manifestations of rhythm causes tensions that pull the observer toward the discovery of meaning in the dance. Rhythm, which may be even or uneven, produces changes in energy and feeling response. Even rhythms, like symmetrical balance, usually promote a sense of continuity, stasis, rest, and sometimes monotony. Uneven rhythms, like asymmetrical balance, may solicit a sense of move-

ment, dynamics, and change. The subsequent meaning of a dance is affected by one's feeling responses to the various aspects of rhythm and its structure.

Rhythm in painting is similar to rhythm in dance and music. The difference lies in the fact that rhythm in painting is a function of spatial organization. Rhythm in music is a function of temporal organization. Rhythm in dance is both visible and audible and emerges from a kinesthetic (or motor) source.

Emergence and Recedence

The concept of emergence and recedence of elements within a work of art is analogous to the concept of figure and ground. Aschenbrenner (1985) wrote extensively on the concept and stated that the artist in any medium makes use of the figure-ground principle in order to focus the attention of the apprehender and emphasize important aspects of the art work. He wrote:

> Sceptics often scoff at the idea that there is any common order that underlies musical composition, pictorial and sculptural design, dramatic and narrative form, the several arts, in short. Clearly, they have not looked very hard, or hard enough. The application of the figure-ground principle, not only to music but to other arts as well, is so completely fitting and natural that what is surprising is only that so little appeal to it has been made. (p. 153)

As examples, Aschenbrenner notes that the painter furthers emergence by providing differences in size, color, and shape. The musician is able to further emergence through the contrast of high and low voices and through the use of timbre. The choreographer isolates movement that is highlighted within a phrase or utilizes a soloist who emerges from a group.

Balance

Balance is termed as the compromise between parts. The artist attempts to achieve this compromise or synthesis in order to create a coherent organization in which the parts and the whole co-exist and do not destroy each other. Balance is achieved in dance through design in the shape of the body or movement, in the use of the dance space, and in the movement itself. The relationship of the body to gravity through the vertical, diagonal, and horizontal planes constitutes an aspect of spatial balance. As Laban noted, movement within the vertical plane is predominantly solid or stable.

The horizontal axis or plane also suggests stability. Labile movement occurs between the vertical and horizontal planes. This diagonal movement is replete with dynamism due to the increase of tension as the body moves out of either the vertical or horizontal plane. The most urgent sense of movement is perceived at the point of greatest imbalance.

It is a choice of the artist to present a pattern of movement, sound, or shape as either symmetrical or asymmetrical. Symmetry, which exists as an identical resemblance between the parts of a pattern, produces an image of minimum tension. Asymmetry, which consists of an inequality between the parts of a pattern, produces an image of maximum tension. Balance is then the coherent relationship between minimum and maximum tensions in an art work.

Development

Development in dance, music, and painting is enhanced by transitions, or gradients, and the flow to the climax (or climaxes) within the piece.

Development in dance is synonymous with continuity. The dance piece is perceived as a happening, an event which unfolds through space and time. Inherent meaning within a dance is revealed through its unique and individual order and flow. The development of the work contributes to the unity and coherence of the piece.

Development in music and painting occurs in analogous ways. Theme development in painting involves elements that are comparable. Unlike the painter, the musician has no visible shape with which to compose, yet the composer does establish regularities early in the work. The first notes of a composition establish a key signature and a time signature, which serve as a frame of reference for the piece. The minimal requirements for a theme in music would then be a series of contrasts in pitch and a series of contrasts in time. Thematic development in music then ebbs and flows from this frame of reference as does development in painting.

Transitions act as bridges between parts binding together the disparate aspects of the art work. Transitions develop from one element or sequence of a work and evolve into another element or

A modern dance class at Kent State University. *Photo by University Photographers.*

sequence. In dance, the transition develops from one movement idea and leads to the next. The individual work determines the exact way in which its parts are related. Transition differs from contrast in that a transition must consist of several steps or intervals that bridge different parts of the art work. Contrast consists of sharply defined opposites. Elements within a work opposing one another provide contrast. Transitions blend together elements and contribute to the development and flow of the work.

Climax is the result of a developmental progression. In dance and music climax is the inevitable result of the development of a section or an entire art work. The artist consciously or subconsciously prepares for the climax and builds toward it. It exists as "the accumulated high point of the piece" (Blom & Chaplin, 1982). A climax is often the result of a crescendo and is usually followed by resolution of some kind. In dance, long choreographies can possess secondary or complementary climaxes used to further the development which builds to a large climax. Climaxes occur as part of the development of a piece.

Studying the Organizational Principles

Dance MATERIAL was designed to interrelate eight selected organizational principles used in the creation of dance, music, and painting. Within the curricular model, each principle of organization is considered in relation to each art form. As the focus of the model, organizational principles are studied first in dance, and dance is considered first in relation to the other two arts. Coherence is the aspect that integrates and connects all parts of an art work in order to produce a holistic entity and is included as an integrator of the other principles of organization utilized. The concept of dynamism, or movement in the arts, connects the creation of dance, music, and painting through movement and thus becomes an additional component of the content area summary.

As a basis for curriculum development, it is suggested that each organizational principle be studied first in relation to dance, then in relation to music, and third in relation to painting. In this way the art forms maintain autonomy, and significant differences as well as commonalities may be discussed. The teaching of the eight organizational principles incorporates dance as an educational focus. Therefore, any of the aspects are first taught through the medium of dance. Aspects are next taught through dance in relation to music, and finally, through dance in relation to music and in relation to painting. The development of a curriculum based on the eight content areas can represent this progression from dance to music to painting.

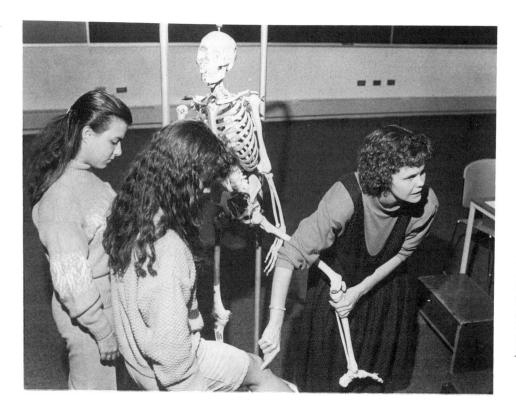

Lynn Deering explains body mechanics as part of the overall dance program at Kent State University. *Photo by University Photographers.*

In order to teach the comparison and interrelatedness of coherence, dynamism, unity, variety, repetition, contrast, rhythm, emergence and recedence, balance (which includes both symmetrical and asymmetrical balance), and development (which includes transitions and flow to climax), an individual principle of organization may be considered. Within a resultant curriculum the organizational principle under investigation would progress through its application in dance, music, and painting respectively. As a result of this sequence each organizational principle would form a component in the total configuration of the curriculum. Each organizational principle exists in relation to all others and thus reinforces the concept of coherence or organic wholeness in the arts. Both the individual principle and the manner in which it is interrelated in the three arts are studied.

Examples of Implementation

The implementation of the content areas within Dance MATERIAL includes the active participation of the student as the creator of dance, music, and painting. An example of a possible implementation could evolve as follows: The instructor could present and discuss the concept of emergence and recedence (figure and ground). Students would explore the concept through the medium of dance. The choreographer can emphasize the movements of one dancer and cause other movement to recede, to receive less focus. The choreographer may create a solo or duet, which emerges as a focal point, while the movement of the other dancers recedes to become background.

Once the students comprehend the concept of emergence and recedence in its manifestation in dance, the concept can be applied to music. Individuals or groups of dancers could be compared to individual sounds or groups of notes. The composer's manipulation of notes could be compared to the choreographer's manipulation of bodies. Once this connection has been discussed and understood, students could investigate the concept of figure and ground in painting and relate the painter's choice of focal points and relationships of figure and ground to the similar process undergone by the choreographer and composer.

Both similarities and differences occurring in the three arts media could be investigated and discussed. This interrelated perspective presents the arts as independent forms that may be compared. Much can be learned by observing how each art form is significant in its own regard and how each organizational principle manifests itself differently in each art.

Dance MATERIAL is designed as a basis for a course of study in dance as an art form, specifically focusing on dance composition. The curricular model interrelates the composition process in the three art types and fosters the development of creativity, collaboration, and aesthetic education. For example, the dancer benefits from a greater awareness of rhythm, music, pattern, and linear design. Possibilities of movement are expanded and enhanced. A more comprehensive awareness of the body as a medium of visual, aural, and kinesthetic expression results. The choreographer is able to better understand and utilize music and visual design in his/her creations. The teacher is able to draw from richer visual, aural, and kinesthetic sources in order to present learning experiences for students. The individual develops a greater understanding of art history, including dance, music, and painting in other epochs and cultures. A study of the organization of form develops critical thinking skills and gives one a point of departure in order to view dance in historic, social, and cultural contexts. As a medium of expression, the study of dance, music, and painting offers the individual a multitude of outlets.

References

Arnold, N. D. (1976). *The interrelated arts in leisure: Perceiving and creating.* St. Louis, MO: C. V. Mosby Company.

Aschenbrenner, K. (1985). *The concept of coherence in art.* Dordrecht, Holland: D. Reidel Publishing Co.

Ball, W. A. (1988, April). Expressing the inexpressible: Developing an aesthetic vocabulary. *Music Educator's Journal*, 53–56.

Blom, L. A., & Chaplin, L. T. (1982). *The intimate act of choreography.* Pittsburgh, PA: University of Pittsburgh Press.

Broudy, H.S. (1972). *Enlightened cherishing: An essay on aesthetic education.* Urbana, IL: University of Illinois Press.

Gardner, H. (1983). *Frames of mind: The theory of multiple intelligences.* New York: Basic Books, Inc., Publishers.

Getty Center for Education in the Arts. (1985). *Beyond creating: The place for art in America's schools.* New York: J. Paul Getty Trust.

Hawkins, A. (1988). *Creating through dance.* Princeton, NJ: Princeton Book Company.

H'Doubler, M. (1940). *Dance: A creative art experience.* New York: Appleton-Century-Crofts.

Hill, A. (Ed.) (1968). *DATA: Directions in art, theory and aesthetics.* London: Faber & Faber.

Humphrey, D. (1959). *The art of making dances.* New York: Rinehart & Co., Inc.

Karpati, A., & Abonyi, V. (1987). Interdisciplinarity in aesthetic education: Ideas, results, prospects. *Journal of Aesthetic Education, 21* (3).

Kushner, T. K. (1983). *The anatomy of art: Problems in the description and evaluation of works of art.* St. Louis, MO: Warren H. Green, Inc.

Laban, R. V. (1971). *The mastery of movement* (3rd ed., rev. Lisa Ullmann). Boston, MA: Plays, Inc.

Laban, R. V., & Lawrence, F. C. (1947). *Effort.* London: MacDonald & Evans.

Munro, T. (1970). *Form and style in the arts: An introduction to aesthetic morphology.* Cleveland, OH: Press of Case Western Reserve University.

National Dance Association. (1988). *Dance curricula guidelines K-12.* Reston, VA: National Dance Association.

Watts, E. (1977). *Towards dance and art: A study of relationships between two art forms.* London: Lepus Books.

Weiss, P. (1961). *Nine basic arts.* Carbondale, IL: Southern Illinois University Press.

**John R. Crawford is in the Dance Unit of the
School of Physical Education, Recreation, and Dance,
Kent State University, Kent, Ohio 44242.**

College/Adult
Beginners

<hr/>

Developing Skills in Dance: Considerations for Teaching Adult Beginners

Carol A. Wood and Susan Gillis-Kruman

Where do successful strategies for teaching dance technique originate? The process of developing skill in movement requires decision making on the part of the teacher. Teachers' decisions may be based on the opinion of the authorities in the field, on tradition, or on the insight that comes from observation and critical analysis. The purpose of this paper is to suggest practical strategies for the teaching of dance. The concepts that will be presented have been drawn primarily from the body of theoretical and research information from the discipline of motor control and learning.

In any movement, the learner plans the movement based upon an action goal. For any movement related activities, e.g., basketball or football, the goal of the movement is related to the outcome rather than the quality of the movement itself. From this perspective, dance as movement is based on a different set of criteria for successful performance. Not only is the successful technical execution of a movement considered but also how the movement is performed in terms of space, time, and energy. Dance movement is internally organized. The outcome is tied to the individuality of the performer. It is this uniqueness that makes dance an aesthetic experience. The individual not only shapes the movement, but makes aesthetic choices about how to use movement qualities to create dynamic and articulate movement that expresses the inner organization and intent of the performer.

Criteria for successful movement performance may include: 1) clarity of the movement articulation; 2) fluidity/ease of execution; 3) awareness of time or temporal change; 4) ability to demonstrate spatial intent; 5) use of body focus/projection, i.e., the ability of the dancer to demonstrate appropriate intensity (focus) with intent; 6) ability to display a dynamic range; 7) correct movement sequence and execution; and 8) adherence to the rhythmic structure of the music.

Many characteristics of dance movement quality emerge only after many hours of training. Therefore, the primary focus of this paper is to present instructor strategies that will enhance the beginning dancer's ability to articulate the movement as well as its fundamental qualitative components, perform the movement sequence correctly, and adhere to the rhythmic structure of the movement. These teaching strategies are based on the skill level/experience of the class are designed to be used for teaching in the studio setting.

Learning Characteristics of Beginners

The task of learning a movement is complicated by the inability of the beginner to manageably reduce the quantity of information needed to perform the movement. Maximum attention demands are placed on the information processing system of the learner because beginners do not have the experience to accurately pinpoint essential information. Characteristics of the beginning dancer that increase the difficulty of learning movement are 1) lack of knowledge about what elements of the movement to focus on, 2) longer time to monitor perceptual input from the visual system and the body, and 3) difficulty in performing simultaneous movement (Spaeth-Arnold, 1981).

During the initial stages of learning a factor that must be considered within any teaching setting is that beginners have extremely limited capacities for attending to information (Gentile, 1972; Fitts & Posner, 1967). For example, when teaching a plié, many pieces of information may be generated by the instructor. Factors for performing a plié with aesthetic quality are numerous and might include the position of the pelvis, alignment of the knees, the relationship of the shoulders and the pelvis, positioning of the rib cage, activation of abdominal muscles, head position, heels in contact or not in contact with the floor, coordination of arm and bending kee, and coordination of movement to music.

When structuring teaching for any beginner, the instructor must remember that beginners are easily overwhelmed by the amount of information that must be remembered for successful performance. Beginning students are not able to adequately focus attention on the relevant aspects of the movement or the critical cues embedded in the teachers' movement instructions. In addition, the student's ability to pay attention to several sources of information (e.g., the position of the legs, arms, tempo, quality, etc.) is severely limited. And the student's memory capacity for movement directions presented by the instructor is restricted due to short term memory limitations (see Miller, 1956). This implies that during early learning, instructions and movement cues from the teacher to the student must be brief. To overcome these problems and aid successful student learning, several strategies may be implemented by the instructor.

Teacher Implemented Strategies

The teacher's responsibilities during the initial stage of learning are numerous. Due to the limited processing ability of beginners, abundant verbalization about the movement is not desired and may actually delay the learning process by confusing the learner. The teacher should attempt to set up the learning environment in a way that is most conducive to the learner.

The first task the teacher faces is describing the goal of the action (Gentile, 1972). For example, in the plié movement previously described, one goal of the movement is related specifically to body alignment. Another subgoal of a plié that may not be readily observable to the learner is the role of plié in preparation and landing for jumps. Once the learner has "gotten the idea" of plié, the learner will approximate a response based on the demonstration by the instructor and past movement experiences. Subsequent attempts at plié allow the learner to refine the response and eventually a plié with correct form is performed.

The second task facing the teacher is structuring the practice environment so that consistent movement patterns are established. Although variations of movement (position or speed) may vary, dance is a movement form requiring that certain lines of the body remain consistent. It is the development of

the consistent movement patterns and the implementation of those movement patterns into movement variations that are critical to the dancer's success.

Rehearsal is defined as a repetition of individual movements and movement sequences. The organization of rehearsal or practice may take many forms. Typical of dance classes, rehearsal of movements is rote as in a ballet barre or stylized warm-up. Dance practice organization should be based on achieving the correct form of the movement and using those movements in conjunction with other movements.

Rehearsal should be structured so that the qualities of the movement are developed in a way that can be repeated in many settings and combinations. An illustration of this effect is a beginning student performing tendu at the barre and at center. Although the pattern of the tendu should be identical in both situations, moving to center often causes the beginner to produce a very different tendu pattern. In each case, the teacher must allow practice of the movement. Variations of consistent patterns that are desirable require the instruction to be designed so that the student practices all of the desired variations (Gentile, 1972; Spaeth-Arnold, 1981).

Clarifying the goal of the task through modeling and demonstration and structuring class practice does not necessarily mean that the learner will attend to the specific characteristics of the movement that are critical. The teacher must also use strategies to focus the attention of the learner on the task (Khaneman, 1973). As a part of the learning process, a beginning student must be able to distinguish the difference between relevant and irrelevant information that is critical to skilled performance.

Cues and Modeling

The teacher's identification of critical elements or cues used to focus the attention of the learner on the relevant information about the movement should be used to circumvent common errors of the movement. How many cues or critical elements should an instructor use? The number of pieces of information is dependent on the skill level of the student. As the skill level of the dancer increases the number of critical elements may be increased due to the individual's increasing efficiency in storing information. For the novice, however, information amounts should be limited to one or two cues. For example, when teaching plié, one might ver-

The teacher must use a variety of teaching strategies and structure the learning environment to facilitate learning. *Photo of instructor Gael Stepanek and students at Teachers College, Columbia University by Otto M. Berk.*

bally cue on the position of the pelvis and the relationship of the knees to the feet. More information might confuse the issue. However, after several practice attempts more information may be given. At the novice level, brevity of information is critical to the learning.

For most teaching, instructors use a model to demonstrate the movement. Modeling is the visual demonstration of skill. The elements of the action are seen directly by the learner. The model can be the teacher, a video tape, or a student. Studies on modeling tend to suggest several implications for instruction. First, learners who receive verbal instructions without a visual demonstration require longer practice to acquire appropriate movement quality (McCullagh, Steihl, & Weiss, 1990.) Second, the timeliness of the demonstration is important. The most effective use of modeling for student learning of movement occurs when the demonstration is presented before the movement attempt. Increases in effectiveness can be gained by modeling again during the practice phase of movement learning (Landers, 1975). Third, the skill level of the model and the correctness of the demonstration are critical factors that will influence the learner. The best possible situation is for a skilled teacher to be a model. If that isn't an option, using a student peer would be the next best situation (Landers & Landers, 1973; McCullagh, 1987).

The teacher must understand that processing demands are very high during early learning and adding nonessential information demands to the learner can be harmful. In many studios, visual information from mirrors adds to the processing load of the beginners. At first, watching the image may disrupt the movement quality and rhythm that

have been previously developed. This disruption occurs because attention tends to be automatically drawn to a highly meaningful source, the individual's image. Many beginners will develop a strategy that shifts the gaze from the mirror to the floor so that concentration can be focused on the movement. Eventually the movement has been practiced sufficiently to allow the beginner to watch her/his image and correct the movement during its execution.

Without realizing the potency of the mirror to the beginner, the teacher may be adding unnecessary demands to the task. For this reason the instructor may want to begin mirror work with static movement that is low attention demanding (e.g., a single movement such as plié, tendu, or a contraction) and progress to dynamic movements which are high attention demanding (e.g., across the floor movement such as leaps, turns, and triplets.)

Teachers may focus the attention of the learner on the appropriate features of the task by applying verbal labels and imagery techniques. The number of cues or stimuli that are verbalized to a student can be reduced by these techniques. Labels are verbal commands used by the teacher to cue subjects on rhythm, body relationships, or movement sequence (Shea, 1977; Ho & Shea, 1978; Magill & Lee, 1987). For example, when teaching a port de bras in ballet class the instructor, rather than counting the positions of the port de bras, (e.g., 1st, 2nd, 3rd, etc.) may label the spatial positions for the movement (e.g., front, high, side, low, etc.). The instructor, by verbalizing the positions of the arms in time with the music, can give the counts of the movement in synchrony with the body positions. Using voice inflection to highlight the critical beats of the movement is also helpful. For example, in teaching a modern dance triplet, the instructor might say "**DOWN**, up, up" or "**ONE**, two, three," accenting the downbeat of the music and initiation of a weight shift. The goal of teacher labeling is to count and voice inflect on the beats while reinforcing specific dance vocabulary or movement quality.

Imagery is a technique whereby a picture of a related concept that describes an aspect of the movement, such as quality, or a representation of some action, shape, and/or feeling is presented to the student. Images allow individuals to draw from previously acquired knowledge so that a linking of movement and image concepts can be used (Hall & Buckholz, 1983). For example, when teaching a plié, certain images may be used to reinforce proper alignment. One image might be of a spine sliding down a fireman's pole. This image should aid the student in understanding the relationship of the alignment to the downward movement of the plié. This image gives the quality of the movement (sliding or fluid) and the visual image of an elongated, vertical spine. Through experience, teachers find various images that evoke the best physical response from their students. Many images may be used to enhance proper quality and shape of movement.

Consolidating

The beginner's ability to "chunk" or consolidate information will increase as practice continues. Discrete movements and movement sequences will be joined together to form longer phrases or combinations specific to the dance technique (Chase & Simon, 1973; Starkes, Deakin, Lindley, & Crisp, 1987). A beginner in any dance form, typically, has difficulty performing arm and leg movements simultaneously. Minimal articulation of the torso is seen during early practice. As practice begins, the learner becomes more familiar with arm and leg coordination and the coarse shape of the movement emerges. Subsequent practice leads to refinement in movement articulation and body positioning in conjunction with the coordination of the arm and leg.

For example, many beginning ballet students have difficulty executing tendu in conjunction with port de bras. The port de bras is particularly difficult because many beginners do not have a good idea of the path of the moving arm, which is moving in a different plane from the moving leg. Also, if the path of the arm extends beyond the peripheral view of the student the student will not be able to

visually monitor the movement. The instructor may also use a verbal cue to encourage students to direct focus on the quality of the port de bras movement, e.g., smooth and flowing, versus the quality of the leg movement, e.g., direct and percussive or vice versa, depending on the errors made.

Feedback

The final goal for productive teaching of beginners is the instructor's role in providing feedback about movements. Following initial attempts at a new activity the learner must use feedback to establish the effectiveness of the movement pattern (Marteniuk, 1976). During early learning the beginning dancer will tend to rely heavily on visual information to guide and modify the movement (Robb, 1968). As skill develops, kinesthetic/proprioceptive information plays an increasing role in movement correction (Fleishman & Rich, 1963). The teacher supplements the learner's internal information sources by providing augmented information about some quality of the movement (e.g., "feel the lengthening and lifting of the torso as you . . ."). During early learning, the learner may not be able to adequately monitor all the internal and external sources of information that provide information about the movement. The teacher's role is twofold. First he/she must guide the learner in developing his/her internal error detection process. And two, the teacher must provide information that is not readily available to the learner.

For example, a beginning student when performing a grande battement at the barre may tend to use visual feedback early in the learning to guide the leg to its proper spatial position and ensure that it returns to fifth position on movement completion. Early learners appear to be unaware of the position of the trunk and pelvis during the movement and the rotation of the standing leg and elevated leg is usually lost. By providing verbal feedback, teachers can focus attention on the inadequacies of the task. Guidance by the teacher that aids the learner in developing a "correct sensation" of a movement might be, for example, verbalizing "level hips, rotated thighs, activated abdominal muscles, or move as if you're reaching to the sky or spiraling upward, or contracting and expanding with each breath . . ." will serve to improve the movement form and quality.

The primary consideration for the feedback, however, is related to the information demands placed on the subject. Providing too much information in the feedback message, as in ororverbalization, may cause the beginner to attend to a non-critical portion of the message. In the statement "You neglected to align your pelvis correctly, you had no turn-out, the movement was jerky, you faced the wrong way and you should have begun on count two," the beginner might only attend to the fact that she/he began on the wrong count and disregard the remainder of the feedback.

Coincidentally, information that is highly precise may also interfere with learning (Rogers, 1974; Magill & Wood, 1986). Care should also be taken that the feedback messages are spaced across the instruction (Lavery, 1962; Schmidt, Young, Swinnen, & Shapiro, 1989). A teacher who provides feedback following each movement attempt may cause the learner to rely too heavily on teacher information as opposed to relying on the student's own internal, proprioceptive sense. If this were the case and the teacher information was withdrawn, performance of the movement may be degraded.

We have attempted to present a variety of teaching strategies that can be easily implemented into studio instruction. Although the focus of this article was teaching adult beginners, many of the same strategies may be applied to teaching students of varying skill level. To facilitate dance development in the studio, the teacher must understand the constraints of the activity being taught and the process of the learner. It is the ambition of the teacher to help the student "learn how to learn." To aid in the process, the teacher must consciously structure the learning environment to facilitate learning.

References

Chase, W.G., & Simon, H.A. (1973). Perception in chess. *Cognitive Psychology, 4*, 55–81.

Fitts, P.M., & Posner, M.I. (1967). *Human performance.* Belmont, CA: Brooks/Cole.

Fleishman, E.A., & Rich, S. (1963). Role of kinesthetic and spatial-visual abilities in perceptual-motor learning. *Journal of Experimental Psychology, 66*, 6–11.

Gentile, A.M. (1972). A working model of skill acquisition with application to teaching. *Quest,* Monograph 17, 3–23.

Hall, C.R., & Buckholz, E. (1982–83). Imagery and the recall of movement patterns. *Imagination, Cognition and Personality, 2*, 251–260.

Ho, L., & Shea, J.B. (1978). Levels of processing and the coding of position cues in motor short-term memory. *Journal of Motor Behavior, 10*, 113–121.

Khaneman, D. (1973). *Attention and effort.* Englewood Cliffs, NJ: Prentice-Hall.

Landers, D.M. (1975). Observational learning of a motor skill: Temporal spacing of demonstrations and audience presence. *Journal of Motor Behavior, 7*, 281–287.

Landers, D.M., & Landers, D.M. (1973). Teacher versus peer models: Effect of model's presence and performance level on motor behavior. *Journal of Motor Behavior, 5*, 129–139.

Lavery, J.J. (1962). Retention of simple motor skill as a function of type of knowledge of results. *Canadian Journal of Psychology, 16*, 300–311.

Magill, R.A., & Lee, T.D. (1987). Verbal label effects on response accuracy and organization for learning limb positioning movements. *Journal of Human Movement Studies, 13*, 285–308.

Magill, R.A., & Wood, C.A. (1986). Knowledge of results precision as a learning variable in motor skill acquisition. *Research Quarterly for Exercise and Sport, 54*, 346–351.

Marteniuk, R.G. (1976). *Information processing in motor skills.* New York: Holt, Rinehart and Winston.

McCullagh, P. (1987). Model similarity effects on motor performance. *Journal of Sports Psychology, 9*, 249–260.

McCullagh, P., Steihl, J., & Weiss, M.R. (1990). Developmental modeling effects on the quantitative and qualitative aspects of motor performance. *Research Quarterly for Exercise and Sport, 61*, 344–350.

Miller, G.A. (1956). The magical number seven plus or minus two: Some limits on our capacity for processing information. *Psychological Review, 63*, 81–97.

Robb, M. (1968). Feedback and skill learning. *Research Quarterly, 37*, 393–405.

Rogers, C.A. (1974). Feedback precision and post-feedback interval duration. *Journal of Experimental Psychology, 102*, 604–608.

Schmidt, R.A., Young, D.E., Swinnen, S., & Shapiro, D.C. (1989). Summary knowledge of results for skill acquisition: Support for the guidance hypothesis. *Journal of Experimental Psychology: Learning, Memory, and Cognition, 15*, 325–359.

Shea, J.B. (1977). Effects of labelling on motor short-term memory. *Journal of Experimental Psychology: Human Learning and Memory, 5*, 179–187.

Spaeth-Arnold, R.K. (1981). Developing sport skills: A dynamic interplay of task, learner, and teacher. *Motor Skills: Theory into Practice,* Monograph 2, 1–81.

Starkes, J.L., Deakin, J.M., Lindley, S., & Crisp, F. (1987). Motor versus verbal recall of ballet sequences by young expert dancers. *Journal of Sport Psychology, 9*, 222–230.

Carol A. Wood and Susan Gillis-Kruman are in the Department of Health, Physical Education, Recreation, and Dance, University of Pittsburgh, Pittsburgh, Pennsylvania 15261.

Student as Teacher, Teacher as Student

Gail Lee Abrams

As a college dance professor for the past 15 years, I have often been confronted with questions about the validity of dance as a field of study at the postsecondary level. College administrators, faculty colleagues, students, parents, and even we, as dancers ourselves, ask about the value of dance in education, the practicality of dance as a possible career choice, and the impact dance can have in personal growth. Although I have become practiced at answering these questions to most people's satisfaction, they have raised other questions about how I might better accomplish my goals as a teacher of movement and convey to my students just how rich a contribution dance can make to their lives.

The Motivation

Many people who have not studied dance assume that it is a very specific, self-contained discipline that may not be particularly applicable within the broader context of a college education. What makes dance so potentially effective as a component of higher education is its interactive, participatory, experiential approach. Although possible, it is certainly not easy to get through a dance class without truly paying attention and actively getting involved. Since so many college classes are taught in a lecture format, in which students can merely sit, take notes, and decline to participate, a dance class can serve as a tremendously challenging, recuperative, and stimulating experience calling on the physical and mental capabilities of the student in a totally unfamiliar way.

In striving to achieve this goal of total involvement, I have been evaluating many of my own teaching methods and have discovered the value of incorporating "self-teaching" techniques into my classes. A few years ago, I noticed that some of my students were treating my dance technique course as simply another academic class; they were lazy and seemed to be "sleep-dancing" through classes at times. Many of them expected to be spoon-fed the material, just as they were in more traditional classes. The syndrome of "show me the movement, and I'll repeat it back" was surfacing more and more, and interactions between students and teacher, and between students themselves, were often mechanical and impersonal.

It also seemed that when students did try to learn movement phrases, they did not really *see* what was important in the movement. Their concern was for the steps, the counts, that is, the quantitative rather than the qualitative essence of the movement. Consequently, their own versions of the movement often tended to be mechanical and externally motivated rather than felt from and connected to internal motivation and kinesthetic sensation. In addition, I wanted to more effectively tap the creative potential of *all* of my students, especially those who were not as technically skilled but who might have wonderful, creative gifts. I began to look for more ways to clarify, and to teach students to clarify, concepts about movement and what it communicates.

It seemed that the best way to solve these problems was to involve students more, not only in the *learning* process, but also in the *teaching* process. This had always been a significant part of my composition classes, but I had applied it in my technique classes less often and more haphazardly. Although I sometimes had students help each other with movement phrases by learning the opposite side in pairs or by observing and correcting each other, and although we often did improvisation and short composition studies, these never seemed fully integrated into my teaching process in a way that really made a difference. I had always felt that as the teacher, I should be responsible for all, or most, of the teaching. Once I began to experiment with different ways of having students teach themselves and each other. I realized that more productive work was being accomplished, students were learning more, and I was learning more and teaching better.

The Methods

There is nothing magical about the specific techniques I have been using, except that they work: they help students understand more about movement, their own learning processes, and themselves. Many of the examples I will give are probably things that many dance instructors already do in their classes. If so, perhaps this will simply provide a new perspective on ways in which they can be effective; if not, I hope they will prove helpful.

Perhaps the most common self-teaching technique is having students coach each other in pairs, after having learned a movement phrase in technique class. The observer gives feedback about what she has seen and what she believes could be worked on, both quantitatively and qualitatively. The coaching process also includes discussion about how the mover *feels* when doing the movement, both on a physical and an expressive level. When the roles are reversed, both students realize that, although they are doing the same basic movement phrase, each puts her own imprint on the movement and claims it as her own, because she has discovered her own personal connection to it. By watching each other, students improve their observational skills; they have to define their own concept of the movement in terms of motivation, shape, quality, timing, initiation, phrasing, etc.

In developing images for herself and her partner, the student becomes accountable for her own movement and the choices she makes. She more consciously recognizes her own tendencies and preferences and gains confidence in her ability to observe, evaluate, and help another. While working as partners, students challenge each other to justify and clarify what they are doing.

Another exercise in observation and clarification involves showing a movement phrase (usually not a counted phrase) and having the students repeat what they have seen after only one viewing. Obviously, they can't really repeat the phrase accurately; the point of the exercise is to find out what aspects of the movement have made the greatest initial impression. Students continue to work on what they remember of the phrase until they have clarified and developed it into their own phrase. Through this evolutionary process, each version becomes something quite different from the original; however, there is also a unity because each version has sprung from the same source. Playing with the various phrases in duets, trios, etc. can yield fascinating results and allows students to work on composition, improvisation, and technique simultaneously.

While observing and guiding the students' working processes, I discover more about each individual's own learning methods. The more I understand how and what each student sees and does not see, and what each student perceives as being important in learning a phrase, the better equipped I am to give constructive feedback to that student. I can speak to her using her own language, and I can introduce her to new concepts from the starting point of things she already understands.

Another way of approaching this is by having students dialogue with themselves while dancing a phrase. I ask each dancer to literally talk to herself out loud; she describes what she is doing, how she is doing it, what she likes and doesn't like about the movement, how she feels when doing it, images that occur to her, etc. In this manner, the student consciously hooks into what she is doing and becomes more fully aware of the physical and mental connections. I also ask each student to identify the moment or moments in the phrase that she loves dancing the most, and to perform those with the fullest energy and commitment possible. Then she is asked to allow that energy and joy to extend itself through the movement that occurs before and after her favorite moment(s), so that eventually the entire phrase is infused with the same life she gave the isolated moment. This not only results in greater enjoyment and fuller performance, it also gives her a greater understanding of kinesthetic connections and movement transitions within a dance phrase.

Asking students to choreograph and teach their own sequences to the class is an effective "self-teaching" method. In most classes, some students will jump at the opportunity to lead class, while others are terrified at the prospect of such responsibility. Once convinced to try it, they generally find it much more fun but also more difficult than they expected. As they see their classmates try to reproduce their movement, the "teachers" learn where they have been unclear, in either time structure or movement quality, initiation, phrasing, or sequence. Their own classmates challenge them to become more articulate as they ask for exactness in the teacher's performance or verbal description of the movement. By observing areas in which the students have difficulty communicating to each other, I learn what concepts I need to focus on more fully within a particular class.

One of the most glaring problems to surface during this exercise has been in the area of rhythmic structure. Students are invariably unable to do the movement the same way twice because they do not understand how to count their own phrases. I have been dismayed to see this occur even in more advanced classes. This has alerted me to the need for more emphasis on rhythmic analysis and music training in my classes, which I accomplish with Dalcroze Eurythmics exercises as well as consultation and team-teaching with my accompanist.

During technique and improvisation classes, the self-teaching method may also take form through the development of a ritual. To promote group unity, I often use this in a "disconnected" class, in which people do not seem to be relating to each other as classmates or as friends. We decide on a particular concept around which to design a ritual; it may be an idea I suggest, or it may be something related to the season, or perhaps a political or social issue. The class brainstorms ideas verbally, tries to find some organization or structure from those ideas, and then breaks into groups. Each group develops its own part of the ritual, and at least some part of the ritual brings everyone together at the beginning, end, or both. Several rehearsals precede the final performance. Discussion about the ritual itself as an effective communication of the chosen concept, and about the dynamics of group process, concludes the class.

In composition class, an excellent assignment in which students teach each other involves random pairing of classmates who will each create a movement study for the other. They frankly discuss their own technical and choreographic strengths, preferences, and weaknesses and give feedback to their partner on the same issues. In creating a study for the partner, each choreographer attempts to incorporate both people's assets into one dance, in order to capitalize on positive features and minimize negative ones. By blending both styles, each is moving in an unfamiliar way and attempting to give up crutches and discover new ways of dancing. Each is also learning to recognize what is good and valuable about her own movement style, which is vital since students often experience extreme insecurity and doubt about their own creative abilities. While watching the final studies in class, it is amazing to see how much each choreographer has grown and how successfully each has been able to

solve the problem. Through this assignment, the students usually achieve a new level of objectivity that greatly enhances and improves their subsequent work.

In addition, I require composition students to schedule "labs" with each other each week (rotating partners throughout the semester) in order to get and give feedback on a more individual basis before showing their work to a larger audience in class. This enables students to refine their work one step further before showing, and gives them more practice in critiquing each other. Consequently, they have more confidence in their ability to talk about movement in greater depth, and their comments quickly progress past the level of "It was really good (but I don't know why)."

Students tie their experiences together through journal writing, a vital component of the self-teaching process. By recording experiences, reactions, observations, and insights about events occurring in and out of class, students articulate, verbalize, and bring to the conscious level many ideas and connections of which they might otherwise be unaware. This written diary provides them with a chronological record of their growth and development, which can be a valuable resource not only during the semester but later on as well. By reading and commenting on the journal at mid-semester, I can encourage students who are on the right track and challenge those who are not to dig deeper or consider other possibilities.

At the end of the semester, all students are required to re-read their entire journal and write a concluding entry, which may be a summation of feelings about the course and their progress, an altered response to something they wrote earlier in the semester, or any other thoughts that may emerge as a result of re-reading. This process serves as a synthesis of everything that has occurred throughout the semester. Through reading the journals, it is clear that students recognize not only how much they have progressed in their dance lives, but also how applicable their experience is to their personal and academic lives.

The Benefits

Although many of the advantages of self-teaching are discussed above, a few others should be mentioned. Initially, I began to use self-teaching techniques more frequently during a semester in which I was teaching over seven hours of dance in one day (fortunately, not every day!). Fear of burnout and a neck injury that semester forced me to find ways of conducting a full class while protecting myself and not cheating my students. Later on, teaching through a pregnancy helped me test and refine other ways of using students to teach each other. I found this to be a tremendous energy-saver, and my teaching style and enthusiasm were quite rejuvenated.

Having students work with each other also freed my eyes so that I could observe more and give more thorough feedback to individuals in the class. As many of us do, I suffered from the "super-teacher syndrome": I must see everything that is going on in the room. I must be able to help everyone at once, and I must know all the answers. Students can, with the right guidance, find the answers for themselves, and often there are several appropriate solutions to a particular problem. Using students to help each other gives rise to many possibilities teachers may not see themselves.

Having students coach each other helped solve the problem of what to do with the rest of the class when I was giving corrections or feedback to one particular student. Occupying the rest of the class in pairs or groups prevented me from losing the attention of the class or stopping its momentum, while promoting class unity and mutual support relationships at the same time. Equalization of skill level among class members also occurred, as each recognized her ability to help another regardless of her technical ability.

For example, one student may not be as technically advanced as another, but she may be an excellent observer, give articulate feedback, or have tremendous creative skills. Thus, students gain confidence in themselves through awareness of their own special abilities, and they gain respect for each other's individual contributions. In addition, respect for their teacher, and for the process of teaching, is enhanced.

Dance is often assumed to be a nonverbal discipline that is experienced solely through the body. This concept must be dispelled, and use of these techniques is one way to do it. Asking students to articulate their body experiences makes light bulbs go on for them in a way that is new and revealing. By consciously thinking through and verbalizing what they feel and see, concepts hit home more quickly and become better integrated, and the student is much more likely to apply her new-found knowledge to her dancing and choreography.

The study of dance can have tremendous impact on the college student by helping to facilitate problem-finding and problem-solving. It also fosters recognition of learning processes, working processes, and studying processes, as well as awareness of how one functions within a group and within interpersonal relationships. These characteristics establish dance as a rejuvenator and builder of the individual, who is then better able to approach the rest of the curriculum with the same sense of connection, vision, and creative insight.

The concept of "student as teacher, teacher as student" can further facilitate significant, integrated, active learning among students, while maximizing our energy, efficiency, and effectiveness as teachers. As teachers, we must each remain the observer, the seeker—the student.

Gail Lee Abrams teaches in the Dance Department, Scripps College, Claremont, California 91711.

Ballet I Curricular Design in Higher Education

Carol J. Soleau

Ballet I curricular design must relate to the context in which the course is taught. In some institutions, dance classes are offered by dance or fine arts departments. Auditions are held to determine placement, and the Ballet I curriculum is designed to span one or ideally two semesters. In other institutions, dance classes are elective choices within a physical education service program. No auditions are held for placement, and therefore the clientele will differ significantly in ability and motivation. Within a typical ten-week quarter system, classes will meet twice a week for an hour or less.

There may be administrative pressure for accountability and the course must incorporate its justification into the curriculum. Furthermore, since many service programs are supported by a fee structure for survival in higher education, an entrepreneurial system is emerging as standard practice. Popularity, not content, determines whether a class is taught or not. The courses which survive must be an enjoyable experience for the students. Such factors create a particular challenge for ballet educators, because the content is traditionally taught in a slow repetitive manner within a formal working atmosphere that can hardly be described as "fun."

The curricular concepts that follow were developed to address the particular situation described above. They can also be applied in classes that are subject to less restrictive conditions.

The initial challenge is to determine those content areas that must be taught, realizing that many students will only take one course in ballet. Students' expectations can help define the goals. For instance, it is safe to assume that young adults taking ballet for the first time are not realistically pursuing a career in the field. Reasons for taking such a course would more likely include improving their physical well-being, including strength, flexibility, balance, and coordination; enhancing their performance level in another sport or physical activity; peer recommendations; or fulfilling a childhood fantasy or fascination with the art form.

Though student expectations should not dictate the goals, they do support the premise that ballet can be accessible to a broad population rather than to a chosen few. It is unrealistic to expect to produce highly skilled technicians, because the per-

Carol Soleau, author, in "Some Other Time," 1990.
Photo from Oregon State University, Corvallis.

84

formance standard takes years of intense training to achieve. Rather, it seems prudent to introduce the technique as part of a tradition including a rich historical background and unique aesthetic properties. Teaching a diverse population clarifies the primary focus. It is to foster an appreciation of the art form and to cultivate the joy of dancing.

The specific technical skills introduced are determined by observing novices, identifying foundational ability competence, utilizing the traditional ballet barre format, and recognizing that Ballet I students can experience the pleasure of dancing. To facilitate teaching, attention is given to accommodating diverse learning styles and to grouping steps into similar shapes. Complex skills are built adhering to the desired timing rather than broken down into parts. Limb preference and directional preference are discouraged in an effort to symmetrically train the body. Skills are taught by directing attention to the placement of the entire body, not by "teaching the feet first."

Though there are other areas that could enhance efficient presentation of material, this paper will limit itself to those described above. The application of selected motor learning research findings and personal experience have contributed to the development of these concepts.

Class Structure

Each class follows a similar format that becomes familiar to the students. The class begins in the center with a warm-up, followed by floorwork, the barre, the center, sequences across the floor, and a center floor closing. The warm-up, floor, and barre take approximately 37 minutes; the center, across the floor work, and closing take 23 minutes. Each class includes the skills that will be introduced, the skills that have previously been introduced and are practiced, brief anecdotes about dance or the meaning of the vocabulary, and traveling sequences that satisfy the students' need for physical exertion.

The separate sections of the class not only keep the students from becoming discouraged in one area, but make the hour feel longer than it is. The students are mentally and physically active due to the brisk pace and the number of skills that are practiced in each class. These skills are often simply variations of one skill, which provides the students with the opportunity to build upon their previous experience. Ideally, this format promotes learning and ensures a sense of accomplishment.

Observation of Novices

Sometimes it is difficult to know where to begin when confronted with a large class of adult novices. Some have had previous experience and some have never entered a dance studio before. Though the list could be endless, I have identified seven areas that seem to pose frequent problems for the beginning level student. These are:

1. An understanding of alignment, placement, and initiating movement from the center of the body.
2. Coordination of body parts to achieve movement efficiency and enjoyment.
3. The use of breath.
4. The timing of movement.
5. Outward rotation of the hip joint that affects overall alignment, particularly the pelvis, knees, and feet.
6. The shape of the pointed foot and weight bearing foot.
7. The use of straight and bent knees in both weight bearing and nonweight bearing exercises.

These concepts are interrelated and occur repeatedly in each class. Several areas need immediate attention, for some students have a preconceived picture of the ballet aesthetic. For example, they will try to force a turn out of the feet that does not reflect the true outward rotation capability of the hip joint. This stance distorts the body and is detrimental to the knees and feet. There is also a tendency to minimize the plié in order to appear to defy gravity. Time needs to be spent on clarifying the adults' capabilities, noting individual differences in flexibility ranges and strength capacities, and insisting that our current knowledge of the body can prevent injuries.

Utilizing Foundational Abilities

In order to keep students from being overwhelmed by the specificity of ballet technique, early classes concentrate on motor capabilities that they already possess, such as walking, skipping, and running both forward and backward. This supports Richard Magill's (1989) findings that foundational abilities underlie the performance of complex motor skills. He reports that Edwin Fleishman (1978, 1982) conducted research that resulted in initially identifying 11 perceptual-motor abilities and 9 physical proficiency abilities. The perceptual-motor abilities, which particularly pertain to ballet, include multilimb coordination and control precision. The physical proficiency abilities, which can be described as physical fitness abilities, include static and dynamic strength and flexibility.

Based on Fleishman's research, ballet curricula could utilize this knowledge to maximize teaching efficiency. It would be pointless and unsafe to teach grand fouetté en tournant in the first class, whereas a grand jeté would be acceptable because it is an extension of running, a foundational motor ability. Sauté attitude en avant could be introduced after practicing skipping, arabesque sautée after practicing hopping. Though the execution may not be perfect, students realize that many complex movements are built upon skills that they have already mastered.

The Barre

The ballet barre is the staple for students of all levels. It must be modified for beginners to ensure safe and correct technical practices. The premise is to warm up the body slowly and thoroughly beginning with large muscle groups and graduating to exercises that require more flexibility, strength, and quickness.

A typical beginning barre format includes: pliés, tendus, dégagés, rond de jambes, adagio sequences, frappés, and grand battements. The exercises are introduced throughout the quarter and can be modified for novices. For example, grand plié can be eliminated if safety is a concern. The important point is to prepare students for dancing.

The barre is not a separate entity. Once the students have an understanding of pliés, tendus, and dégagés in combinations, they possess the fundamental skills for many variations of elevations and traveling steps.

Traveling vs. Center Floor Combinations

Clearly, all basic technical skills cannot be taught at the beginning level and choices have to be made. I choose to focus on preparations for large traveling movement combinations (grand allegro) rather than sustained movement combinations (adage) or quick center floor elevations (petit allegro) based upon observing the abilities of the majority of beginners.

Adage requires a strong center, flexibility, strength, balance, and concentration. Petit allegro requires speed and articulate legs and feet.

Traveling combinations, on the other hand, allow the students to experience the exhilaration of dancing in spite of their limited technical backgrounds.

I also curtail the practice of turning skills to three or four minutes in every lesson to slowly develop "spotting" techniques, because there is a wide difference in proficiency levels among beginners in executing this particular skill. Those who like to turn practice constantly on their own. Those who don't, complain of dizziness and disorientation and easily get discouraged. Since the course might be students' only exposure to ballet, an effort is made to minimize frustration caused by introducing skills that are enjoyed by only a portion of the class.

Different Learning Styles

Another area that can expedite learning is the use of imagery, particularly kinetic imagery. Though it has become a common practice in teaching dance, it is clear that images must be meaningful to the learner. In fact, imagery may produce negative results among some learners, who respond better to verbal explanations and visual modeling practices. In order to reach the broadest population, I experiment with a variety of approaches. Demonstration is the most popular method of teaching. This can be accompanied with a straightforward verbal explanation as well as with several carefully chosen images.

For instance, in teaching battement tendu quatrième devant, I give the following explanation. "Keeping both legs straight, slide the gesture leg forward leading with the heel until it has to lift off the floor. Begin to arch the foot through the instep and ball of the foot until the toes are stretched, and they are not weight bearing. To return, slide the foot back leading with the toes. Relax the toes and the ball of the foot until the heel is released onto the floor and continue sliding the foot back to the original position."

For some, the following images might help to produce the desired result. "Feel yourself lifted out of the legs from deep inside the pelvic region. A gentle force propels the leg forward from behind the buttocks smoothly sending energy down and forward, encasing the back of the leg. Brush through the floor as if it was covered with powder, feeling as if the foot could travel through the floor until it is fully extended. Draw the leg back from deep inside the abdominals, again brushing through powder until the starting position is reached." Useful information is imparted in both explanations, and the different cues may reach a larger proportion of the class.

Grouping Technical Steps by Shapes

Another principle that seems to facilitate learning among beginners is to group the teaching of technical steps into similar shapes of the body as a whole. This is based on the theory that beginning level students have difficulty in coordinating bent vs. straight leg combinations. For example, the placement of sur le cou de pied will be taught in the same class as frappés, jetés dessus and dessous, and finally, skipping with the foot in a reasonable proximity of the sur le cou de pied position. Sur le cou de pied and battement retiré are practiced before pas de chat is introduced, and glissade derrière is taught in the same class with grand jeté à la seconde. Glissade and pas de chat are never taught in the same class. The starting and ending points are the same, but the intent and desired shape of the legs during the execution are quite different. I combine glissade and assemblé together, which is less confusing and easier for beginners to grasp.

Alternative Teaching Methods

A common practice among dance teachers is to "break down" complex steps or patterns, allowing the student to experience a degree of success in early stages of practice. My premise is to "build" complex movements, adhering to the timing of the ultimate goal.

For instance, I introduce assemblés as follows. At the barre the tendus are (count 1) plié, (count 2) tendu, (count 3) plié, (count 4) and straight. Dégagés will be taught as plié for 2, brush both legs straight for 2, in first and in 3rd position à la seconde. The timing will then be taught as "and 1' (plié brush close plié). After several other exercises to warm up the feet, assemblé dessus is practiced facing the barre in 3rd position. Immediately following, assemblé dessous is practiced. Later both are rehearsed in the center. In the following class, the dégagé combination will be practiced en croix in preparation for assemblés en avant and en arrière, giving the students the kinesthetic feeling for the many variations of assemblés, but these will not be further developed at the beginning level.

Lesa R. Broadhead instructs ballet students in the dance program at Kent State University's School of Physical Education, Recreation and Dance. *Photo by University Photographers.*

The choice to introduce assemblé dessus and dessous together is a conscious one. Ballet is supposed to be symmetrically practiced, and in many cases it is not. Typically, the left hand is placed on the barre first, followed by the right hand. Turns tend to be taught to the right first, followed by the left. Assemblé dessus is taught first, as is jeté dessus, and glissade derrière. My premise is to try to minimize preferred limb preference and preferred directional preference by practicing both equally. Though fewer steps will be taught at the beginning level, ideally, the students will be more habitually balanced in their approach to the art form.

Finally, I never teach "the feet first." Demonstrations include attention to the placement of the entire body. Students can immediately observe the final expected execution. The initial port de bras may be simple, but it must be modeled. The concept of "putting it all together at the end" wastes time. The students must reprocess the information. Also, teaching in parts requires altering the timing of the breath and the overall timing of coordinating the body limbs.

Cultural Components

Though much of the course is devoted to acquiring technical proficiency, I also allow time for including the cultural, historical, and aesthetic aspects of the art form. All the terms are introduced in French and the class is provided with written English translations of the terms. The students are required to take a vocabulary quiz during the sixth week, rather than at the end of the term when they will no longer be using the information.

I encourage the class to attend a live ballet performance. If this is not possible, films are shown outside of class time. Students are provided with written guidelines to aid their critical assessment of the performance they observed. Pictures of well-known ballet artists and choreographers are shared with the class, as well as short explanations of the

history of selected ballets. The students particularly enjoy Sandra Noll Hammond's (1982) description of a 19th century ballet barre. They are interested in the progression of the art form. The technical skills they learn, combined with their brief exposure to ballet's past as well as its present, instill in the students a respect for the difficulty of the medium, as well as an appreciation of its evolution through time.

Summary

The curricular design that has been introduced grew out of the necessity to survive within a system that values the popularity of a course more than its content. The fact that it must be aimed at a diverse population, must be taught within a strict time limit, and must satisfy the needs of the students, mandates that priorities are established. The challenge is to maintain the integrity of the course. Identifying and utilizing foundational abilities, grouping technical steps by shapes, and employing alternative teaching methods aid in teaching efficiency. Structuring the class into many segments, as well as utilizing the barre as the means to achieve freedom of movement, ensures that a majority of the students will experience a level of success. Introducing students to the rich cultural history of the art form helps to keep its traditions alive.

The fact that the course must be designed to appeal to a broad population has also produced positive results. Many students will experience an introduction to ballet who may not have taken the course because of its elitist reputation, or its gender biased history. Some of these students will be motivated to further their studies. They will know what to expect and will be physically and mentally prepared to improve their technical movement vocabulary. Most important, ballet curriculum will survive in higher education, for students have learned through experience to appreciate its value.

References

Fleishman, E.A. (1978). Relating individual differences to the dimensions of human tasks. *Ergonomics, 21,* 1007–1019.

Fleishman, E.A. (1982). Systems for describing human tasks. *American Psychologist, 37,* 821–834.

Hammond, S.N. (1982). *Ballet: Beyond the basics.* Palo Alto, CA: Mayfield Publishing Co.

Magill, R.A. (1989). *Motor learning concepts and applications.* Dubuque, IA: Wm. C. Brown Publishers.

Carol J. Soleau teaches dance in the College of Health and Human Performance, Oregon State University, Corvallis, Oregon 97331.

Serving a Broad Dance Community in Higher Education

Eleanor Weisman

The development of dance curriculum at the university level is most frequently focused on the dance major. Dance educators face the challenge of training future dance performers, teachers, and choreographers. However, there is another aspect of dance education to be addressed, the role that dance can play in the general education of all college students. Besides the specialization of the dance major, a general study of dance would be a beneficial component of higher studies just as English composition and the sciences are part of every student's education.

Many state education departments and arts councils are developing arts curricula that address the issue of providing arts education for all students in the lower grades. The Wisconsin Department of Public Instruction states:

> All people need the guided, comprehensive experience of dance as a fine art in their lives. The dance experience for most people should be a joyous one, with emphasis on the process rather than on the product professional dancers stress. Dance is not just for the elite who can afford expensive study in private studios. Everyone should know the joy of moving freely and unselfconsciously so as to reveal a unique personality. . . .
>
> As the demand for educational excellence grows around the country, teaching the easily transmitted forms of dance will no longer be sufficient. Educators will have to expand their own potential in order to expand that of their students as well. (Bryant-Weiler, Mills-Maas, & Nirschl, 1988, p. 2)

We higher education dance educators must also expand our curricular objectives to include the general student population in appropriate dance programs.

As we move into the 21st century, we recognize the importance of the physical, mental, emotional, and spiritual aspects of the human individual. The physical fitness craze has been running strong for many years now, and many university students take time out of their class schedules to exercise at their school's physical education center. This is definitely a step in the right direction, but an exercise regime does not necessarily provide the same benefits that a dance experience can—most importantly, the joy of self-expression through movement.

Educational theorist Howard Gardner (1983) writes of seven human intelligences in his book *Frames of Mind:* linguistic, logical/mathematical, spatial, musical, bodily-kinesthetic, interpersonal, and intrapersonal. The specialization that occurs in higher education usually focuses on the linguistic and the logical/mathematical intelligences. Many college students find themselves under stress and intense pressure from this concentration on specific learning styles. Student at the University of South Dakota have asked me to present Yoga and stress release programs because they need recuperation from their high-paced lifestyles. Instead of focusing on only two of the intelligences, higher education must celebrate the wholeness of the human being. Dance and movement education is an exploration of our kinesthetic intelligence that also develops our other six intelligences, and as such could be a foundation of a liberal arts education.

Dance classes can be designed quite naturally to address all the intelligences and to challenge students at all levels. A dance session might use verbal images for movement motivation and place them in a structured sequence (linguistic intelligence). The sequence could be performed to different pieces of music or with the dancers creating their own accompanying sounds (musical intelligence). A logical/mathematical experience can be explored by setting specific rhythmic counts, then cutting the counts in half, doubling them, etc. Spatial reasoning can be challenged by changing the directions, levels, and facings of the sequence as well as by creating group formations. Group work also develops interpersonal intelligence, while the encouragement of each student to commit to the movement and to make it his/her own self-expression can foster the intrapersonal.

Exploration of one's self and one's relationships with others becomes increasingly more valuable (and often more difficult) as a person matures. College students frequently tell me they find dance classes based on conceptual experiences to be therapeutic. Certainly most college students will cognitively grasp basic concepts easily, but physically is another matter. As their physical ability increases, older students can explore more complex spatial pulls, including off-vertical movement, more complex use of movement and language through poetry, and movement and music through canons, rounds, accumulations, etc. For a college student who is a beginning dancer, classes that are challenging conceptually as well as physically may be much more rewarding than a dance class that focuses on imitation and learning steps. In essence, dance is a way for a student to better understand and express him/herself, to better communicate with others, and to better function in and with the environment.

If dance is defined as the artistic or creative aspect of movement, then dance education is a method to teach creative thinking through our kinesthetic intelligence. This type of education need not stop at the lower grades but can continue throughout higher education. Students of business management, for example, learn skills of negotiation and team-building. Those same skills are used nonverbally in group dance improvisation. Dance/movement training based on group improvisation can provide instruction in communication through mirroring, syncronicity, eye contact, touch, spatial arrangement and patterns, order of moving, and individual expression, as well as leading and following.

The development of nonverbal communication skills leads to self-confidence, respect for the uniqueness of the individual, and successful teamwork or ensemble. Dance improvisation exercises relate to the skills taught for conflict resolution. We all need to be able to express ourselves, to listen to others, and to celebrate our differences and our similarities. When we are able to do so in the movement space of a dance studio, we may also find it easier in the political, social, and business environments.

Dance is a way to cross cultural barriers. We can learn about people with very different backgrounds by spending a dance class session exploring an Irish jig or an African welcome dance. We use these objectives as reasons why dance education is so valuable in grades K-12; they arc even more acutely true for older students who will soon be our policy makers.

If we look at primary cultures with tribal society organization, we see that dance was often a communal activity. Members of all ages would perform in ritual and festive dances. We learn from these societies that dance is not necessarily only a performing art, but has value as a participating art. In *History of the Dance in Art and Education*, dance scholars Richard Kraus, Sarah Chapman-Hilsendager, and Brenda Dixon (1991) state, "Among lineage-based cultures, then, one of the great purposes of dance has been to establish social unity and provide a means of collective strength and purpose" (p. 19). From the Lakota wacipi (powwow) to the European folk dance gathering, dance events provide safe environments for community interaction. Physical, social, and even spiritual needs can be met through community dance.

More recently, in the first half of this century in Europe, Rudolf Laban developed what he called "dance for the layman." He choreographed large group pieces and coined the term "movement choir" to describe them. The dancers were lay people with little or no dance training. Vera Maletic (1987) writes of Laban's ideas in *Body-Space-Expression*:

> Laban conceived of movement choirs as a medium providing an experience of togetherness, as community through dance: "Thousands of people can now experience the benefit of the rhythm and flow of dance, not only as spectators but also an active players in the joy of moving." However, he emphasized that besides the shared experience of the joyful movement, the crucial task of the movement choirs was to maintain a sense of humanity in a dignified form. He saw choral movement not as one of the many ways to achieve body-mind education but as the only possible way—for adults and children alike. (p. 14–15)

If our education system is to address the education of the "whole person," then certainly dance/movement must be part of the learning process.

When our higher education student body studies dance with this participatory aspect, there will also be a greater need for more technically trained performers and teachers. Again quoting from Maletic:

Dance curriculum at the higher education level must be broad enough to serve the community as well as the individual student. *Performance of Soleau's "Black Widow," 1991, Oregon State University photo.*

Laban also realized that lay participation in these movement choirs led to greater appreciation of theatre dance, so his promotion of the dance form enabled him to solve several pedagogical problems at "one blow." (p. 14–15)

We increase our audience for dance performance when we expose nonskilled movers to participation in dance through their own experience of it. Our dance curriculum at the higher education level must be broad enough to serve the community and the needs of the individual who is not a trained dancer, but rather a well-rounded individual.

One Approach to Community Education

As the only dance faculty person in the Theatre Department of the University of South Dakota, I founded the USD Moving Co. with community service in mind. I teach large, beginning-level classes

to students with little or no previous dance background and realize that involving as many students as possible in positive dance experiences is my goal. I introduce technique through the body therapies, specifically Bartenieff Fundamentals of Movement™ and Body-Mind Centering™, while concentrating on improvisational skills. As I am also a certified movement analyst, I use Laban movement analysis to create a full range of movement experiences, and I borrow Laban's idea of movement choirs to structure large group improvisational pieces.

The USD Moving Co. came into existence in the spring of 1990. Its purpose is to provide a format for dancing together. Membership is open to the entire university community—students, faculty, and staff. Movers need not have dance experience nor be enrolled in dance classes. We provide a service to the University by performing at various functions. For example, 18 of us (including three faculty members) performed on Earth Day 1990. The philosophy of the company is reflected in our work. We value teamwork and the worth of the individual within the group. At our first concert performances, audiences were surprised by the individualism and freedom in the movement and by the large number of performers. The responses soon became "that looks like fun; I'd like to do it, too." Dance class enrollments and the number of participants in the USD Moving Co. continue to grow (from 35 students in fall 1989 to over 60 in spring 1991). It is obvious that there is an interest in and a need for this type of dance activity. In fact, students frequently give up free time on Saturdays and Sundays to meet to dance together and rehearse.

Besides developing a dance curriculum for the talented and select group of skilled dancers and dance teachers, we must also create a dance curriculum that is an enabling experience for all students. This could be a participatory Dance Appreciation course similar to Music or Art Appreciation courses already offered at many universities. Naima Prevots offers a Dance and Society course at the American University in Washington, D.C. I suggest that similar courses with a basis in dance as a *participating* art be developed.

Perhaps we dance educators will rally to promote bodily/kinesthetic intelligence courses as part of the core requirements for all students. Dance is an activity that touches many aspects of being human, not just the physical. By creating a holistic dance curriculum for a broad population of higher education students, we will better educate citizens for the global environment of the 21st century.

References

Bryant-Weiler, V., Mills-Maas, J., & Nirschl, E. (1988). *A guide to curriculum planning in dance.* Madison, WI: Wisconsin Dept. of Public Instruction.

Gardner, H. (1983). *Frames of mind.* New York: Basic Books, Inc.

Kraus, R., Chapman-Hilsendger, S., & Dixon, B. (1991). *History of the dance in art and education.* Englewood Cliffs, NJ: Prentice Hall.

Maletic, V. (1987). *Body-space-expression.* Berlin: Mouton de Gruyter.

**Eleanor Weisman, formerly in the Theatre Department
at the University of South Dakota, is now a doctoral candidate
in the Dance Department at the Ohio State University,
Columbus, Ohio 43202.**

Teaching
Choreography

The Integration of Process and Craft in the Teaching of Modern Choreography: A Historical Overview

Carol M. Press

"The only way to master choreography is by choreographing" (Nadel, 1978, p. 81). This is obviously the case, but what choreography is depends upon how one understands it. Additionally, one's understanding of choreography affects one's approach to teaching, for teaching methods represent acknowledged, and unacknowledged, philosophies and theories about the practice of choreography and the creative process in general. Therefore, when establishing curriculum for courses on modern composition or choreography one must again face the philosophical question: what are the constitutional elements, the "stuff" of modern choreography? The answers a teacher has to this question should give the basis for course designs and assignments, reflecting a philosophical and aesthetic understanding of choreography.

Such a task should not be taken lightly. Modern dance was founded upon ideas of integrity for the individual subjective response, giving validity to the subjective, when much of our world has become overwhelmed with objectivity. I view the act of choreographing modern dance as a creative activity that gives "ordered external expression to internal imagery, feelings, and ideas that are unique in some way for that individual" (Sarason, 1990, p. 1). Psychologist Seymour Sarason (1990) asserts that "artistic activity is . . . observable in all young children in all cultures on this earth" (p. ix). However, he expresses concern for the lack of artistic activity in most American adult lives: "The satisfaction that comes from making something, and being made and formed by it, is missing in the lives of most people" (p. ix).

Creative activity can be nurtured, fostered, developed, and evolved in the young adults who take our choreography classes, experiences that are lacking in the teaching of many other disciplines, which often revolve around large lecture halls and purely factual objective information. Dance contains the propensity for much more. Indeed, literature professor Roger Shattuck states: "A college of arts and sciences that establishes a department of dance in its midst will be doing more to extend the meaning of education than can be done through any other single innovation" (Shattuck in Smith, 1990, pp. 207–208). To philosophically concern ourselves with the creative aspects of modern dance when teaching, choreography teachers can extend a special and important opportunity to ourselves, our students, the university and college, and society as a whole.

However, historically, not all modern dance artists/teachers have philosophically agreed upon what the "stuff" of modern choreography is. Indeed for many years choreographers/teachers seemed to be divided between two camps of thought—those who spoke about craft, the objective principles and rules of composition and those who spoke about process, the subjective motivation and creative modes of working. I define objective as that which is motivated by external forces, and subjective as that which is motivated by internal forces ultimately connected to one's unique creative individuality. Great choreography possesses both realms; the integration of these realms in the choreography classroom is also essential. But I contend that craft used most beneficially in the classroom and in art must transcend objectivity; it must be seen as an outgrowth of the subjective. Only then can a choreographer truly maintain artistic integrity and become what Paul Taylor describes as "an arbiter between form and expression" (Taylor in Tobias, 1985, p. 54). The following is a brief historical

overview of these issues in the teaching of modern choreography.

The dichotomized division that had developed between these two realms, craft and process, the objective and the subjective, can clearly be seen in Martha Coleman's 1949 interview of Louis Horst. Horst proclaims that form is primary in dance and defines form as "the application of traditionally accepted rules" (p. 128). Strongly influenced by his musical background, Horst applies musical forms such as ABA thematic development and theme and variation to dance composition. He taught students that form developed from objective and external "devices of manipulation" (p. 128) of movement. Horst considers the subjective content of the dance secondary. Indeed, he says, "If an artist has command of form, he need not be concerned so greatly with content" (p. 128). Horst's approach is concerned with an objective understanding of choreography through "traditionally accepted rules." Additionally, if one comprehends and follows these rules, content is not very important. It is not clear what exactly Horst means by content, but since he separates it so specifically from the objective rules, we can infer that content is concerned with the more subjective realities of choreography as experienced through movement.

Horst, as we all are, is partly a product of his historical time. Part of his emphasis upon structure resulted from his concern with modern dance as a new art form, filled with the potential for self-indulgence. Horst felt that emoting on stage was not art. Art had to transform subjective experience into an entity, a dance, that could exist beyond the choreographer. In other words, to go on stage and emote may be one form of self-expression, but to make that event art one must have formed that self-expression. Horst (1954) says: "Your material must be sublimated to form and stylization or symbolization into a work of art. Until that takes place, it is only self-expressionism" (p. 2).

But to see Horst's view solely as a historical phenomenon is too limited. Jean Erdman, also concerned with self-indulgence, dealt with the issue differently from Horst. In 1952 Erdman, also interviewed by Coleman, argues that dance must evolve from a "seed idea" (p. 52). She says the choreographer must "turn for inspiration . . . to the greater outer and inner world of life, ideas, feelings, and experience. The critical task is to bring this world to focus in moments of realization and then project the realizations into communicative forms" (Erdman, 1948, p. 40). Both working during the same historical period, Erdman appears to be seeking a greater integration between idea and form than Horst.

Coleman's 1950 interview of Alwin Nikolais suggests another individual attempt to integrate process and craft. Nikolais is not comfortable with the separation of content and form. He states that the idea, which includes the subjective content, is primary, and develops "from the impress of the universe upon the artist and his perception of it" (p. 148). The subservient structure or form "must serve to manifest the idea" (p. 148). Nikolais does not advocate the use of prescribed musical forms, but instead believes that "dance should strive for its own forms" (p. 149). To do this he encourages the use of improvisation. Nikolais implies that there is a dynamic interaction between content and form with *content forming the form*. Thus the use of the form is no longer objective, but subjective, part of the continuum between idea, content, and form.

In sharp contrast to Nikolais, Eva Desca's essay published in *Dance Magazine* in March and May of 1952 clearly isolates form from idea and content—

for Desca form need not have subjective significance. In section one of the essay, Desca asserts her most basic rule for choreographing: all dances have a beginning, middle, and end. She suggests an ABA or ABC schema. Desca (1952, March) suggests that one choose movements that end in *ing* such as "running, hopping, skipping, jumping, sliding, leaping, turning" (p. 29). She says that if a student chooses three *ing* words and works out smooth transitions between the actions he/she will make a dance. There is no importance placed upon subjective content, until the very end of her essay, where she suggests stereotypical moods, such as gay or solemn, or character studies. She offers the example of character study done on Paul Bunyan. Desca advises one "might use striding, chopping (of wood) and pulling (of trees), all done in a very exaggerated manner, as would be fitting for a man of his exaggerated size" (p. 30). Desca's approach suggests a nonthreatening formula that emphasizes the objective and ignores subjective meaning.

Continuing in this objective vein, but on an eminently more sophisticated level, is Doris Humphrey's book, *The Art of Making Dances*, published in 1959. The book is a clear testimony to craft, outlining four basic elements of choreography as "design, dynamics, rhythm, and motivation" (p. 46). Her approach places motivation last. The following are Humphrey's directions for isolating the craft concept of space designs:

> To realize these ideas, the student is asked to bring in space designs for the single body. That is, he is to prepare several symmetricals and asymmetricals, both in oppositions and successions which do not move in space or time (except for the simplest transitions from one to the other) and are not motivated, but are merely exercises for the manipulation of line, in order to become familiar with the ideas of their organization. (p. 59)

There are several philosophical implications in Humphrey's statement: craft can be experienced objectively and is best, initially, taught objectively; there is, consequently, a right and a wrong way to explore an element of craft; and by studying objective choreographic craft, students will, on their own, grasp the connections between craft and the making of meaningful art.

The teaching and writings of Robert Ellis Dunn during the early 1960s, immediately following the publication of Humphrey's book, exemplify the revolt against such craft-oriented approaches to choreography. His students comprised the new avant-garde and were called the Judson Dance Theatre. "In general, the students who attended [Dunn's classes] were dissatisfied with composition courses; these, they felt, were too structured for genuine innovative exploration" (McDonagh, 1970, p. 77). Dunn specifically did not want to replicate the mistakes he felt other choreography teachers made: "I had seen both Doris [Humphrey] and Louis [Horst] give recipes for things, which I thought were very stultifying" (Dunn in McDonagh, 1970, p. 79). Instead he tried to implement teaching methods that encouraged individual and unique choreographic development in his students.

Dunn specifically promoted class discussions while not evaluating or judging the students'

works. However, students previously trained to expect objective evaluations based upon external rights and wrongs can find the lack of such judgment frightening. A teacher choosing this path must be aware of the emotional demands placed upon the students as well as the teacher, as Dunn himself discovered:

> There was a great deal of anxiety and some hostility toward me, which I had to get used to, because they had expected an evaluation and I saw how thoroughly people were trying to fill the recipe. And there was simply no recipe to fill for me. (Dunn in McDonagh, 1970, p. 82)

During this same time the books of Alma Hawkins, *Modern Dance in Higher Education* and *Creating Through Dance*, originally published in 1954 and 1964, respectively, centered upon process and the exploration of teaching methods that promote creativity in the classroom. Specifically, Hawkins is concerned with the establishment of a constructive educational environment. Her books are filled with encouragement to teachers to provide a safe, structured, yet permissive atmosphere in class, to accept students' individual creative growth, to respect and encourage a supportive peer group, to help clarify choreographic principles when they become relevant, and to assist students in drawing their own aesthetic generalizations.

These latter two points demonstrate Hawkins' attempts to integrate process and craft in a meaningful way into her classes. She advocates the introduction of choreographic principles when they become *relevant* to the student, and help students, *themselves*, to draw aesthetic generalizations. Surely, Hawkins (1964) must have been aware of the effects of dichotomizing craft and process and of the necessity for integration when she wrote: "As a craftsman the dancer may construct a sequence of movements, but as an artist he creates an organic entity" (p. 5). Most especially, Hawkins, in sharp contrast to Humphrey's approach, believed that "from the very beginning the student should experience dance as a creative art" (1982, p. 119). Additionally, Hawkins clearly states that the self plays a vital role in the creative process:

> The creative process starts with the self, and the self remains the controlling agent throughout the process, which ends with the expression of the self. . . . Creative expression through dance may also bring about a new response to self. As the student works to create or mold something that is his own, he must clarify his feelings and sort out and organize his ideas. Through this process he gains a new awareness of self and a feeling of integration. (1982, pp. 64, 92–93)

Still during the 1980s the dichotomy between craft and process and their relation to teaching can be seen. In Melissa Nunn's 1982 article, "A Method to the Madness," she attempts to deal with students in her modern choreography classes who have strong backgrounds in ballet and jazz. Nunn devises dances that are literally equivalent to doing choreography by numbers or as she puts it, "standard compositional formulae" (p. 13).

For instance, to demonstrate the concept of shape, she suggests that the students from ballet pick eight familiar shapes, four of which must be on a high level, four on a middle level, devise eight count transitions, hold the first and last shape for eight counts and all other shapes for four. The same type of recipe is suggested for jazz and modern dance students. But there is no inauguration of dance as a uniquely creative activity.

Nunn has found a way to deal with her own tension as teacher, a situation many can empathize with, but her way of so doing has robbed her students of the opportunity for creative endeavor. Additionally, Nunn, acknowledging the strong influence of Horst upon her, takes the proposition "that the principles of good composition remain the same, that it is only the style of their application which changes" (p. 14). But over time, as individuals' subjective and creative endeavors engage principles of composition, these principles do change. For example, with the continually sustained and repetitive spinning in some of Laura Dean's work, it is doubtful that Dean would agree with Doris Humphrey's assertion that "monotony is fatal; look for contrasts" (1959, p. 159). *Creativity is constantly forming and reforming form.*

Even back in the late 1960s Judith Dunn (1967) expressed concern that teachers were taking what Horst and Humphrey had taught and transforming "these concepts into absolute dogmas which blind them" (p. 50). Without a philosophical awareness of this pitfall Dunn proclaims that "a dogmatic teacher can praise a student choreographer for 'being able to handle large groups' or for 'mastery of ABA form' without even realizing that these dances, composed by 'the rules,' may also be creatively insipid" (p. 50).

Avoiding such a pitfall, Alice Trexler's 1981 article, "Making and Dancing Improvisational Games," attempts to design situations where her students can experience play as an important aspect of creativity. By approaching choreography not as formulae but as a creative activity, she chooses what is for her (and for many—see the work of psychoanalyst D.W. Winnicott [1982] for an example) a basis element of creative work—play. From this philosophical base Trexler forms her assignments to help initiate her students into the experience of creative play. She sees the teacher's role as designing a place for his/her students to start their own subjective processes, instead of handing out formulae. From this vantage point a future choreographer has the basic tool of play to begin his/her own journey to discover and explore form.

The 1980s have continued to bring a greater exploration of the relation between craft and process. Insightful examples are the books by Lynne Anne Blom and L. Tarin Chaplin, *The Intimate Act of Choreography* (1982) and *The Moment of Movement* (1988). For these teachers the avenue to understanding choreography is the tool of improvisation. Through this process students are provided the opportunity to discover the relevance of choreographic concepts by direct manipulation of the medium—movement. Implied in Blom and Chaplin's methods is the notion that students gain access to the understanding of dance-making as an inner-directed activity by experiencing concepts through improvisation. And craft is not taught as objective truths, but as elements of choreography to be explored.

Penelope Hanstein (1986) in her doctoral dissertation, *On the Nature of the Art Making in Dance: An Artistic Process Skills Model for the Teaching of Choreography*, suggests a complete philosophical rethinking. Her concern is not with objective craft, but with objective skills that allow individuals to subjectively engage in process. Such skills as "thinking, perceiving, and forming" (p. 150) are applied to basic activities involved in choreographing such as idea finding, problem finding, idea shaping/forming, idea transforming, and solution finding. In Hanstein's work, process, with its ultimate connection to craft, becomes explicit within the choreography classroom.

My own research (Press, 1990) centers on a psychoanalytic understanding of the choreographic process from the perspective of the self and healthy narcissism. More specifically, I have sought a theoretical model for creativity from the works of Heinz Kohut (1971, 1977, 1978, 1984, 1987), considered the father of psychoanalytically informed self-psychology. Kohut's writings concern narcissism, one's relation to self, in pathology and health. Kohut argues, in contrast to Freud, that narcissism is not something to overcome, but something that goes through tempering transformations, which, in health, continually form our ideals, drive our ambitions, and allow us to partake in meaningful fulfilling activities.

Photo of Providence College Dance Co. by Alan Bean.

Kohut cites five examples of mature healthy transformations of narcissism: creativity, empathy, the ability to accept one's eventual death, humor, and wisdom. Kohut believes that creative engagement must come from a healthy aspect of the self. Additionally, he firmly states that there exist inherent psychological stresses in the creative process, that these are not pathological in nature, and that there are significant avenues available for artists to cope with these psychological risks.

I have used a Kohutian model for creativity to examine the writings of several modern choreographers to illuminate the role and needs of the self and the attendant risks to the self that are involved in the choreographic process. Such a theoretical understanding of process provides the basis for an educational environment that respects, and is attuned to respond to, subjective creativity. A vocabulary for classroom discussion of process, and not just craft, is supplied.

Applying these insights to understanding the psychodynamics of the choreography classroom, I have examined the educational milieu, the roles of the peer group and teacher, the use of dialogue and improvisation, the place of the teaching of choreographic form, and the importance of phase-appropriate teacher responses. In conclusion I assert that the relational aspects of the choreography class—the student's relation to self, to the teacher, to the peer group, and to the emerging art work; and the teacher's relation to self, to the individual student, the group, and the choreographic

99

process—significantly promote or limit an evolution of the creative process.

Additionally, these insights have led me to a greater appreciation of craft. Craft now has its niche, its home, in a subjective, meaningful relation to process. Significantly, such work is complementary to the work of individuals like Blom, Chaplin, and Hanstein, who are also searching for better ways to integrate process and craft.

To approach the question of the integration of process and craft, or lack of it, in the teaching of choreography, one must first become aware that his/her teaching methods do represent a philosophy concerning this issue. Teaching methods do imply answers to such questions as: What is craft? What is creativity? What can be taught about them? And the implied answers to these questions express philosophical beliefs about the individual's involvement in creative work. Perhaps most importantly, a philosophical examination of one's teaching methods opens the door for teaching itself to become a more enriching and vital creative process for the teacher. Without such personal creative involvement in teaching, the teaching of a creative form loses its dynamic potential and succumbs to rote and recipe.

References

Blom, L., & Chaplin, L. (1982). *The intimate act of choreography*. Pittsburgh: University of Pittsburgh Press.

Blom, L., & Chaplin, L. (1988). *The moment of movement: Dance improvisation*. Pittsburgh: University of Pittsburgh Press.

Coleman, M. (1949, November). On the teaching of choreography: Interview with Louis Horst. *Dance Observer*, pp. 128–130.

Coleman, M. (1950, December). On the teaching of choreography: Interview with Alwin Nikolais. *Dance Observer*, pp. 148–150.

Coleman, M. (1952, April). On the teaching of choreography: Interview with Jean Erdman. *Dance Observer*, pp. 52–53.

Desca, E. (1952, March). How to compose a dance, part I. *Dance Magazine*, p. 29.

Desca, E. (1952, May). How to compose a dance, part II. *Dance Magazine*, p. 30.

Dunn, J. (1967, November). Judith Dunn and the endless quest. *Dance Magazine*, pp. 48–51, 66–67.

Erdman, J. (1948, April). Young dancers state their views: As told to Joseph Campbell. *Dance Observer*, pp. 40–41.

Hanstein, P. (1986/1987). On the nature of art making in dance: An artistic process skills model for the teaching of choreography. Doctoral dissertation, Ohio State University. *Dissertation Abstracts International, 47*, 3640A–3641A.

Hawkins, A. (1964). *Creating through dance*. Englewood Cliffs, NJ: Prentice Hall.

Hawkins, A. (1982). *Modern dance in higher education*. New York: CORD.

Horst, L. (1954). Louis Horst considers the question. *Impulse*, pp. 1–6.

Humphrey, D. (1959). *The art of making dances*. New York: Grove Press.

Kohut, H. (1971). *The analysis of the self: A systematic approach to the psychoanalytic treatment of narcissistic personality disorders*. Madison, CT: International Universities Press.

Kohut, H. (1977). *The restoration of the self*. New York: International Universities Press.

Kohut, H. (1978). *The search for the self: Selected writings of Heinz Kohut: 1950–1978* (Vols. 1–2), P. H. Ornstein, Ed. New York: International Universities Press.

Kohut, H. (1984). *How does analysis cure?* A. Goldberg & P. E. Stepansky, Eds. Chicago: University of Chicago Press.

Kohut, H. (1987). *The Kohut seminars on self psychology and psychotherapy with adolescents and young adults*, M. Elson, Ed. New York: Norton.

McDonagh, D. (1970). *The rise and fall and rise of modern dance*. New York: Outerbridge & Dienstfrey.

Nadel, M. H. (1978). The process of creating a dance. In M. H. Nadel & C. N. Miller (Eds.), *The dance experience: Readings in dance appreciation* (pp. 74–81). New York: Universe Books.

Nunn, M. (1982). A method to the madness: A basic system of dance composition. *Dance Teacher Now, 4*(4), 12–14.

Press, C. (1990). Heinz Kohut's psychoanalytic theories of the self and creativity: Implications for the choreographic process in modern dance. Doctoral dissertation, Columbia University, Teachers College.

Sarason, S. (1990). *The challenge of art to psychology*. New Haven: Yale University.

Smith, P. (1990). *Killing the spirit: Higher education in America*. New York: Viking Penguin.

Tobias, T. (1985, April). A conversation with Paul Taylor and George Tacet. *Dance Magazine*, pp. 54–60.

Trexler, A. (1981). Making and dancing improvisational games. *Contact Quarterly, 6*(3/4), 13–15.

Winnicott, D. W. (1982). *Playing and reality*. New York: Methuen.

Carol M. Press is an artist-in-residence for the Santa Barbara County Schools, Santa Barbara, California 93105.

Observation and Criticism in the Choreography Class

Moving beyond "I don't know if it's art, but I know what I like."

Larry Lavender

In the "Evaluations" section of her book *Dance Composition—A Practical Guide for Teachers* (1976, pp. 92–98), Jacqueline M. Smith lists over 50 questions one might ask about a dance. These questions have to do with the dance as a whole, the movements, the emotional content, the action, effort, space, staging, music, performance, etc. They are all good questions. But immediately following this list Smith tells us:

> Inextricably bound with intellectual reflection an any level are the feelings of pleasure that an aesthetic work of art evokes in an onlooker. Each person experiences this pleasure in varying ways and in different degrees, but—in judging art—it is the fundamental criterion. Above all, therefore, the most important question to ask the viewer and the composer in relation to his own work, is whether or not the work was pleasing. *Did you like it*? If the answer is yes, there is, perhaps, no need for further evaluation, except that it can become a useful learning process to understand why it was appreciated. If the answer is no, then probably reasons for its "failure" can be found by asking *some* of the questions. (p. 98)

Smith is correct that asking her questions can be a useful learning process and can lead to the discovery of why and how a dance succeeds or fails, but I think she is mistaken on several very important counts. First, pleasure is not the fundamental criterion in judging art, nor is "Did you like it?" the most important question to ask viewers or composers. Finally, whether the answer to that question is yes or no, there is need for further inquiry in order to justify one's answer.

Smith appears not to recognize that in addition to the practice of producing small dances, or "studies," there are two other distinct practices in which choreography students must gain proficiency. The first is *observation*: open-minded, pre-reflective looking at dances and dancing. This practice must be taken seriously in order for Smith's questions to be of any use when reflecting upon a dance. The second practice is *criticism*: articulating and justifying judgments of the works presented to and observed by the class. The primary educational imperative for teaching observation and criticism to choreography students is that in a class of, say, ten students, each must act as an observer/critic nine times for every one time his or her own work is presented.

However, choreography teachers ordinarily devote great amounts of class time to exploring movement and producing studies, leaving little time for the specific development of observation and critical skills. Undoubtedly there are many reasons for this. Many teachers may not realize how good observation and criticism inform creativity. Teachers may assume that these skills are secondary or develop sufficiently by themselves as students produce and discuss studies. Or there may be wide acceptance of the "Did you like it?" principle of evaluation, coupled with uncertainty about how students might learn to be good observer/critics. None of these reasons justifies failing to move students beyond noting the kind and degree of pleasure they feel and stating whether or not they "like" a particular work.

Choreography students can learn to be good observers through the discipline of mentally setting aside artistic prejudices and personal feelings in order to fully *see/experience and describe* the dance presented. This means that both practical and conceptual knowledge, as well as what Bertram

Jessup (1960, p. 54) terms "felt-appreciation," are not permitted to condition observation.

Students can develop skills in the practice of criticism by first being taught to listen to and choose carefully the words and statements of ordinary discourse about dance and the other arts. Through disciplined observation and careful use of ordinary language students can learn to provide good reasons for the aesthetic judgments they make about their own creative work and that of others. Surely this will enrich the students' creative efforts—which is the primary objective of the choreography class—and enhance their overall fitness as dance professionals.

I have been referring to the use of ordinary language. Let me demonstrate how ordinary language conditions both observation and criticism.

Imagine a choreography class. A student shows a dance and awaits comments. The teacher asks the group, "What did you see in the dance?" or Smith's question, "Did you like it?" The two questions differ greatly in terms of the context they set for discussion. The first question calls for language describing the dance and implies the need for sharp observation. The second question asks only for an explanation or account of what the students think or feel. If teachers habitually open discussion with the second question, the students' observation skills become dulled and narrowed by the blinders of likes and dislikes.

I submit, contrary to Smith, that a precise and cogent answer to the first question is of considerably greater educational value than *any* possible answer to the second.

Suppose one of the students, Tom, says, "I liked it, it was very good. It made me feel happy." Responses like this are typical even when the teacher has asked, "What did you see?" Many teachers might not recognize that their question has not been answered or will choose to ignore it. Tom might be invited to elaborate on his response. He does so by giving a more detailed account of the feelings he gained from the piece.

What has Tom accomplished? He has stated an aesthetic judgment (that the piece is a good one) and given an explanation—or psychological report—of his happy feelings or emotions. If this proves acceptable to the teacher, other students may join in with psychological reports of their feelings. According to Smith this is satisfactory when the students' comments amount to praise. I argue that it is wholly unsatisfactory to "evaluate" the dance by offering psychological reports. Jessup (1960) speaks to this point:

Inadequate response may also be described as failure to respond to the work as object and to use it rather as a trigger to set off memories, feelings, and sentiments which are related to the object only by psychological privacies or eccentricities of the individual beholder. In that case the taste is directed not upon the object but upon the recalled and outside incidents and interests of the beholder's life. (p. 58)

Now suppose Tom says. "Oh, I hated that dance! It was dull, I was totally bored." Again he offers no information about the dance, but he makes a judgment that it was dull and reports his boredom as proof of this claim. Here is where Smith, to her credit, would begin asking Tom questions *about the dance*. Apparently Smith would recognize that further inquiry is needed because Tom's boredom is a "psychological privacy or eccentricity." But if an account of Tom's boredom calls forth Smith's questions, so should an account of his pleasure. In both instances Tom's claims are about himself, not the dance.

Any passerby can watch a dance and answer the question, "Did you like it?" The question nearly always elicits passionate responses. If the teacher is seduced by this and forgets to bring the discussion back to the dance, it is unfortunate for Tom if he intends his educational experiences to enable him to articulate responses that are more sophisticated and relevant than those of any passerby. It is also unfortunate for the choreographer, who recognizes that his or her dance is being praised or denigrated on the strength of Tom's claims of happiness or boredom. The choreographer needs to learn which specific aspects of the dance have brought forth a particular judgment from one observer/critic. Tom needs to learn how to transform his self-reflexive responses into critical statements that may be valuable to his colleagues. Neither of these needs can be satisfied until Tom learns to provide good reasons to justify his judgments.

Let me offer assurances to choreography teachers who may recoil at the idea of their classes drifting away from specifics of choreography and becoming bogged down in language analysis. No such drifting is necessary or imminent. To determine if a reason is a *good* justification for a judgment is not a matter of convoluted jargon or lengthy and confusing talk. Reasons are good when they specify something in particular about the dance that can be verified either by seeing the dance again, or upon reflection. As David Ecker (1967) writes, "Thus, justification is terminally nonlinguistic; and the crucial criterion of the success of written and oral criticism is apparently its referential adequacy, its ability to make in some way more adequate one's perception of what is there" (p. 7).

This means that rather than drifting away from important choreographic issues, the *good reasons approach* anchors the discussion firmly in the immediate vicinity of these issues as they pertain to the dance under consideration. Thus language analysis alone does not tell us a reason is good, but it does tell us right off the bat if what we are hearing from Tom is a reason or a report of feelings.

Suppose Tom says, "I didn't like it, I thought it was dull. The movement was too slow and faced the back too much. I felt bored." Here we have a judgment with reasons and a psychological report. The class must check the referential adequacy of Tom's reasons to determine if they are good ones. What is important to the class is not that Tom is bored but that he judges the dance to be dull because of its speed and the performer's facing.

Now the teacher can maximize the educational value of the discussion by inviting class members to consider their own observations of the dance in order to support or dispute Tom's judgment. This is what Alan Tormey (1979), in the tradition of Immanuel Kant, describes as testing critical claims to see if they can be *corroborated* through direct inspection of, or reflection upon, the art work in question. While aesthetic judgments are not open to *confirmative* (true/false) tests, they are nonetheless testable on the basis of their acceptance among independent judgers. Happily, the impossibility of objectively verifying critical claims need not force us to embrace Smith's "Did you like it?" as the primary question of criticism. There is fertile ground between scientific verification and unbridled relativism.

Perhaps a student disagrees with Tom and describes aspects of the dance in order to claim that it is successful. Others may corroborate Tom's claim that the dance fails, and the teacher can ask them (and Tom) to suggest how the dance could be improved. All the students are certain to benefit from this kind of discussion.

We can see that judgments justified by good reasons generate discussion valuable to the choreographer. Psychological reports provide no claims inviting debate. If someone says "I like it" and another says "I don't like it," the two claims are equally true and there is no disagreement. The difficulty with psychological reports is that we cannot know whether or to what degree they derive from the dance or from factors in the personality of the observer. While it may be interesting to conduct psychological inquiry into the causes of feelings, the choreography teacher is not a psychologist, and criticism requires good reasons that refer directly to the work in question. Psychological reports have critical value only when the teacher is willing to help the student discover and articulate the reasons for the judgment implied by his or her remarks.

Some educators will disagree, claiming that psychological reports should be allowed and encouraged as vehicles through which students may discover valuable information about themselves. This argument holds that discouraging explanations and accounts of feelings is tantamount to cutting students off from vital aspects of their personal inner reality. Such protests are well-intentioned but mistaken.

When a student's dance is about to be presented, the rest of the class assembles in order to practice observation and criticism. After the dance is shown, gently steering critical discussions away from explanations of feeling-states and toward the reasons for the judgments implied by such explanations is *not* detrimental. What is detrimental is to allow students to practice observation geared toward feeling-level responses as if such responses are the basis of criticism. Directing discussion toward the justificatory level of judgments is precisely how the proper relationship between observation, criticism, and feeling-level responses is discovered. Of course feelings are important, but accounts of feelings must not become a substitute for criticism. Similarly, in discussing the practice of creating dances, the value of the choreographer's feelings and inner inclinations can best be ascertained by trying to discover their influence upon creative choices and decisions.

However, many teachers are likely to defend psychological reports as a sufficient critical response. Let me briefly sketch out two habits of mind that may account for this. First, although most artists and critics have discarded the Greek theory of art as mimesis or representation in favor of a theory of art as subjective expression, art (especially dance, because the human body is its instrument) remains burdened by a central problem inherited from the mimetic theory. This problem is the assumption that the work of art, by definition, *says* or *means* something in particular. Consequently, discussions of art tend to begin with the psychological question, "What is it saying?" or "What does it mean?" The only way Tom thinks he can answer with authority, apparently, is with an account of what the work says or means to him. Thus self-reflexive interpretations, when delivered as explanations of feeling-responses, subjugate observation and description in discourse about art.

Further muddying the waters is the more general problem of ambiguity in speech. Arnold Isenberg (1949) notes that in everyday conversation the distinction is seldom made between *explaining* and *justifying* our critical responses to art (or to anything). The chief reason for this is that "some statements about the object will necessarily figure both in the explanation and the critical defense of any

reaction to it" (p. 660). Isenberg urges that a careful distinction be made in critical language between the purpose of criticism and that of psychology. The first step for teachers in making this distinction is to continually remind students that observations governed by feeling-responses produce descriptions and judgments that are inadequate if they focus upon the critic's feelings instead of the work of art.

The second habit of mind that I believe accounts for the seeming importance and finality of feeling-responses to art is the hedonistic criterion or phi-

Larry Lavender, author, rehearses Lara Lyddon in "Brush the Neck and Shiver," 1987, New York University.

losophy of art such as found in George Santayana's *The Sense of Beauty* (1896). Santayana makes a strong case for the pleasure principle as a theory of art. The crux of this theory is that the good and beautiful (in nature and art) give pleasure while the bad and ugly bring forth displeasure. Since we perceive through our senses, what better barometer can there be for judging the value of art but the pleasure/pain response? We have seen that Smith embraces this view in principle. An example of this view put into critical practice is a passage (written nearly 100 years after *The Sense of Beauty*) from a recent *New York Times* article by Anna Kisselgoff (1990). Discussing the rise to fame of choreographer Mark Morris, Kisselgoff writes:

> At his worst, his step-for-note bias can drive an audience into glazed-eye agony. . . . But at his best—and he is getting better—he can make the public overlook the choreography's formal underpinnings and sweep the entire house into a glorious groundswell of happiness. (p. 11)

Comments like these justify the judgments—"worst" and "better"—with accounts of the alleged feeling states of the audience. Choreographers following this lead often find themselves sacrificing ambiguity, mystery, risk, and innovation in a desperate effort to make their audience "feel good."

But feeling good is an objective and a value whose arena is more that of entertainment than art—unless we consider these arenas as absolutely identical. If this is the case, Suzi Gablik's lament that "art's value tends to be defined, not by its spiritual, intellectual, or emotional content, but by its economic worth" (1984, p. 39) is a sad statement of fact, and all artistic activity and all art criticism is properly subsumed by hedonism.

I believe educators must avoid acceding to hedonistic habits of mind that reduce art to a fetish or commodity of pleasure—however natural and ordinary it may have become to think of art this way. Hedonism takes us no further than the feeling-response level, the very point at which we must teach students to *begin* the practice of criticism. Moreover, unless educators strenuously avoid basing judgments about art upon *any* single theory or set of values, they risk entrapping students in shrill and fruitless attempts to defend the objective truth or falseness of critical claims.

If we recognize that choreography students should practice disciplined observation leading to serious critical discourse about dance and the other arts, the next step is to teach them how. David Ecker (1980, pp. 14–16) articulates a procedure grounded in Husserlian phenomenology for conducting aesthetic inquiry in the classroom or studio setting.

Ecker's procedure is as follows: Everyone observes the performance attentively, ignoring all extraneous stimuli. This is TIME 1. During TIME 1 observers are expected to set aside feeling-responses, theories, and all terms and presuppositions of value which precondition and prejudice observation. This setting aside—which is the discipline of the practice of observation—prevents observers from mentally interrupting the flow of the dance and fragmentizing its inherent totality.

TIME 2 is a four or five minute period of reflection during which the observers jot down what has been observed during TIME 1. This dovetails nicely with the practice of keeping a class journal that many teachers ask of their students. Teachers will find that TIME 2 notes become more descriptively rich and less self-reflexive as students learn disciplined observation. During TIME 3, observations are shared and the range of differences of perception and of judgment of the dance is discovered. Judgments are articulated and justified during TIME 3 discussion. By rooting TIME 3 discussion in TIME 2 observations, which themselves are rooted in the TIME 1 experience, the discussion stands a good chance of remaining focused on relevant points concerning the dance. Of course, the teacher must occasionally steer the discussion to assure relevancy.

Ecker's procedure can be introduced and employed without disrupting the manner in which choreography classes ordinarily view and evaluate works. Teachers need not alter their methods of presenting improvisations or creative assignments, and no unwelcome jargon or extensive training in phenomenology is required.

David Ecker and Eugene Kaelin's "ladder" of aesthetic inquiry (1972, p. 267) facilitates TIME 3 discussion by schematizing the level of discourse on which relevant comments occur (see Figure 1). Ecker and Kaelin place the object/event—in our case a dance study—at the foundation of their ladder:

| META-THEORY |
| THEORY |
| META-CRITICISM |
| CRITICISM |
| OBJECT/EVENT
Aesthetic Experience |

Figure 1. Ecker/Kaelin ladder of aesthetic inquiry.

Accordingly, it is upon reflection of the TIME 1 experience of the object/event that the observer/critic begins to formulate aesthetic judgments. Evaluative remarks referring directly to the dance study are on the rung of *criticism*. For example, an observer might say, "The ending of the dance is much too abrupt." Another observer might reply, "I think that to characterize the ending as too abrupt is a mistake because. . . ." Remarks of this kind that dispute (or support) critical claims are termed *meta-criticism*. Discussions of creative approaches or principles of value that may account for the various critical and meta-critical statements fall on the level of *theory*. For example, "The most successful dances communicate something very clearly to the audience." In response to this one might say, "The notion that a dance must 'communicate' something is untenable because. . . ." Remarks such as these that assess some aspect of one or more theories are termed *meta-theoretical* remarks. There is no rung on the ladder for psychological reports.

Although the rungs of the ladder are distinct, all teachers can attest that student discussions are likely to be fluid, and individual statements containing ideas corresponding to more than one rung are likely to emerge. Of course, it would be absurd to interrupt a discussion to note the position on the ladder occupied by each statement. But introducing students to the ladder can help them to discover how the various kinds of statements one makes about art differ from one another, and how each kind of statement operates in a discussion of a particular work of art. As students become familiar with the levels of aesthetic inquiry, their critical statements should become more acute and their discussion as a whole more focused. If a particular statement is ambiguous or confusing, pausing to note which rung the statement ostensibly occupies can be useful.

It is not particularly difficult to devise choreography assignments. There are books full of them. Nor is it difficult to base judgments of a dance upon personal feelings. But choreography students are entitled to more than mere exposure to the rudiments of dance craft and the feeling-responses of their teachers and peers. Students deserve training in disciplined observation and critical discourse in order to develop as choreographers and as articulate spokespersons for the dance. The choreography class, with its steady supply of student-created dances, is the ideal arena in which to center such training.

References

Ecker, D. W. (1967). Justifying aesthetic judgments. *Art Education, 20*, 5–8.

Ecker, D. W. (1980). Introduction: Instituting qualitative evaluation in the arts. In D. W. Ecker (Ed.), *Proceedings of the First Summer Institute on Qualitative Evaluation in the Arts* (pp. 1–16). New York: New York University Division of Arts and Arts Education.

Ecker, D. W., & Kaelin, E. F. (1972). The limits of aesthetic inquiry: A guide to educational research. *Philosophical Redirection of Educational Research,* 71st Yearbook, Part 1, pp. 258–286.

Gablik, S. (1984). *Has modernism failed?* New York: Thames and Hudson.

Isenberg, A. (1949). Critical communication. In W. E. Kennick (Ed.), *Art and philosophy*, 2nd ed. (pp. 658–668). New York: St. Martin's Press.

Jessup, B. (1960). Taste and judgment in aesthetic experience. *The Journal of Aesthetics and Art Criticism, 19*(1), 53–59.

Kisselgoff, A. (1990, November 11). Divining the mystique of Mark Morris. *The New York Times*, p. 11.

Santayana, G. (1896). *The sense of beauty.* New York: Charles Scribner's Sons.

Smith, J. M. (1976), *Dance composition: A practical guide for teachers.* London: A & C Black.

Tormey, A. (1979). Critical judgments. In W. E. Kennick (Ed.), *Art and philosophy*, 2nd ed. (pp. 620–630). New York: St. Martin's Press.

Larry Lavender teaches dance in the Communications Arts Department, at New York University, New York, New York 10003.

Faculty Issues

Tenure and Promotion of Dance Faculty

Jessica Wood

The tenure debate rages on within academic circles. There are valid concerns as to why tenure should be abolished or why tenure should remain. Proponents of the abolition of tenure have offered numerous alternatives, some of which are interesting and credible. Those in favor of retaining tenure ardently defend its import as a safeguard to academic freedom, job security, and institutional stability and as a means of ensuring quality faculty.

However interesting this debate may be and despite one's personal views, most faculty find themselves in a position whereby the earning of tenure is critical to their career in academe. If tenure is denied, the "up and out" clause forces the nonrenewal of that faculty member's contract. A junior faculty member who does not understand the concept of tenure or promotion is ill-equipped to make a viable application for a change in status (Hanstein, 1990). In view of the significance of tenure, a closer look at the institution of tenure is warranted.

Academic tenure is "an arrangement under which faculty appointments in an institution of higher education are continued until retirement for age or physical disability, subject to dismissal for adequate cause or unavoidable termination on account of financial exigency or change of institutional program" (Keast & Macy, 1973, p. 256). Any tenured faculty member is guaranteed, by the privilege of tenure, the right to the legal action of due process in a dismissal for cause. Due process and tenure protect the academic freedom of the faculty.

The award of tenure is a decision about the future quality, content, and direction of the educational program in tandem with the prevailing economic and budgetary considerations (Keast & Macy, 1973). The decision to grant tenure is based not only on the excellence and promise of the candidate but also on other institutional concerns. Granting of tenure has serious financial implications. It can commit institutional resources for salary and benefits that could exceed \$600,000 over a 30-year period (Seldin, 1980). A denial of tenure could occur not because of reservations concerning the candidate, but rather on the basis of the needs of the academic program or fiscal priorities (Kirschling, 1978). Theoretically, separation from an institution as a result of denial of tenure carries no professional stigma (Keast & Macy, 1973).

The tenure review process characteristically involves a pyramid of reviewing committees. The process begins in the academic department with peer and departmental chair review and evaluation of the candidate. If the department finds the candidate worthy of tenure (or promotion), the candidate's document is forwarded to the dean of the appropriate college for review and evaluation. The procedure continues on to a campus-wide tenure review committee, the president, and finally the board of trustees for official approval. At each step, the decision to grant or deny tenure is made and a negative decision at any level will terminate the process and result in a denial of tenure. By far the most crucial decision is that of the campus-wide tenure review committee. Because of the long-term commitment of institutional resources, tenure decisions are subject to a more strenuous, thorough, and critical review than are other personnel decisions.

It is at this level of evaluation that the applications of dance faculty are often subject to misunderstanding based on ignorance of the discipline, devaluation of evidence of merit, and consequentially the denial of tenure. This disturbing fact points to the imperative need for dance faculty to become involved in institutional governance through membership on varied campus-wide committees. It is only as a fully participating affiliate of such institutional mechanisms that the dance faculty can begin to make instrumental changes that will facilitate their success in gaining tenure and/or promotion.

109

Generally, the tenure or promotion decision is based on three areas of endeavor: teaching, scholarship, and service. The granting of tenure is contingent upon proof of excellence in all three areas and evidence of intent to continue working at a high level of quality. The burden of proof of excellence is the responsibility of the candidate. The weight or value of each component may vary depending upon the mission of the institution, the mission of the academic department, and the role of the candidate within the department. Specific criteria for tenure and/or promotion are best determined by the faculty of each academic department by clearly defining the institutional criteria as they relate to the standards of each discipline.

"While dance as a field of study has become an accepted part of academics, considerations for retention, promotion and tenure of dance faculty have not taken into account the nature of the discipline" (Beal, Rosenberg, & Sandback, 1986, p. 15). To do this "the general categories of teaching, scholarship and service should be more narrowly defined by the dance faculty at the academic component level" (Hanstein, 1990, p. 3).

At most universities and colleges, scholarship has emerged as the leading criterion for awarding tenure and promotion (Beal, Rosenberg, & Sandback, 1986). Scholarship is most widely considered to be manifested by research and publications. This interpretation of scholarship is too limiting in scope for any institution in which art making is an integral part of any of its disciplines. The creation and performance of dance is central to the discipline and therefore, it must be considered a vital part of the evaluation of dance faculty for tenure and/or promotion. The Association for Theater in Higher Education in their "Guidelines for Evaluating Teacher/Artists for Promotion and Tenure" states that "all faculty who have public performance responsibilities should be evaluated, at least in part, on their level of achievement in these responsibilities" (1987, p. 39).

To actively lobby for the inclusion of creative endeavors in the definition of scholarship, the dance faculty must become involved in campus-wide committees that deal with such issues. As a committee member, the dance representative will be in place to initiate change and to educate the other faculty about the field of dance. Most faculty from other areas will have little prior knowledge or experience of dance. This is a difficult, delicate, and possibly politically explosive assignment. Therefore, it might best be undertaken by a dance faculty member with tenure.

It is possible that art making has been omitted from scholarship because of the difficulty in evaluating the work. The other scholarship components of research and publication have established methods of documentation that are relatively noncontroversial and are generally accepted. The documentation and evaluation of creative endeavors and the articulation of the basis for evaluation is the responsibility of the dance faculty and the dance chair (ATHE, 1987).

Documenting Creative Endeavors

Documentation of artistic accomplishments should include a videotape of the performance. Incorporation of the entire body of work in the video portion is beyond the scope of the tenure/promotion committee's responsibility to review such massive information. Two or three works representative of the body of dances are suggested. Committee members will be familiar with the amount of time, energy, and effort it takes to write an article or book, but they will have little or no information about the choreographic process. If the committee views only the performance, the product might appear effortless (Beal, Rosenberg, & Sandback, 1986).

To guard against this perception, the documentary video might also include segments of the choreographer in the process of creating the movement vocabulary for the dance and rehearsals at the beginning, mid-point, and near the end of the rehearsal period. Needless to say, the video must be of high quality. Depending on the length of the work, a dance might be equated with an article or a book.

Articles vary in value as evidence of scholarship. An article published in a juried journal is weighted more than one published in a nonjuried journal. This distinction can be translated to creative endeavors to differentiate between on-campus performances and off-campus performances. Contributions to on-campus performances have merit; however, contributions to off-campus performances will undoubtedly be considered stronger evidence of accomplishment in creative endeavors. Works that are performed by invitation or in a juried concert will be held in higher regard.

To augment the weight of on-campus performances, an outside adjudicator can be invited to review and evaluate the artistic merit of a specific work or works. The dance department should assemble a list of dance knowledgeable people in the geographic area from which the choreographer would choose an adjudicator. If budgetary consideration permits, an adjudicator, possibly with professional credentials from outside the geographic area, would be brought to campus to review and evaluate the choreographer's work. A standardized form for evaluation is suggested. Any narrative the adjudicator might wish to add to the evaluation should be attached to the form. The same evaluative form should be completed by the dance department chair and selected dance faculty.

A list of organizations that offer opportunities to have choreography adjudicated and selected for performance within the geographic area of the institution and nation-wide should be compiled by the dance faculty. Submitting choreographies to these organizations on an annual or biannual basis is recommended. Choreographies accepted for performance sponsored by these organizations should be equated with a juried article. Any choreography should be considered juried when another institution, dance company, or reputable organization accepts the work for performance.

The promotion/tenure documentation should include a video tape, evaluation by the adjudicator, chairperson, and peers, and a written statement that the choreographer prepares including information that will

1) Provide adequate information about the work: title, number of dancers, length of the work, music.
2) Indicate under what circumstances the work was choreographed or performed: Was it an invited performance, an adjudicated performance, or an off-campus concert produced by yourself or a group of fellow artists with or without external funding.
3) Provide a statement of your artistic intention, purpose, or vision.
4) If a self-evaluation is appropriate, discuss briefly how a particular work resulted in significant growth for you as an artist, discuss audience reaction, . . .
5) Include review of criticis . . . .
(Hanstein, 1990, pp. 7–8)

Even when a provision is in place to include creative endeavors as a part of scholarship, publications often must be included in the scholarship portfolio if dance faculty are to be successful in the promotion/tenure process (Beal, Rosenberg, & Sandback, 1986). The need for publications is more critical for the dance faculty who hold PhD degrees than for those who hold MFA degrees.

The teaching component involved in the tenure/promotion review process needs to be clearly delineated in regards to the structure of the discipline. For example, the teaching methodology of a technique class is different from the teaching methodology of a choreography or academic class. Most universities and colleges use standardized student evaluations that may not be applicable or appropriate for use in determining the teaching qualification of dance faculty. The dance faculty and dance chair are encouraged to create, or adapt, a student evaluation instrument that will measure the ability of the instructor for each category of class taught in the department.

Evaluating Teaching Performance

The two basic purposes of faculty teaching evaluations are to improve faculty performance (a formative function) and to assist in making equitable and effective academic personnel decisions (a summative function) (Miller, 1987). Any evaluation instrument should "seek information which can be utilized in a formative and summative manner" (Seldin, 1980). Within the instrument, questions to elicit information for both functions should be included.

Peer evaluation of teacher competency by classroom visitation is part of the comprehensive review of any faculty for promotion/tenure. This method of evaluation is most effective when it "involves friendliness and interest as well as critical and instructional purpose" (Seldin, 1980, p. 68). The observer is best prepared when supplied in advance of the visitation with a course outline and an outline of the material for that day. A pre-observation discussion allows the faculty member who is being evaluated ample opportunity to prepare the visiting faculty member to view the class. A post-observation discussion would facilitate the opportunity to share the insights of the visiting faculty with the faculty member who is being observed. A standard peer evaluation instrument will ensure that all faculty are assessed on the same criteria. In addition to these evaluations of teaching, it is helpful to include in the promotion/tenure document course syllabi that contain a course outline, objectives, methods of student assessment, and course assignments (Hanstein, 1990).

The service component is divided into service to the institution and service to the profession. Membership on departmental and institutional committees or the faculty senate and varied recruitment activities are all aspects of institutional service. Leadership roles in professional organizations, participation on the board of a dance company, production organization, or arts council participation are avenues for service to the profession.

In general, the service component of the promotion/tenure triad is similar to the service component in other disciplines. Therefore, it needs little translation to those outside the field.

The American Association of University Professors suggests that a pretenure faculty member should come up for tenure after a probationary period of not more than seven years of full time employment at the university or college. The pretenure years are most constructively regarded by the institution and faculty member as years of development of the teacher/artist/scholar and not merely an extended period of screening (Smith & associates, 1973). In some instances, credit for years of service at a previous institution (or a previous award of tenure) may shorten the pretenure period. Each faculty member on pretenure status "must be informed of the standards and procedures employed in making decisions about reappointment or tenure" (Bledso, 1988, p. 9).

An annual or end of semester review of the work and progress of a probationary faculty should be conducted by the dance department chair. The annual review process is initiated by the chair, who evaluates in writing the faculty member in terms of teaching effectiveness, scholarly/creative endeavors, personal growth, and institutional and professional service. This evaluation is then given to the evaluated faculty member to read and to assess. A conference is then set to discuss the specifics of the critique. Afterwards, the faculty member may respond, in writing, to any aspect of the content of the evaluation. Both statements become part of the personnel file (Georgia State University Faculty Handbook, 1989). This system guarantees the awareness and involvement of the faculty member in his or her progress toward promotion/tenure long before the seven year deadline.

If, during the annual review, an area of weakness or concern is pointed out, a four-step guide to strengthen or correct the weakness is then suggested. First, the probable cause must be determined and described; second, possible solutions are presented; third, implementation of the suggested solutions are determined and rated for possible success; and fourth, the results are described at a later date. Because each of the four steps is written, the procedure deals with concrete matters specifically and constructively. It is then the faculty member's responsibility to implement the improvement plan (Karman, 1969).

A statement of the pretenure faculty's role in the department and the expectations of his or her role will clarify the status of each area of evaluation in the annual review (Hanstein, 1990). A written "job description" summarizes the role, responsibilities, and the priority of each area of assessment. The process of delineation of role, annual review, and four-step improvement plan are all "mile markers" on the road to promotion/tenure. Do not allow them to be passed over. Insist on each one.

The same criteria are generally utilized for promotion and tenure. "Promotion criteria focus more on the merit of the instructor's professional and scholarly contributions and promise, the criteria for tenure focus more on the long-term worth of the instructor to the university" (Miller, 1987, p. 92). Promotion through the ranks of instructor, assistant professor, associate professor, and professor varies at each university. It is contingent upon not only the above-mentioned criteria but also years of service in the rank and academic credentials.

Women Faculty Face Negative Factors

The fact that the majority of dance faculty are women can be and probably is a negative factor in the application for promotion/tenure. Although women have increased in number as undergraduates and PhDs since 1964, "women remain disproportionately underrepresented in the tenure ranks of academe. In 1988–89, only 49% of female faculty held tenure, compared to 71% of male faculty" (Vandell & Fishbein, 1989). More women are being hired, but at lower ranks, and they are promoted at a slower rate than their male counterparts. When hired, women are further handicapped in their progress toward promotion/tenure in that their teaching loads are heavier than their male counterparts. In addition, their course load is generally comprised of lower level courses. The teaching of graduate students and research are more highly valued activities in consideration for advancement or tenure. In conjunction with lower rank and a less desirable and excessive teaching load, the scholarship a female faculty produces is often downgraded. "Numerous studies have shown that articles attributed to women are given lower 'grades' than identical articles attributed to men" (Vandell & Fishbein, 1989).

For women dance faculty, this poses a double bind. First, the scholarship in the form of creative endeavors is still considered less important than traditional scholarship of a written nature. Second, the gender of the candidate affects negatively the evaluation of her work. Consequently, dance work of a feminist nature or choreographic material on female themes would probably be a poor choice to document as evidence of scholarship. This sad fact serves to illuminate the magnitude of the work left to do to facilitate the understanding and reappraisal of the discipline of dance and the status of women in the university.

Women's professional service is often judged differently from that of men's and it may even go unrecognized. Service to any woman's organization, whether on- or off-campus, is subject to devaluation through the claim that such involvement is political activity. Conversely, men's involvement in groups such as the Jaycees is likely to be considered valuable service (Vandell & Fishbein, 1989).

Not only do women faculty have to face prejudice in every area of evaluation for promotion/tenure, they will also be negatively affected by the "tenure crunch." The "tenure crunch" refers to the large number of faculty tenured in the 1950s and 1960s, which resulted in many departments and institutions being top-heavy with tenured faculty—mostly men. Therefore, the number of tenure appointments is reduced by the enlarged number of tenured faculty. Some departments may be so overtenured that no possibility of granting tenure to another faculty member exists.

The American Association of University Women recommends these strategies for women faculty:

> Develop a ten-year career plan including research and networking . . . an excellent research portfolio must be supplemented by faculty allies for the tenure review process.

> Join women's groups such as AAUW that provide expertise and support from outside academe. Collect data about the gender distribution of tenure-track and nontenure-track slots on your local campus and write letters to or schedule a meeting with administration officials to voice your concerns and explore solutions. (Vandell and Fishbein, 1989).

As women, the majority of dance faculty begin the tenure/promotion process from a disadvantaged position. The lack of knowledge about the discipline of dance on the part of faculty from other fields and the resistance to the inclusion of creative endeavors as scholarship combine to place the application of dance faculty in peril. Dance as a discipline must specify standards and methodologies to measure excellence in creative endeavors that reflect the same rigor of judgment applied in other disciplines.

Evaluation of faculty is an ongoing process and does not end with tenure or promotion to the rank of professor. The time and effort put into learning about the promotion/tenure system can only enhance the applicant's ability to prepare a cogent, cohesive, viable document to send to the committee. The research and creativity involved in putting forth a strong resolution that artistic endeavors be considered part of scholarship and the education of faculty outside of dance form a mission that will impact on all applications of dance faculty now and in the future.

References

Association for Theater in Higher Education. (1987). *Guidelines for Evaluating Teacher/Artists for Promotion and Tenure*. New York: the Association.

Beal, R. K., Rosenberg, L. K., & Sandback, P. R. (1986). Meeting retention, promotion and tenure criteria: Suggestions for dance faculty. *American Dance: A Journal of The American Dance Guild, 1*, (1).

Bledsoe, G. B. (1988). Entering the profession: Advice for the untenured. *National Education Association: To Promote Academic Justice and Excellence*. Washington, DC: National Education Association.

Georgia State University Faculty Handbook. (1989). Atlanta, GA: Georgia State University.

Hanstein, P. (1990). The evaluation, promotion and tenure of dance faculty: Establishing credibility in the academic community. Paper presented to the National Dance Association meeting in New Orleans, LA on March 29.

Karman, T. A. (1969). Faculty evaluation. *Liberal Education, 55*.

Keast, W. R., & Macy, Jr., J. W. (1973). Faculty tenure: A report and recommendations by the Commission on Academic Tenure in Higher Education. San Francisco: Jossey-Bass, Publishers.

Kirschling, W. R., Ed. (1978). *Evaluating faculty performance and vitality: New directions for institutional research*, Vol. 4, No. 4. San Francisco: Jossey-Bass Inc., Publishers.

Miller, R. I. (1987). *Evaluating faculty for promotion and tenure*. San Francisco: Jossey-Bass Inc., Publishers.

Seldin, P. (1980). *Successful faculty evaluation programs: A practical guide to improve faculty performance and promotion/tenure decisions*. Crugers, NY: Coventry Press.

Smith, B. L. & associates. (1973). *The tenure debate*. San Francisco: Jossey-Bass Inc., Publishing.

Vandell, K. and Fishbein, L. (1989, December). Women and tenure: The opportunity of a century. *American Association of University Women*.

Jessica Wood is a graduate student in dance at Texas Woman's University, Denton, Texas 76201.

Management Competencies for Dance Administrators in Higher Education

Erlyne F. Whiteman

The discipline of dance in higher education has undergone many changes in the past decade and it has been difficult to meet all the challenges necessary to accommodate these changes. The development of management competencies for dance administrators in higher education may help to meet some of the demands for the future. Lloyd E. McCleary (1973), a specialist in the field of management competencies in educational administration, stated that "No group can claim professional standing without explicit statements about what constitutes competency in that field and the means by which it can be obtained and assessed."

The development of management competencies for administrators in the fields of physical education and leisure studies has most recently been addressed by various theses and dissertations and by a number of books and journals. Sport management, in particular, has been defined as management that relates to "sport, exercise, dance, and play" (NASSM, 1987).

In order to assess management competencies for dance administrators, the Delphi technique was utilized to create a consensus of views about both general administrative areas of responsibilities and specific competencies related to these general areas. Five dance pioneers (Alma Hawkins, Elizabeth Hayes, Araminta Little, Aileene Lockhart, and Betty Toman) were involved in a pilot study to determine the ten major administrative areas, using the thesis by Ronald Paris (1979) as a model. Forty-five dance administrators across the country participated in the Delphi study, which is a three-round questionnaire developed by Olaf Helmer and Norman Dalkey in 1951 to determine solicitation of expert opinions through the use of a controlled feedback system (Helmer, 1968). Fifty competencies were developed from the first questionnaire. Thirty-five of the original group of experts completed all three rounds of questionnaires and came to a consensus of views on 25 of the 50 competencies.

Management Competency Development

Prior to the 1950s, the history of management thought in physical education and its related fields pertained more to principles of administration than to management competencies. As early as 1954, R. A. Snyder and Harry A. Scott "detailed a competency-based approach to professional preparation" in physical education and allied fields, but according to Earle F. Zeigler and G. S. Bowie (1983), the concept was ahead of its time and did not make an impact (p. 14).

It was not until 1975 that the duties and responsibilities of physical education, recreation, and health administrators were expressed in terms of competencies. John Foley (1975) analyzed a number of competencies for these administrators at the elementary and secondary levels. Twenty-one critical duties were identified that could be related to administrators in higher education in subsequent research.

A comprehensive research study on management competency was developed for physical education and sport by Ronald Paris in 1979. With Zeigler as his chairman, he analyzed competencies viewed by selected educational administrators in physical education and sport. As a result of the final analysis, six major areas of general administration were identified with five to ten specific competencies delineated under each. This model was utilized in the research for dance administrators in higher education. In 1983, Zeigler and Bowie published the first major textbook on *Management Competency Development in Sport and Physical Education*, utilizing information from Paris (1979) and other research from business administration and the newly developing field of sport management. In addition, the first issue of the *Journal of Sports Management* addressed the concept of management competency for sport in four of its articles, overviewed by Janet Parks and Gordan Olafson (1987).

Development of Dance Administration

Historically, the foundations for dance administration began as early as 1926 when Margaret H'Doubler created the first dance major within the department of women's physical education at the University of Wisconsin. The new major led the way for other pioneers in the 1930s and 1940s. Much of the literature of this formative period focused on the place of dance in education, giving support to the need for educating students at all levels in the discipline of dance.

It was not until the 1960s that the issue of dance administration as a field of inquiry came to the attention of the National Section on Dance of AAHPER. The Section created a platform for dance as a discipline in higher education, separate from physical education, in which they saw a need for the development of leadership standards for the training of dance educators. As the Section developed into a Division by 1970, the need for the development of professional competencies for dance educators was identified and later refined by 1974 in AAHPER's *Professional Preparation in Dance, Physical Education, Safety Education, and School Health Education*. The report was specifically designed to identify the unique characteristics of dance as a discipline and to suggest guidelines and competencies for the training of dance students in the areas of teaching and leadership.

However, it was not until the mid-1970s that the literature specifically addressed the need for training in the tasks, responsibilities, and practices of dance administrators. A number of articles appeared in *Dance Magazine* from 1975–1983 on administrative issues for both professional companies and educators at the college and university level. In one such article, Ruth Solomon (1983) discussed the role of the university dance administrator as one who had "grown up with and through the program" (p. 67), but had no experience or training specific to the new role.

While many dance administrators in higher education and dance company directors in the professional world tended to learn the administrative role on the job, recent literature reported in *JOPERD* suggested that the process might be expedited by some professional training. Susan Lee (1984) discovered a trend away from "the cottage industry approach to dance management" (p. 75) toward training in law, art management, and business management that was specific to the discipline of dance. She forecasted that dance administration would become an expanding market in the future. Based on these concerns, Alma Hawkins, one of the pioneers in dance education, founded CODA (Council of Dance Administrators) and in 1985 developed some standards for helping "young administrators understand the role of chairperson and accompanying problems and how to deal with them" (Fichter, 1985, p. 18). A conference was held in June 1985 to outline the various responsibilities, specifically delineating tasks, responsibilities, and practices unique to dance administrators, the results of which were published in the report, *Dance Administration, Themes and Directions*.

Articles in *JOPERD* by Barbara Ebenstein (1986), Louanne Norwood and Terry Worthy (1986), and in *Spotlight for Dance* by Mary Ella Montague (1987) all indicated a trend toward the addition of administration and management courses within graduate and undergraduate programs in the United States. Ebenstein specifically expressed a need for doctoral degrees to fulfill the need for training for department chairpersons in dance in higher education.

Analysis of Management Competencies

In order to identify some of the general and specific management competencies needed by dance administrators, a modified Delphi technique was utilized to gain some consensus among dance administrators in various settings in higher education across the United States. Five dance pioneers participated in a pilot study to determine ten general areas of administrative responsibility (Table 1). Fifty dance department chairpersons across the United States were asked to participate in a pilot study of three rounds of questions to determine specific tasks and skills for each of the ten general administrative areas. Forty-five agreed to participate, while only 35 actually completed all three rounds. Thirty-four institutions of higher learning were represented in 23 states across the country. Departmental housing varied from physical education, to theatre or fine arts, to independent departments of dance. Twenty-one of the administrators

Table 1. Dimensions of General Administrative Areas of Responsibility

Dimension (D)	Description of Dance Administrator
Artist (D1)	Has had experience as dancer-choreographer in educational setting
Communicator (D2)	Conveys information effectively about dance as an art & discipline
Educator (D3)	Has had teaching experience
Facilitator (D4)	Is an ombudsman, collaborator, counselor, negotiator, intermediary
Motivator (D5)	Is an encourager, supporter, initiator
Planner (D6)	Organizes and initiates
Resource Developer (D7)	Helps to develop human, physical, & financial resources
Public Relations (D8)	Has expertise in dealing with various types of publics for the enrichment of the program
Scholar (D9)	Encourages & initiates research
Visionary Leader (D10)	Is a role model in dreaming the feasible & impossible dreams for the future of dance education

had either a PhD or EdD and all belonged to a number of professional dance-related organizations. Responses by this panel of experts were combined and categorized into 50 competency items, 20 of which were calculated as falling within a 75 to 100 percent consensus. The medians, interquartile scores, and deviations are shown for these competencies in Table 2. Conclusions were drawn in light of the consensus reached that competency training is essential for dance administrators and that further research is needed in order to accomplish this task.

Recommendations for further research are suggested in light of the findings of the study and include: additional Delphi investigations that might reveal some information as to why a greater consensus did not occur on more competencies; investigations that might also reveal differences in views about competencies between dance administrators in various settings, comparing dance programs within physical education to independent departments, or to fine or theatre arts departments; and investigations into programs at the graduate level that presently offer degree programs in dance administration.

References

AAHPER (1974). *Professional preparation in dance, physical education, recreation education, safety education, and school health education.* Washington, DC: AAHPER.

Ebenstein, B. J. (1986). A PhD in what? A survey of doctoral programs in dance. *JOPERD, 57*(8), 18–21.

Fichter, N. S. (Ed.). (1985, June). Dance administration, themes and directions. In *Proceedings of the CODA Conference on Dance Administration.* Monticello, IL: Council of Dance Administrators.

Foley, J. F. (1975). An analysis of the duties and responsibilities of selected administrators of health, physical education, and recreation in New York State. Doctoral dissertation, Indiana University. *Dissertation Abstracts International*, 36, 36A.

Helmer, O. (1968). *The use of the delphi technique in problems of education innovations* (D-3499). Santa Monica: The Rand Corporation.

Lee, S. (1984). Dance administrative opportunities. *JOPERD, 55*(5), 74–75, 81.

McCleary, L. (1973). Competency-based educational administration and application to related fields. In *Proceedings of the Conference on Administrative Competence* (pp. 26–28). Tempe AZ: Arizona State University, Bureau of Educational Research.

Montague, M. E. (1987). Beliefs, fears, biases. *Spotlight on Dance, 13*(3), 1,8.

NASSM. (1987). Management memos. *Journal of Sport Management, 1*(1), 87.

Norwood, L., & Worthy, T. (1986). Dance teacher evaluation: Current methods and criteria. *JOPERD, 57*(2), 85–87.

Paris, R. H. (1979). *An analysis of management competency as viewed by selected educational administrators in Ontario physical education and sport.* Unpublished master's thesis, University of Graduate Studies, London, Ontario.

Parks, J., & Olafson, G. (1987). Sport management and a new journal. *Journal of Sport Management, 1*(1), 1–3.

Snyder, R., & Scott, H. (1954). *Professional preparation in health, physical education, and recreation education.* New York: McGraw Hill.

Solomon, R. (1983). Dancer into administrator: Chairing the department or life at the top. *JOPERD, 57*(2), 66–67.

Zeigler, E. F., & Bowie, G. S. (1983). *Management competency development in sport and physical education.* Philadelphia: Lea & Febiger.

Table 2. Analysis of Management Competencies for Dance Administrators

Competency (D1-10)	Percent Essentiality	Q1	Q3	d
Hires quality teachers & performers* (D1)	91.7	5.00	5	3
Is adept at verbal, written & visual skills* (D2)	97.2	5.00	5	0
Communicates/interprets polices & decisions (D2)	91.7	5.00	5	3
Is current as a pedagogue (D3)	75.0	4.25	5	2
Makes things happen (D4)	88.9	5.00	5	4
Resolves conflict with human relations skills (D4)	91.7	5.00	5	3
Facilitates meetings with group management skills (D4)	88.9	5.00	5	4
Advises/counsels with listening skills (D4)	80.6	5.00	5	7
Encourages risk, growth, & change (D4)	86.1	5.00	5	5
Sets the tone for work habits, expectations, & artistic standards* (D5)	88.9	5.00	5	4
Recognizes contributions in teaching, scholarship, & choreography* (D5)	91.7	5.00	5	3
Encourages cohesiveness (D5)	94.4	5.00	5	2
Leads department in budget making & grant funding (D6)	91.7	5.00	5	3
Leads department in development of schedules, curriculum, & productions* (D6)	75.0	5.00	5	8
Leads department in planning new facilities & equipment (D6)	80.6	5.00	5	7
Leads department in policy-making decisions (D6)	94.4	5.00	5	2
Leads department in long & short-range plans (D6)	97.2	5.00	5	0
Works with higher administration on budgetary support (D7)	97.2	5.00	5	0
Recruits qualified faculty, staff, & students (D7)	88.9	5.00	5	4
Encourages development of teaching & artistic talent in faculty & students* (D7)	77.8	5.00	5	3
Helps to shape individual & public opinion about dance* (D8)	88.9	5.00	5	4
Stays current with educational philosophy & theory (D9)	75.0	4.25	5	1
Develops a mission statement for department (D10)	75.0	4.25	5	4
Keeps informed of societal trends (D10)	77.8	5.00	5	8
Empowers faculty & programs (D10)	88.9	5.00	5	3

Note: 50 competencies were initially developed in Round 1, from which the above 25 were analyzed and agreed upon in Rounds 2 and 3, where for all entries: $N = 35$, the median = 5 (highly essential), Q1-Q3 = 75% of scores, d = # people outside the consensus, * = competencies unique to dance, and D = general administrative dimensions from Table 1.

Erlyne Whiteman is assistant professor of physical education and dance, Westmont College, Santa Barbara, California 93108-1099.

Benign Neglect: Issues in Mentoring

Kelley Pierce-Byrd

The worlds of business and leadership have coined a phrase, "benign neglect," and generally apply it to noninterference with the careers of their professionals—doing no harm but also doing no good. It seems odd, then, that these worlds, having long recognized the importance of mentoring the inexperienced, should excuse their neglect of these individuals with the use of the term "benign" when, in fact, this type of neglect appears much more malignant in nature.

It is the purpose of this paper to examine the concept of mentoring, highlighting its importance in the careers of young professionals, particularly those in higher education and specifically those untenured faculty members in university/college departments of dance. Further, the concept of neglecting mentoring will be explored through a malignancy model that demonstrates a connection between the health of the dance discipline in higher education and the career health of those artistic professionals which comprise its faculties.

Mentoring has its formal beginnings in Greek mythology, dating back to the time Odysseus was preparing to depart on his famous journey, the Odyssey. He entrusted his son Telemachus to his friend Mentor, who had agreed to raise and educate the boy, taking the role of "trusted counselor and guide." A fascinating twist to this tale, often omitted by modern writers, is that Mentor was reported to be the goddess Athena in disguise, making that first mentor a powerful woman.

Mentoring is, in its largest context, a relationship between a more experienced professional and a novice. Shirley Chater, president of Texas Woman's University, describes mentoring as a "mutually beneficial process . . . a personally interactive process," a process that "does not end" formally but extends across time and throughout careers. Although no single definition has been agreed upon, the act of mentoring suggests the process as the teaching of "a young person valuable lessons along the way" and the participants as "willing to enter into a one-on-one relationship over time as friend, advisor, teacher, coach, listener, and resource person" (Stephan, 1989).

Mentoring Defined

Psychologist Daniel Levinson devised an excellent model describing the roles and functions of a mentor (Levinson, 1987). In the Levinson model, the mentor acts as a teacher in order to enhance the protege's skills and intellectual development. As a sponsor, the mentor influences the protege's ability to enter into the discipline and make advancements. When in the role of host and guide, the mentor is the protege's contact with the inner social circles of the discipline, introducing and tutoring the protege in the values, customs, resources, and personalities of that group. The mentor is the protege's exemplar, the role model whom the protege emulates as well as the counselor to whom the protege may turn in times of stress. The anchor of this model is found in the mentor's role as "promoter of the dream," a term that brings images of shared goals and connects/coordinates the mentor's functions.

Linda Philips-Jones further divides mentoring into primary and secondary roles (Philips-Jones, 1982). As the primary supporter, the mentor enters willingly into a relationship that is both personal and emotional. The mentor has the power to make things happen for the protege, helping the proteges advance their career significantly, and provides "the blessing," a crucial element. The secondary supporter is typically a peer who offers support and encouragement yet is, to an extent, limited because of his/her own "junior status." It is the role of the primary mentor that then appears to be the most significant, exerting the greatest influence on the protege.

In general, the role of the mentor promotes professional development through the sharing of

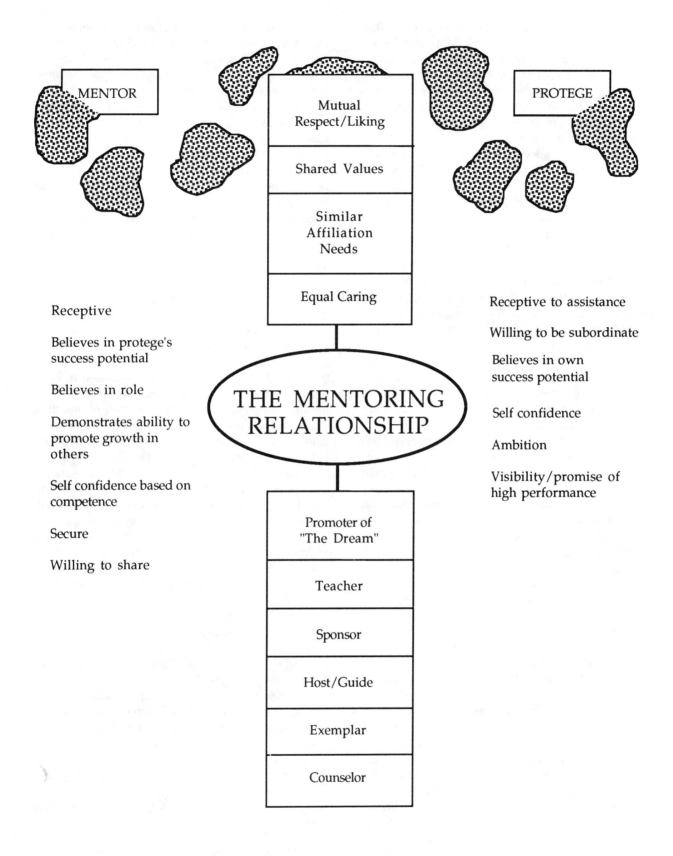

MENTOR

PROTEGE

Mutual Respect/Liking

Shared Values

Similar Affiliation Needs

Equal Caring

Receptive

Believes in protege's success potential

Believes in role

Demonstrates ability to promote growth in others

Self confidence based on competence

Secure

Willing to share

THE MENTORING RELATIONSHIP

Receptive to assistance

Willing to be subordinate

Believes in own success potential

Self confidence

Ambition

Visibility/promise of high performance

Promoter of "The Dream"

Teacher

Sponsor

Host/Guide

Exemplar

Counselor

Figure 1. "Stepping Stones": A Model of Mentoring

knowledge. The protege's career is advanced as the mentor provides exposure and visibility at the work place as well as the social setting. The protege's professional competence is confirmed through the mentor's efforts and the mentor becomes the honest friend who not only will career plan with the protege, but will provide truthful evaluation of progress and contributions.

Because of the special nature of mentoring, the roles of mentor and protege are only for certain individuals. Proteges must be receptive to assistance and hold the belief that the mentor can help. They must be willing to take the subordinate role, not to infer subservience, for a great deal of self-confidence is necessary to assume this role. But also they must be accepting of guidance, feedback, and critical review of performance, trusting the mentor to lead the way. Further, they must be ready for a mentoring relationship on a personal basis. Proteges must believe they can be successful, confident in their abilities, and driven by an ambition to succeed. Although having the desire and ability to accept the power and risk resulting from this relationship is essential, these attributes are moot if readiness and promise of high performance are not made visible to a potential mentor.

Mentorship, as well, requires a very special individual. Receptivity or desire for the process is essential. It has been demonstrated that mentor relationships that develop on their own initiative prove to be the longest lasting, most beneficial, and most satisfying (Stephan, 1989). Mentors believe the protege can succeed and therefore make a wise investment in taking this protege under their wing. They generally believe leaders are responsible for the development of talent and skills in the inexperienced and have demonstrated an ability to promote growth in others, relating particularly well to those with less experience. The personality profile of a mentor includes a self-confidence based on competence, a security with self and position (Zey, 1984), a willingness to share (Stephan, 1989), and a joy in the talents of others. E. Paul Torrance, educator, describes the mentor as idealistic, nonviolent in philosophy, relaxed, patient, thorough, vital, and witty (Torrance, 1984).

The ingredients that blend the mentor and the protege together begin with mutual respect and liking. The mentor and protege demonstrate to each other shared values and a similar need for affiliation. Furthermore, the relationship is cemented in an equal depth of caring, both participants investing the same amounts in the mentoring process (see Figure 1).

The benefits of mentoring are not reserved for the protege but rather further the theme of "relationship," in that both parties may gain from the mentoring experience. Through their interactions, both gain insights, knowledge, and satisfaction from the relationship. Promotion of an individual follows a two-way street and while the mentor promotes the protege, the protege responds with promotion of the mentor (Philip-Jones, 1982). Ego gratification for both parties is available, the protege as they make career gains and the mentor as the gains are made possible through them. Significantly, the power and influence of both protege and mentor are increased as a direct result of the mentoring process (Kram, 1985).

The Malignancy Model

How then is a lack of mentoring malignant? To better explain this phenomenon, it is helpful to look at a modified systems model (see Figure 2) frequently used in the medical profession. The premise of this template takes into account that multiple factors affect the general state of health. A single neglected component compromises the whole organism. In a malignant condition a unit becomes dysfunctional due to the disease process, and due to the interrelatedness of all the systems, the disease affects all other units. When the condition is neglected, the disease seeds itself to additional and seemingly unrelated units, compromising the entire organism. The end result is a sickness of the whole organism multiplied in swiftness and morbidity by the number of units invaded.

It stands to reason that if the inexperienced dance faculty member is deficient in any one unit, it affects the whole performance of this individual. Does it not also stand to reason, if the malignancy template is followed, that the deficiencies may seed and cause the demise of this individual at a faster and more deadly pace?

It therefore becomes quite clear that to ignore a young faculty member's deficiencies and inexperience (benign neglect), to deny him/her mentoring, is to place him/her in danger of failure. The potential losses are multi-fold. Not only does the individual lose his/her position in higher education but higher education loses an artist whose potential was never realized. The students lose, the art form loses, the dance department loses, and no one wins.

It further becomes clear that any one deficient area affects the whole "well-being" of that faculty member. This is where mentoring becomes crucial.

Just as a person seeks a physician for a check-up of all their systems, so it is equally desirable (indeed, imperative) that the untenured faculty member seek those with more experience, more practiced insight, and more personal distance for a "check-up."

Perceived Expectations Survey

In a small survey conducted during the fall semester 1991 within the Texas Woman's University Programs in Dance, six faculty and five graduate students with university level teaching experience were questioned as to their perceived

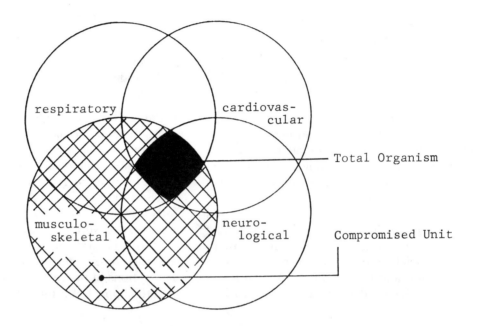

If the systems model is applied to the career of a young professional in higher education it might appear as follows:

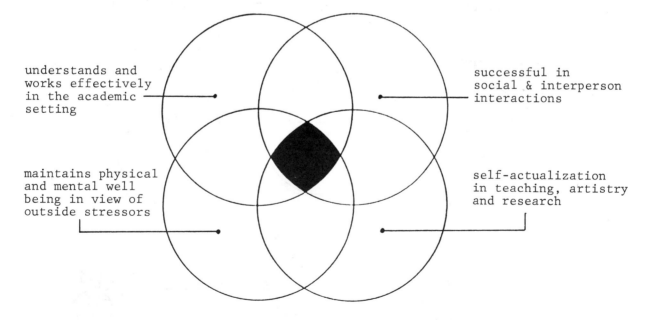

Figure 2. Systems Model of Young Professionals

expectations of untenured (junior) faculty members. Responses were received from 10 of the 11 surveyed.

The survey instrument was divided into four sections. The initial section developed a profile of the respondent, involving information regarding the number of years served as a junior and senior faculty member and any previous experience in a mentoring relationship.

The second section posed questions concerning the respondent's knowledge of a university work situation *prior* to becoming a faculty member juxtaposed against what each respondent felt was necessary to know before beginning a faculty career. This section presented 33 separate questions ranging from publication concerns to committee membership, political functioning, and personal interactions. The final question was structured so as to allow any additional responses not present in the survey. Questions were responded to with a check mark beside each applicable area.

The third section explored each respondent's expectations of the junior faculty member, posing various questions regarding areas for growth, scholarship, teaching performance, and service to the department and the university. A total of 18 questions were included with a final question allow-

ing for independent responses. Responses fell into seven general categories:

1. Growth in teaching skills/curriculum innovation.
2. Publication in professional journals/presentations of papers.
3. Creative (dance) works/presentation of creative works.
4. Growth in committee skills/interaction with other departments.
5. Membership/service in professional organizations.
6. Student recruitment/advising.
7. Attendance at social/political functions.

Categories 1 through 4 were deemed as those areas needing the most guidance. If these categories are placed in a systems model, it becomes clear how complex the position of a dance faculty member is (see Figure 4).

The final section required written responses, answering questions that called for an opinion. The respondents were asked to consider which expectations of a junior faculty member were most critical and therefore might require "the most guidance." Perceptions of the role of a mentor were asked for and the appeal of a formal mentoring system was

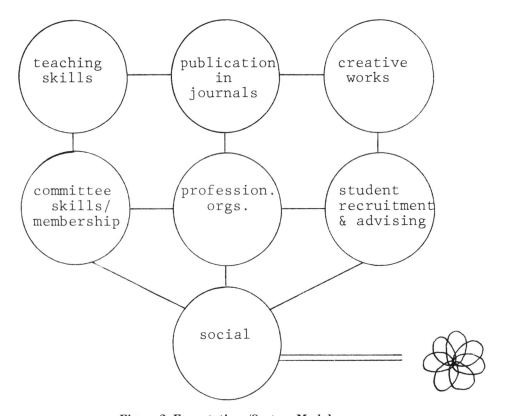

Figure 3. Expectations/System Model

appraised. As a final question, the concept of mentoring as a feminist issue was posed with thought toward exploring this in future investigations of mentoring.

Survey Results

The Texas Woman's University dance department appears to have a clear sense of mentoring needs and functions most important to the growth of the untenured faculty member. In general, they see the role of mentor for a dance faculty member as:

- Facilitator
- Colleague
- Provider of professional advice (career)
- Involving the junior faculty member in the inner circles (social and political)
- Communicator of the "myths" and "symbols" of the institution
- Technical advisor (curriculum, grant writing, teaching, research, and publication)
- Role model
- Perspective monitor (personal and professional)
- Confidante/friend

These areas match professional literature in content with the added dimension that all of these functions must be doubly applied—both in the academic and in the artistic worlds in which the dance faculty member must function. In light of the comprehensive roles perceived of the mentor, it seems that within dance in higher education the need for a guide is imperative.

It is not within the scope of this paper to prescribe the implementation aspects of mentoring; however, the TWU survey proved itself overwhelmingly in favor of the process. Again consistent with professional literature was the thought that mentoring was best implemented on an informal basis, allowing mentoring relationships to develop along "sincere and sensitive" lines.

Although academic competition between faculty members (tenured or not) is traditionally regarded as strong, the belief that the system of a department is healthy and productive only when all the components are likewise healthy and productive may assist in reconciling this phenomenon. It is perhaps noteworthy, and most certainly a topic due further consideration, that although women were not perceived as traditional mentors in the TWU survey, the nature of mentoring embraces feminist thought and practice. In the male dominated world of higher education, where role models and mentors are largely not available to women, the fact that dance faculties are largely female provides an excellent resource for future study and consideration.

References

Kram, K.E. (1985). *Mentoring at work: Developmental relationships.* In *Organizational life*, Glenview, IL: Scott, Foresman.

Levinson, D.J. (1987). *Seasons of a man's life.* New York: Ballantine Books.

Philips-Jones, L. (1982). *Mentors and proteges.* New York: Arbor House.

Stephan, N.L. (1989). *Mentoring and the superintendency: Critical functions relationship factors, and outcomes.* Unpublished doctoral dissertation. Seattle University, Washington.

Torrance, E.P. (1984). *Mentor relationships: How they aid creative achievement, endure, change, and die.* Buffalo, NY: Bearly Ltd.

Zey, M.G. (1984). *The mentor connection.* Homewood, IL: Dow Jones-Irwin.

**Kelley Pierce-Byrd is a graduate student in the
Dance Department at Texas Woman's University,
Denton, Texas 76201.**

PURPOSES OF THE AMERICAN ALLIANCE FOR HEALTH, PHYSICAL EDUCATION, RECREATION AND DANCE

The American Alliance is an educational organization, structured for the purposes of supporting, encouraging, and providing assistance to member groups and their personnel throughout the nation as they seek to initiate, develop, and conduct programs in health, leisure, and movement-related activities for the enrichment of human life.

Alliance objectives include:

1. Professional growth and development—to support, encourage and provide guidance in the development and conduct of programs in health, leisure, and movement-related activities which are based on the needs, interests, and inherent capacities of the individual in today's society.

2. Communication—to facilitate public and professional understanding and appreciation of health, leisure, and movement-related activities, and to disseminate the findings to the profession and other interested and concerned publics.

3. Standards and guidelines—to further the continuous development and evaluation of standards within the profession for personnel and programs in health, leisure, and movement-related activities.

4. Public affairs—to coordinate and administer a planned program of professional, public and governmental relations that will improve education in areas of health, leisure, and movement-related activities.

5. To conduct such other activities as shall be approved by the Board of Governors and the Alliance Assembly, provided that the Alliance shall not engage in any activity which would be inconsistent with the status of an educational and charitable organization as defined in Section 501 (c)(3) of the Internal Revenue Code of 1954 or any successor provision thereto, and none of the said purposes shall at any time be deemed or construed to be purposes other than the public benefit purposes and objectives consistent with such educational and charitable status.